PEOPLE who COUNT

Population and Politics, Women and Children

Dorothy Stein

EARTHSCAN
Earthscan Publications Ltd, London

First published in the UK 1995 by
Earthscan Publications Limited

Copyright © Dorothy Stein, 1995

A catalogue record for this book is available from the British Library

ISBN 1 85383 279 0 (HB)
ISBN 1 85383 233 2 (PB)

Typeset by BookEns Ltd, Royston, Herts.
Printed and bound by Biddles Ltd, Guildford and King's Lynn
Cover design by Dominic Banner

For a full catalogue of publications please contact:

Earthscan Publications Limited
120 Pentonville Road
London N1 9JN
Tel: 0171 278 0433
Fax: 0171 278 1142

Earthscan is an editorially independent subsidiary of Kogan Page Limited
and publishes in association with the World Wide Fund for Nature and the
International Institute for Environment and Development.

Contents

201

Acknowledgements

The production of a book that crosses so many fields and specialties necessarily places its author in many debts, both to the usual assortment of patient and obliging friends, colleagues and publishing professionals, and to a large number of strangers who give their time, information and expertise for no other reason than kindness. In the present work, several members of both categories have earned my thanks in more than one capacity. My gratitude goes first to Basia Zaba who supported and encouraged my first attempts to organize my arguments, and to David Kellogg, who translated the Chinese material and read and criticized the entire manuscript. Thanks also to Meera Abraham, Root Cartwright, Graham Clarke, Tim Dyson, Vibhuti Patel and Burton Stein, all of whom read and commented on several of its parts. For supplying me with information and material, whether on request or spontaneously, I am grateful, in addition to those listed above, to Jon Anson, Garnette Bowler, Rosamund Ebdon, Jia Gailian, Melvyn Goldstein, John Guillebaud, Jo Hanson, Ann Laybourn, Liu Ruping, Neil Thomas, Angela Thomson, Myron Weiner and David Willey. And finally, thanks to Jo O'Driscoll and Jonathan Sinclair Wilson of Earthscan, with whom it has been a pleasure to be associated. All errors are of course my own responsibility.

PART 1
Positions and Politics

Chapter 1

Population, resources and rights

If politics makes strange bedfellows, procreation politics surely produces some of the strangest of all pairings. One month before the long-awaited UN conference on population and development, the papal envoy in Teheran visited the deputy foreign minister (and brother of the president) and urged that the two heads of state collaborate in insisting on changes to the prospective conference plan of action. The proposed alliance between the head of the Roman Catholic Church and the government of Iran is only one of a succession of unlikely associations that crop up in almost every issue that affects the growth, decline or classification or distribution of large groups of people, whether in immigration, natural increase, genocide, infertility, contraception, sterilization, abortion or adoption. But this particular collaboration was remarkable not only because of the generally hostile relationships between Christian and Islamic establishments in the past, but because, within the past four years, the Shi'ite mullahs, who control the government of Iran and disapproved of the use of contraceptives after the 'Islamic' revolution there, have instituted a population policy of which the Catholic Church can only disapprove. Becoming alarmed at rates of natural increase that had reached 3.9 per cent, they are now importing contraceptives and denying state benefits to children of birth order greater than the third. Vasectomy is also encouraged.[1] The policy is,

---

1)   Akbar Aghajanian, 'Recent fertility trends in Iran', paper presented to the 1990 Meeting of the Population Association of America in Toronto, Canada, p 21.

except for the recommended family size, remarkably similar to that of the much-deplored Chinese.

FERTILITY VERSUS POLICY

Officially, Britain, the United States and most other developed countries have no domestic population policies outside of admittedly restrictive immigration and refugee legislation. Those industrialized countries who do have policies, such as France, Germany and Israel, make attempts to stimulate population growth. But even in countries without official birth-stimulating policies, the social, cultural, media and even medical climates tend to be pronatal. Yet the actual behaviour exhibited by industrialized populations all over the world (of whatever predominant religion) is in fact at variance with conventional attitudes. Although the exact figures change slightly with the source, the consensus is clear and in fact unanimous: fertility rates in the industrialized nations have tumbled to the point where almost all are now below replacement (an average of slightly over two children per woman). Almost one in six women in these countries chooses to be childless, even more have only one child, and few aim for more than two.

Between 1965 and the mid 1970s, the 'total fertility rate' (TFR), or number of children born to each woman on the average fell from 2.8 in the UK to 1.8, and since then has been fairly steady. In Sweden the corresponding rates are 2.4 and 1.8 (though this seems to be rising); in the United States, 2.9 and 1.8; in Japan 2.14 and 1.8. Italy, which in 1965 reported a TFR of 2.55, last year reported an all-time national low of 1.27. Canada and Australia also have TFRs in line with those of the UK and the USA. Interestingly too, in these countries, Catholic contraceptive use rose from 50 per cent in 1955 to 88 per cent in 1982, and Catholic and non-Catholic fertility rates are now similar.[2]

These statistics do not necessarily mean that the population – even aside from possible immigration – is decreasing. In fact, the UK population, which was slightly over 57 million in 1989, is still rising and predicted to hit 60 million in 2010. Eventually, of course, if current rates keep up, and even if death rates drop, the increase will halt and the numbers will slowly begin to decline.

---

2) Jean Bourgeois-Pichat, 'The Unprecedented Shortage of Births in Europe', in *Below Replacement Fertility in Industrialized Societies*, K Davis, MS Bernstam, R Ricardo-Campbell, eds, Cambridge: Cambridge University Press, 1987, p 5 with 1975 figures for the UK and Sweden adjusted from 2.0 to 1.8.

THE POLITICS OF POLICY

In the 1960s and 1970s, the United States was in the forefront of international efforts to encourage developing countries to adopt population limitation policies, both through government agencies and the activities of such organizations as the Ford and Rockefeller Foundations, the Population Council and the International Planned Parenthood Federation (IPPF). The United Nations Population Fund (then the United Nations Fund for Population Activities, UNFPA) was actually founded at American instigation over the general indifference of the UN. This activity was a marked development over the 1959 statement to the press by President Eisenhower that 'I cannot imagine anything more emphatically a subject that is not a proper political or governmental activity or function or responsibility', and John Kennedy's flip and famous remark that 'overpopulation is other people's children'. Richard Nixon, Gerald Ford and Jimmy Carter all supported assistance to birth control programmes in poor countries (though of course none of them would have dreamt of recommending a population limitation policy at home).

Created in 1969, the UNFPA became the second largest donor of international population assistance after the American government itself, providing support to other agencies as well as directly to projects in over 140 countries. Although by the early 1980s, the United States was contributing only about 25 per cent of UNFPA funds, it was frequently critical that the UN was not devoting enough effort to family planning. Yet in 1985 the American government decided to withhold all contributions to UNFPA on the grounds that widespread forced sterilization and abortion occurred in China, and the Chinese programme itself, with its incentives and penalties and psychological pressure, was inherently coercive.

In reality, the decision represented a conjunction of the two great obsessions of the American right wing: communism and abortion. But it was justified by appealing to a long-held belief among Americans that their country existed on a moral plane above others. Jesse Helms, now Chair of the Senate Foreign Relations Committee, then co-author of the Kemp–Inouye–Helms amendment on which the justification of the defunding of the UNFPA was based, announced that: 'The family is a divine institution which precedes the state and has rights superior to the state. Accordingly, no power on Earth ... has the authority to dictate to married couples in China or elsewhere that they can have only a certain number of children.' Interestingly, no such denunciations were then made of Romania's draconian pronatalist policies and practices.

The divine right of family decision-making abroad did not include the right to abortion. The political 'New Right' (which included the efforts of the Catholic hierarchy), balked in its attempts to halt legal abortion at home, succeeded in including association with abortion services as a rationale for defunding the International Planned Parenthood Federation. This action was called the 'Mexico City policy' because it was formally enunciated at the World Population Conference at Mexico City in 1984.[3] As for the issue of population itself, the Reagan administration declared it to be a 'neutral factor' in economic development. Within days of his inauguration, William Clinton, the new Democratic President, revoked the policy, thus performing a second volte-face within ten years. (The attempted alliance between the Vatican and mullahs was probably an outgrowth of the Holy See's loss of its powerful old American allies.)[4]

The United States and Iran are not the only governments to have suddenly reversed their population policies in recent years. The most appalling case was that of Romania, where in 1966 abortion and birth

---

3)   In addition to the special singling out of China as the perpetrator of a coercive programme, the policy stated that no US foreign aid may be given to any organization that performs abortions, advises women on abortion or lobbies on behalf of abortion rights – even if these activities are supported by non-US funds. Challenged by the Planned Parenthood Federation in the American courts, the Mexico City policy was upheld by the United States Supreme Court in June 1991. While in force, it led to a decrease in the availability of other forms of contraception: some funds have been diverted from organizations such as Planned Parenthood to, among others, Catholic organizations that advocate only the rhythm method and abstinence. Although technically the policy applied only to private groups (non-governmental organizations), some governments, such as that of Bangladesh, dependent on US foreign aid cut down their abortion services in fear of American reprisals – to the point of refusing to treat women suffering from botched abortions. In addition, pressure from conservative groups has led to the shutting down of research into alternatives to abortion. See John Morgan 'Exporting Misery', *Scientific American*, August, 1991, pp 8–9; also, 'Documents: USAID/UNFPA discord over support for China's family planning program', *Population and Development Review*, March, 1986, pp 159–62. In 1988, Reagan's Attorney General, Edwin Meese, overrode a decision of the State Department and granted political asylum to three Chinese couples who 'feared persecution' over their refusal to comply with the single-child policy. It has also been pointed out that at the same time as the US was withholding funds from the UNFPA, it was opposing sanctions against South Africa's apartheid policy. See Barbara Crane and Jason Finkle, 'The United States, China and the United Nations Population Fund', *Population and Development Review*, 15, March, 1989, pp 23–59.

4)   Jason Finkle and C Alison McIntosh (eds, *The New Politics of Population*, New York: The Population Council, 1994, pp 9–10) point out that 'To understand the politics of family planning within the UN system, it is important to realize that the United Nations is not a hierarchical organization, but a loosely connected system of autonomous and quasi-autonomous councils, commissions and agencies ... [F]or many years the specialized agencies had considered population as too sensitive an issue to grapple with.' Hence population activities were isolated, or quarantined, in their own special fund. Various governments are free to contribute or withhold contributions to UN activities according to whether this suits their own internal political considerations. Thus, the United States was able to exert a paramount influence over the Security Council, while owing the UN a billion dollars, as well as to withdraw or contribute to such specialized agencies and UNICEF and UNFPA, as it did under Reagan and Bush.

control were made illegal almost overnight, and remained that way until the equally sudden changes demanded by the Romanians at the end of 1989 when they overthrew Ceaucescu. In general, however, the changes in the population policies of developing countries have been from complacency, indifference or encouragement, to concern over high birth rates, especially in Africa and Latin America.[5] Countries that shifted to viewing their fertility levels as too high include Algeria, Bangladesh, Ethiopia, Jordan, Nigeria, Peru, Sierra Leone, Tanzania, Vietnam and Zimbabwe. Countries that limited or restricted their citizens' access to contraceptives decreased from 15 in 1976 to six in 1989: Cambodia, Iraq, Laos, Mongolia, Romania and Saudi Arabia. As of 1993, Mongolia was among those listed as viewing its fertility levels as too high, and Romania now offers government support for contraception as well as legalized abortion. On the other hand, Malaysia and Singapore have swung from anti- to pronatalist policies.[6]

Like those who consider their populations too low, governments who view their birth rates as too high usually do so from economic considerations, believing that growth is hindered by the need to support large numbers of children. Only very recently have considerations of diminishing natural resources been listed among the acknowledged concerns of any country.

POLITICS AND POPULATION

The strange and, it must be said, often uneasy alliances among interest or conviction groups on the issues of population and birth control, cannot be analysed along the usual left–right lines. Even among those who consider themselves socially conservative, in fact, even within the Vatican itself, opinions are divided. In addition to the implicit rejection of the papal ban on contraceptives, reflected in the low fertility rates of Catholics in industrialized countries, a recent report issued by the Pontifical Academy of Sciences in Rome, alarmed at the rising global population, urged couples to have no more than

5)   But John Rowley (' "Population no problem", say Egypt's cabinet ministers', *Terra Viva*, Cairo, 8 September, 1994, p 4) reported that a survey taken of Egyptian government officers found only half of them, from cabinet ministers on down agreed that Egypt had a population problem, despite the government's official policy and the publicity afforded by the Population Conference then taking place.

6)   Data for the period 1976–89 from Joseph Chamie, 'Trends, Variations and Contradictions in National Policies to Influence Fertility', in Jason Finkle and C Alison McIntosh, eds, *The New Politics of Population*, New York: The Population Council, 1994. Information for 1993 from the Population Reference Bureau.

two children.[7] Some economic conservatives, such as Julian Simon, assert that increasing population growth and density can bring nothing but benefits and prosperity to countries thickly populated, while others fear the threat of increasing immigration from abroad and the proliferation of teenaged and single mothers more than they do freely available family planning and abortion.

On the left, population as an issue was derided for many years – and still is in some quarters – as simply the proven-wrong opinion of the reactionary Thomas Malthus. Any suggestion that population density or rapid growth could itself generate, as well as result from, poverty, was hotly denounced as a distraction from the identification of maldistribution as the true cause of human (and environmental) misery. More recently, the most populous country on earth, with a long-established Communist government, instituted, and has maintained for a decade and a half, the most ambitious antinatal programmes of all, and a number of other avowedly socialist governments, among them Vietnam and Cuba, preceded or followed the Chinese with restrictive family planning policies.

Nevertheless, many on the left, in concert with militant free marketeers, still decry family planning programmes as the sinister arms of a world-wide conspiracy which includes western governments, particularly that of the United States (despite its recent chequered history), the UN, private foundations and NGOs (non-governmental organizations), the educated élites of developing countries, medical workers, academics and researchers, pharmaceutical companies and other manufacturers of contraceptives. These groups are suspected of caring less about the people they claim to be serving, or the environment, than about making profits; advancing their own careers; feathering their nests; keeping down the number of 'others' at home and abroad (a motivation that has been termed 'genocidal'); and reducing immigration pressures.[8] Many feminists have also viewed with suspicion even the new attention to the welfare of women, since they feel it is motivated primarily by a wish to

---

7)   *Catholic Herald*, 17 June, 1994. The Pope has agreed that parenthood should be 'responsible', but under no circumstances should responsibility be achieved by any means except periodic or long-term sexual abstinence, which alone are at present doctrinally approved. See also John Hooper, 'Pope's stance on birth control undermined by Vatican report', *Guardian*, 11 June, 1994.

8)   Interestingly, one of the most vehement and accusatory denunciations of the 'birth control industry' is contained in Jacqueline Kasun, *The War Against Population*, San Francisco: Ignatius Press, 1988. Kasun, both a free-market economist and believer in eternal moral absolutes of the Jesse Helms school, lists dozens of governmental and private agencies at which to point the finger.

decrease fertility, which uses their betterment as a means rather than an end in itself.[9]

Of course, it could equally be argued that rapid population growth serves the interests of a sinister combination of western business and military leaders, who see in continued population growth a proliferation of cheap labour and new customers, reasons to aid expensive and grandiose development schemes, and a justification for continuing to fund large standing armies and high levels of weapons manufacture and research. It also justifies a brisk arms trade with Third World governments to handle any restlessness among the increasing numbers of the relatively or absolutely deprived. In fact, if the volume of funding is taken as evidence of sinister or self-interested intent, surely the evidence for 'evil pronatalist' conspiracy over-whelms that for the 'evil antinatalist' one.[10]

Yet a pronatalist conspiracy is never discussed. Why not? Because almost everyone is in it. In any attempt to understand and analyse the politics of population, account must be taken of the basic assumptions of right, left and centre, feminist and patriarchal stances, which are all still pronatalist – to such an extent that it has been difficult for any of the parties to acknowledge that increasing numbers of women themselves are less than convinced about the virtues of having more than a couple of children at most. It is an important part of the argument of this book to show that, contrary to widespread assumptions, low fertility rates are not only beneficial to women, children, society and the environment, but are the preference of women themselves.[11]

---

9) See, for example, Ruth Kelly, 'Putting emphasis on women cuts no ice with feminists', *Guardian*, 21 July, 1994, p 13.

10) More specific evidence of the erratic behaviour of the western nations in population matters may be found in the 1992 decision of the United States Agency for International Development to cut the distribution of condoms to Pakistan because of American concerns about its nuclear programme (*IPPF Open File*, February, 1993, p 17; *New York Newsday*, 14 December, 1992), and, more recently, in the threat posed to Cuba's population control policy by the American embargo (Laura Pallares, 'US Embargo Threatens Cuba's Population Policies', *Terra Viva*, 8 September, 1994, p 3).

11) The percentages of women polled who did not want any more children than they had at the moment has increased over the past 20 years in a wide range of countries in Europe, Asia, Latin America and Africa. In Senegal, for example, the increase was from 8 to 17 per cent; in Peru it was from 61 to 73 per cent. Even historically in Europe and America, the long sustained decline in fertility preceded declines in infant mortality (Malcom Potts and Shyam Thapa, *Child Survival: The Role of Family Planning*, New York: IPPF, 1991). The authors point out that, in addition to contraceptive use and child survival having a mutually reinforcing effect on each other, the awareness of the availability of contraception itself stimulates a decline in the number of children desired.

POPULATION AND DEVELOPMENT

At the World Population Conference held in Bucharest in 1974, many developing countries (even some who were already implementing policies to limit population growth at home) insisted that 'development is the best contraceptive', a position that has since achieved the status of dogma to compassionate people across the political spectrum, even as the impossibility of indefinite population growth gradually sank in. 'Development' in this sense refers to economic development, and means not only increased agricultural production, but primarily industrialization: the production of enough goods and services – and employment in such production – to supply the means and wants not just of the rich and middle classes but of the broad mass of the population.

The slogan as a whole refers to the theory of the 'demographic transition'. Any problems of population and poverty, global or regional, are ideally supposed to be cured by following, at an accelerated pace, the model of Europe's century-long stately progress to its current low birth rates (though the problem of poverty even there was never really solved). Death rates drop thanks to improved health, public health and nutrition and, after a certain period, would-be parents lower the number of children they calculate they need in order to supply the family labour and old age support they want. In industrializing societies, people move into cities and housing shortages combined with rising aspirations for their children cause further reductions in fertility.

Unfortunately, in trying to pursue an industrializing strategy, many Third World countries borrowed heavily and, following collapses in the prices of the commodities they were supposed to export to repay the loans, now find themselves heavily in debt. In consequence, in the past two decades, the relative and even the absolute economic position of the Third World has changed mostly for the worse. Many countries find themselves repaying in interest more than they receive in aid. Far from developing, much of Africa has gone backwards. But even in parts of Asia where economies have grown, there are several problems with the 'demographic transition' model, both conceptually and practically.

In the first place, the historical model is incomplete. The 40 million people who left Europe and migrated, mostly to the New World, in the 19th and 20th centuries are usually forgotten in 'development' formulas – especially since immigration today is less and less popular with the prospective recipient countries.[12] In the second

---

12) Estimates vary, but one claim is that the present population of the British Isles, about 65

place, 'development' is measured by an increase in Gross Domestic Product (GDP) or average per capita income.[13] To the extent that this measures national wealth at all, it obscures the inequality of distribution within the country. A better measure, which would give some indication of economic inequality, would be found in median income, which is that below which half the population is to be found. In conditions of economic inequality, the average income is higher than the median, and, in fact, increasing inequality has been a characteristic of many 'developing' economies.[14] But to have any effect on population growth, according to development theory, prosperity must reach the lower parts of the economic pyramid, where the bulk of the people are.

Then too, the very strategy for development which was urged by the World Bank and the IMF (International Monetary Fund) upon developing countries is increasingly questioned (though it continues to be pursued). These institutions have often made the necessary loans contingent upon 'structural adjustment programmes' in the recipient countries, which include the cutting of food subsidies and social expenditures, as well as concentration on the production of goods for export, programmes that are particularly detrimental to the welfare of the poorest. Moreover, the industries encouraged and set up in these countries depend for their general success on manufacturing costs lower than those available in more advanced economies. Thus many new industries find themselves in competition with each other to supply the cheapest and most docile labour (often that of young women and children), with the least stringent of health, safety and environmental standards.

Still another problem with the 'development' model is that the very

––––––––––––––––––––––––––––⟡––––––––––––––––––––––––––––

cont.

    million, would have been as high as 90 million had it not been for emigration (J Le Fanu, 'Must life mean death', *Sunday Telegraph*, 15 August, 1993).

13)   Geoffrey McNicholl ('Economic Growth and Low Fertility', in K Davis, MS Bernstam, R Ricardo-Campbell, eds, *Below Replacement Fertility in Industrialized Societies,* Cambridge: Cambridge University Press, 1987, p 222) points out that in 'mature economies', where much of the workforce 'have jobs for which productivity is a social and accounting convention rather than a material fact', actual GDP becomes rather meaningless; it is an extrapolation from a factory metaphor for production.

14)   John Stanley ('For South, common cause and concern', *The Earth Times* [Published by *Al-Ahram* and the *New York Times*], 10 September, 1994, p 3) cites complaints that the structural adjustment programmes demanded as a condition of further credit by the World Bank has destroyed the middle class in Africa, leaving only the very poor and the very rich. Edward Goldsmith also pointed out that taking money as the measure of the economic health obscures such developments as the decrease in jobs by 5 per cent in Spain in a period in which the economy doubled ('Opinion', BBC Radio 4, 25 September, 1994). A similar trend has been taking place in the United States, where, according to the Bureau of the Census, the median family income in 1993 was $44 less per week than it was in 1989. In 1993, despite 3 per cent economic growth, the median income fell by 1 per cent (James Fallows, 'The Republican Promise', *New York Review of Books*, 12 January, 1995, p 6).

changes that were the supposed engine of falling birth rates in the wealthy countries are now seen by environmentalists as spelling future catastrophe, not only for those countries themselves but for the whole world. In fact, if 'development' by this definition – the continued production of more and more goods, with the attendant use of raw materials, water and other basic resources, and the accompanying pollution that manufacture and consumption generates – could continue indefinitely, there would be no need for concern about any level of world population. In other words, 'overpopulation' is relative only to the long-term ability of the earth to sustain the needs of the human inhabitants (and sometimes a thought is spared for other species as well).

And, finally, the increasing inequality of distribution which is at present a feature of 'development' in both North and South is considered by many to be not only immoral in itself, and unsustainable, but environmentally inefficient, since the wasteful consumption of the wealthy does little to sustain the human population compared to the environmental deterioration it causes.

POPULATION AND ENVIRONMENT

About one-quarter of the current global population of 5.6 billion lives in the 'developed' (that is, richer) part of the world. Annual additions over the next decade at least will be about 97 million, over 90 per cent of this in the poorer parts. But population size is only one ingredient in the ways in which people occupy their available space, consume available resources and generate pollution, which may or may not be confined to the locality they inhabit, and indicate the current state of overcrowding. In most respects, Europe, Japan, and the rest of the 'developed' world are far more 'overpopulated' than the poorer parts of the planet.

A number of different sorts of calculations of the size of a 'sustainable' population (one that could live indefinitely on local or global resources) have been attempted. Often, and crudely, they include only estimates of caloric requirements. For example, one estimate concluded that 1.7 billion could be sustained at American dietary levels, and 6 billion with universal vegetarianism.[15] Another,

---

15) Whether (and for how long) overall world food production (ignoring for the moment the crucial question of its availability to the currently underfed) can keep up with the growing numbers of people has been a matter of considerable debate. While a presidential candidate, in 1980, Ronald Reagan claimed that 'There are studies showing that, using American levels of farming worldwide, the earth can support a population of 28 billion' (Marshall Green, *Population and Development Review*, June, 1993, p 313), conveniently

and somewhat more sophisticated, calculation transforms food, fuel and other necessities into energy equivalents. The most usual way at present of calculating the effect of human population on the environment, or, conversely, its 'carrying capacity' in terms of human freight (that is, neglecting any consideration of other species except as they might affect or be affected by human beings) is as a product of number of people, the average rate of consumption per person and the 'impact' per unit of consumption, which includes waste products and other forms of pollution. For example, a recent Swiss study calculated that Switzerland, with a relatively energy-efficient economy, imports 3.5 times as much energy equivalent as it exports. Were it to live on its own renewable resources, then, the Swiss population would have to be a fraction of what it is to live in its current average style.[16] An American study concluded that if rigorous conservation, efficiency and a shift from fossil fuels were instituted, the United States could support a population of 200 million – compared to the current 253 million – at a 'high' standard of living. On a global basis, the world could maintain about 1.5 billion at the same standard.[17] And wealthy western countries are not the only reckoners of carrying capacity: in the opinion of its policy makers, the optimal population of China would be between 600 and 700 million, a size which they once hoped to reach in the next century – and half of what it now is.[18]

Rates of consumption vary both within and between countries. A British or Japanese baby, for example, is about six times the environmental disaster that a Chinese baby is, but only about four times as threatening as one born in Brazil, and about half as bad as one born in the United States. Or, generally speaking, 20 per cent of the world's population consumes 80 per cent of its resources, and wastes and pollutes accordingly, or rather much more, which may be far more critical in the long run. Thus, for the moment at least,

<hr />

cont.

ignoring the inputs and consequences in terms of such things as water, fertilizer, chemicals and pollutants, of American levels of farming. More believably, Amartya Sen (*New York Review of Books*, 22 September, 1994, p 66) and Tim Dyson ('Population Growth and Food Production: Recent Global and Regional Trends', paper presented to the British Society for Population Studies, 1 September, 1994) argue that food production per capita has increased in all regions of the world except Africa and the Americas since 1982, and that overall world food production is continuing to outpace population.

16) Gonzague Pillet, *Towards an Inquiry into the Carrying Capacity of Nations*, Report to the Coordinator for International Refugee Policy, Federal Department of Foreign Affairs, September, 1991.

17) D Pimentel, R Harman, M Pacenza, J Pecarsky, and M Pimentel, 'Natural Resources and an Optimum US and World Population', unpublished paper, Department of Entomology, Cornell University, Ithaca, New York 14853, USA, 5 April, 1992.

18) Susan Greenhalgh, 'Population Studies in China', in Dudley Poston and David Yaukey, *The Population of Modern China*, New York: Plenum, 1992, p 32.

overconsumption, overpollution and hence overpopulation are global problems whose sources are to be found in the developed world.

But the situation is unlikely to remain static. The emerging Chinese middle class, like that of India and the wealthy élites of all underdeveloped countries, is set to follow western middle-class consumer patterns as closely as possible. In China, a decision was made a decade ago to provide much of the population with refrigerators. More than 100 refrigerator factories were built. The fraction of Beijing households owning a refrigerator rose from roughly 2 per cent to 62 per cent during 1981–86. Unfortunately, an inefficient refrigerator design had been chosen – thereby committing China to billions of dollars worth of electric capacity to serve those appliances. And they all use environmentally unfriendly CFCs as coolants.[19] Recently, moreover, the Chinese government has decided to encourage greater private car ownership, which now amounts to only one out of twenty. Plans are that by the end of the decade, China will be producing 3 million vehicles a year, up from the current 1.3 million, but half of them will be cars, up from one-quarter during the current year.[20]

Human beings now appropriate one-quarter of the solar energy captured by photosynthesis, and even this is not enough.[21] Furthermore, non-renewable and slowly renewable resources, such as soil, water and fossil fuels are being consumed much faster than they are being replaced. In the United States, as in Africa and Asia, desertification threatens to prove the predictions of Malthus, who concluded that food production could not continue to expand indefinitely with the expansion of the population, in a new and unexpected way: food supplies may not long continue to increase at

------

19)   See Amory Lovins, 'Energy, People and Industrialization', in Kingsley Davis and Mikhail Bernstam, eds, *Resources, Environment and Population*, New York: Oxford University Press, 1991, p 112. Lovins' aim was to show how much better 'market oriented economies' do than 'centrally planned' ones. China has the highest agricultural energy inputs in the world – unavoidably, since the land has been overfarmed to feed its vast population, and yields only what is put back into it in terms of fertilizer and soil preparation. On the other hand, rich countries that deal in 'invisibles' and 'services', and rack up lots of notional GNP out of little in the way of goods produced, would appear to use less energy than countries whose economies are primarily agricultural or industrial, so perhaps the comparison is unfair. Qu Geping, Minister of State for the Environment gives somewhat different dates and percentages. He points out, however, that on average, China consumes less than one ton of coal (the major industrial and domestic fuel) per capita per year, while an average American goes through ten tons annually.

20)   John Gittings, 'China's car syndrome', *Guardian Society*, 5 October, 1994, p 5.

21)   See *Global Population – What's New?*, Colorado Population Coalition, September, 1992; PM Vitousek, PR Ehrlich, AH Ehrlich, and PA Matson, 'Human appropriation of the products of biosynthesis', *Bioscience*, 36, no 6, pp 368–73, 1986. All such figures are only rough approximations and vary considerably across estimators, with some estimates up to 40 per cent.

all, let alone 'arithmetically'.[22] However the calculation is approached, other than that of mystical dependence on the intervention of technology as yet undeveloped, the doubling of the present world population that is almost inevitable before stabilization can occur is almost certainly unsustainable in the long run.

Environmental politics   All of these calculations and the assumptions on which they are based have been used recently for political purposes. Carrying capacity calculations that are confined to single countries, such as those of Pillet (whose Report was to the Swiss Coordinator for International Refugee Policy) are readily used as arguments for ever-tighter immigration policies.[23] These arguments have been made even more baldly by Virginia Abernethy, who also maintains that 'unequal distribution, both within and among nations, is a sine qua non of conservation in a world of growing populations'.[24]

The disproportionate consumption of developed countries has been a repeated charge made by underdeveloped countries in economic difficulties. The answer of the governments of the wealthy nations to this is usually swift and clear, as when President Bush announced before the Rio Summit that 'The American lifestyle is not

———————————————◇———————————————

22) The concentration on food as a measure of sustainability has deflected attention from the more basic problem of water, which is needed not only in itself but as a necessary input in agriculture, industry, waste disposal and for the prevention and treatment of disease conditions. Only countries as rich as Saudi Arabia can afford to supply a significant amount of their people's water requirements by desalinating sea water. The work of Malin Falkenmark has insistently pointed to the multiple threats that a growing population and environmental mismanagement pose to future water resources, especially of the requisite quality. Water scarcity especially threatens Africa and Asia in the next 20 years. Moreover, human activities on the land reduce its ability to store rainfall. These catastrophically limiting effects on the planet's carrying capacity will make themselves felt before those of global warming. See Malin Falkenmark, 'Landscape as Life Support Provider', in Francis Graham-Smith (ed), *Population – the complex reality*, London: The Royal Society, 1994.

23) Gonzague Pillet, *Towards an Inquiry into the Carrying Capacity of Nations*, Report to the Coordinator for International Refugee Policy, Federal Department of Foreign Affairs, September, 1991. Dropping the notion that immigration should be limited for the benefit of the world in general, the editor and several contributors to a book sponsored by an American organization called 'Negative Population Growth' adopt a bunker mentality instead: 'We cannot solve all the world's problems', and attempt instead to consider what sort of very limited immigration would be most beneficial to the United States. (Lindsey Grant, *Elephants in a Volkswagen*. New York: WH Freeman, 1992; see Epilogue and Vernon Briggs, 'Practical Confrontation with Economic Reality: Mass Immigration in the Post-Industrial Age'.) No consideration is given to the extent to which past or present American policies have contributed to immigration pressure.

24) Virginia Abernethy, 'The "One World" thesis as an obstacle to environmental preservation', in Kingsley Davis and Mikhail Bernstam, eds, *Resources, Environment and Population*, New York: Oxford University Press, 1991, p 327. Her reasoning is that only the rich have the technology and means to conserve – assuming that cleaning up can always be made less costly than what is produced, an assumption becoming increasingly dubious in the nuclear and other toxic industries.

up for grabs.' It is one thing to give lip-service to the control of particular atmospheric pollutants, such as carbon dioxide or lead, but quite another to entertain the severe changes and restrictions that either redistribution of wealth or a sustainable use of resources on a global scale – let alone both – would entail.

Conservation in rich countries has been treated, at best, as a kind of extravagant indulgence, affordable only in the most prosperous of times.[25] This was indicated, for example, when during the recession of the early 1990s, the percentage of the UK Green Party vote plummeted from a protest-inspired high of 15 per cent in the European elections of 1989 to less than 1 per cent in the general election of 1992. All the major political parties have endorsed economic 'growth' only along conventional lines. In October, 1994, the British Prime Minister held out the possibility of doubling national 'living standards' in the next quarter-century as a presumed vote-getter.

There are few real signs of a trend toward 'rigorous conservation', in either the developed or undeveloped parts of the world. Indeed, in Britain, since the 'green' Mrs Thatcher was replaced by 'grey' John Major, government cuts have largely undone the few measures that might have led to increased energy efficiency and lowered emission levels (for example, grants for loft insulation), and the rate of UK greenhouse emissions was actually rising before the recession put something of a damper on it.[26]

Environment and population   The connection between population size, density and growth and environmental deterioration is still by no means universally acknowledged. In the run-up to the 1992 World Conference on Environment and Development held at Rio de Janeiro, environmentalists as well as feminists, and even environmentally-concerned feminists showed themselves divided or hesitant on the matter. Oxfam, among the most respected of the international aid

---

25) Arguments that free trade and unrestricted market competition lead to the efficiencies and savings associated with conservation are restricted at best and disingenuous at worst. They do not consider the circumstances, both economic and regulatory, which would make the necessary investments in relatively benign technologies profitable, nor the economic and political power differentials that permit the transfer of pollution to poorer people and parts of the world. See, for example, Jagdish Bhagwati, 'The Case for Free Trade', *Scientific American*, November, 1993; Amory Lovins, 'Energy, People and Industrialization', in K Davis and MS Bernstam, eds, *Resources, Environment and Population*, New York: Oxford University Press, 1991.

26) The announcement in March, 1993, that a 17.5 per cent sales tax would be applied to domestic fuel and lighting on the pretext that it would help reduce emissions is thought by many to be an exercise in cynicism, since the poor, whose incomes go disproportionately on such expenditures already ration themselves. Meanwhile, the government actively tried to encourage the purchase of automobiles by revoking the car tax and building roads, supposedly to stimulate the economy.

agencies, was reluctant to pronounce on population policy at all.[27] The Women's Environmental Network (WEN) devoted one of its information leaflets to discussing the imbalance between rich and poor consumption and inveighing against incentives and disincentives applied to sterilization and contraception. The leaflet concludes, albeit without supporting evidence: 'It is a myth that excess population causes environmental degradation.'[28] The Green Party itself, although, alone among British political parties, it has population policies, has become notably reluctant to talk about them.[29]

The environmentally concerned media are also generally silent on the issue of population. The January/February 1992 issue of the *Ecologist*, devoted to the subject of women and the environment and produced under feminist control, contained not a word about population or contraception. A documentary put out by the producers of the prestigious history series, 'Time Watch', was devoted to debunking the myth that the American Indians were 'the first conservationists'. Nevertheless, as the voiceover mentioned, there were some 30 million bison left when Europeans first invested the plains and shortly thereafter drove the herds to near extinction. In like manner, forests and streams teamed with wildlife and fish under the insouciant predations of the North American Indians. No explanation was given, let alone any mention that the Indian population, after 50,000 years of habitation still amounted to no more than half a million people. Then 'Costing the Earth', a 'green' BBC Radio programme announced the nomination of Lynda Chalker, the Overseas Development Minister, as 'Eco-villain of the Year' on the basis of her wish to increase the British contribution to the UN Population Fund.

The separation of population from other environmental issues was evident at the Rio conference itself, where, in the end, the only legally binding documents to emerge from it were those on climate change and biodiversity. The first was weak in setting standards for curbing

---

27) For example, an Oxfam supplement to the London *Observer*, 7 March, 1993, on 'Poverty' focused on Zambia as a case study of the more general plight of black Africa. Among articles on drought, debt, AIDS, the collapse of the copper market, music and the absence of any form of old age support (including family), there was an occasional passing mention of population growth, but no real discussion of the problem, and no mention of family planning programmes.

28) 'Population: An Ecofeminist Perspective'. No mention was made of child welfare or development, except for the suggestion, under 'What you can do': 'Celebrate children: think about your family as valued members of society who enrich the whole world, not simply as "family property".' Under 'Power for the Poor', however, a much longer statement explained how much economic value even young children can contribute to their families.

29) The 1994 Green Party conference, held two weeks after the Cairo conference, voted down, by a 60 per cent to 40 per cent majority, a proposed resolution backing the 'Programme of Action' which had emerged from the ICPD.

carbon dioxide emission levels. The second, which was supposed to conserve endangered plant and animal species, was twisted by the United States and the United Kingdom into a treaty on the commercial exploitation of living organisms.[30] Population had disappeared from the agenda of the meeting.

POPULATION POLICY AND INDIVIDUAL RIGHTS

The paucity of population discussion at Rio was to some extent rationalized by reference to the Cairo conference that was to follow, where, if any place, the question of population and its connections with environmental issues would presumably be taken up in detail. In the event, the Cairo conference agenda was largely set, not by those concerned with the environmental impact of population, but those obsessed with the moral/religious implications of sexuality; the theme of global economic redistribution, unsuccessfully broached by the developing world in Rio, was even less in evidence.

But even if that had not been the case,the long-running debate between 'population controllers' and 'redistributionists' is still carried on as if each side believes the other argues its cause as the exclusive solution to the problem of sustaining the world's human population. Both sides, however, seem to assume implicitly that nations, ethnic and religious groups, families and even individuals would prefer to reproduce without limit if it were not for economic, political or environmental restraints, and, where these restraints operate, any policy that advocates the slowing, stabilization and decrease of populations must necessarily conflict with the rights of the individual. That this is not the case is a still overlooked implication of the new dimension that has recently come forcefully into the population debate and did become an important part Cairo's hard-fought plan of action: that of gender.

---◇---

30) At the final plenary meeting, two 'optimistic' points were stressed. The first was that at least some agreement had been reached at Rio between North and South, and an extra $2.5 billion had been pledged in aid, out of the $125 billion estimated as necessitated by Agenda 21. Shortly afterwards, severe cuts were made in the British aid budget (£250 million) and the European Community (*Observer*, 27 September, 1992, p 2). The second was a comment that the ozone hole had been announced in 1974, and, a comparatively simple scientific problem, it had taken almost 20 years to:

1) get taken seriously;
2) find the cause and suggest what to do about it (reduce CFC and CO2 emissions); and
3) start to do something about it.

Shortly afterwards, newspapers reported that the ozone layer was thinning faster than predicted and the increased ultraviolet radiation is expected to cut crop yields of such vegetables as peas, barley and oil-seed rape by one-fifth (Paul Brown, *Guardian*, 26 September, 1992, p 7).

Women's rights   The new emphasis on women's rights, in economic and other areas as well as in reproductive matters, is an outgrowth and development of the more general sets of human rights conventions and protocols on which many of the UN agencies and functions are founded. The very concept of 'human rights' is, like 'democracy', sometimes criticized as an attempt to foist western values (or, rather, an idealized version of western values, behind which western countries hypocritically pursue their own interests) upon quite disparate cultures. Others point out that the values of social justice and human dignity may be found and selected from many cultures and religions, just as they are found among other western values with which they may be inconsistent in some contexts. In any case, the application of human rights to women has been one of the most contentious areas among the national signatories to international human rights conventions, and was a cause of contention at Cairo.

The 1948 Universal Declaration of Human Rights holds that 'men and women of full age ... have the right to marry and found a family.' The somewhat vague wording neatly obscures the identification of who should have the overriding right in cases of disagreement: the intention of Article 16 was to keep the prying arm of the law outside the domestic arena. Twenty years later, the Teheran World Conference on Human Rights also declared that 'Parents have a basic human right to decide freely and responsibly on the number and spacing of their children.' But the 1979 Convention for the Elimination of All Forms of Discrimination Against Women (CEDAW) pushed past this point to assert that women's rights do not stop within marriage, and even raised a question mark over such gender-based practices 'justified or condoned on the basis of custom, tradition or religion' as female genital mutilation and wife-battering. In particular, the convention is contravened by laws requiring a woman's husband's consent to her receiving any form of health care, including contraceptive services.[31]

--------------------------------◇--------------------------------

31) For further information on CEDAW, see Rebecca Cook, *Women's Health and Human Rights*, Geneva: World Health Organization, 1994. Signatories and would-be signatories have placed more reservations on those provisions which apply to women's rights within marriage and the family than to any others. As of 1 January, 1994, 130 countries had become party to the Convention, including China and a number of Muslim countries.

CEDAW was signed by the American President Carter in 1980 and transmitted to the Senate for ratification, but not further acted upon until later in 1994. As of 1987, Papua New Guinea, Turkey, Japan, South Korea, Taiwan and Tanzania, among others, barred women from receiving examinations, contraceptives, sterilizations or abortions without husband's consent. In Turkey, the spouse's consent is required for either partner to receive family planning help, but in most cases it is only the husband's consent that is at issue. A survey of health officials from 10 African countries and Haiti in 1985 found that in eight of them

FEMINISM AND FAMILY PLANNING

The dire consequences of the denial of women's reproductive rights have been starkly revealed in the results of Ceaucescu's coercive population policy in Romania. In 1966, the regime suddenly declared abortion and family planning illegal, and the birth rate almost doubled in one year. Women found themselves without any of the resources necessary to cope with the increase (even nappies and baby carriages were in short supply), and desperately turned to illegal abortion in large numbers. Thereafter, birth rates began to decline, but maternal mortality rates more than doubled, with 85 per cent of the increase attributable to abortion. Although in theory they had to submit to checks every three months to ensure that they were not using birth control, in practice many women managed to avoid all gynaecological examinations, so that Romania now has the highest rate of cervical cancer mortality in Europe. In the year following the contraceptive ban, infant mortality rates also increased by one-third, largely as a consequence of the abandonment or neglect of unwanted babies. Surviving infants also suffered. As Naila Kabeer observed:

> The other tragic casualties of the policy were the thousands of children placed in institutional care. Most of them came from the economically most vulnerable subgroups: gypsies, young, unmarried or single mothers; the physically and mentally ill. In other words, it appeared that poverty conditions in combination with large family sizes were the key factors associated with the institutionalization of children. A study conducted by Unicef and the Romanian government comments on the human tragedy of the unwanted child ... abandonment, child abuse and neglect, failure to thrive, depression and mental illness in later life, maternal feelings of incompetence, postpartum depression and development delay.[32]

———————————————◇———————————————

cont.

husband's consent was required for sterilization, but not vice versa. Ethiopia, where clinics had been turning away 16 per cent of women who requested contraception, removed this requirement in 1982; clinic utilization then increased by 26 per cent. It has been estimated that if all the women in subSaharan Africa who stated they want no more children were supplied with effective contraception, between 5 and 18 per cent of maternal deaths could be prevented. Thus, it has been argued that requiring spousal consent jeopardizes a woman's right to life. Spousal authorization requirements may exist as well in ministry of health regulations and clinic guidelines even where not in domestic law – in Nigeria, for example. Interestingly, a survey found 79 per cent of doctors in the US required wife's consent to vasectomies and 50 per cent required husband's consent to tubectomies. See Rebecca Cook and Deborah Maine, 'Spousal Veto over Family Planning Services', *American Journal of Public Health*, 1987, vol 77, pp 339–44.

32) Naila Kabeer, *Reversed Realities: Gender Hierarchies in Development Thought*, London: Verso, 1994, pp 196–7. Not even mentioned in Kabeer's list is the AIDS epidemic that later

So far, however, only opponents of abortion who consider that to be born is always a benefit and conservatives who maintain the superiority of the two-parent family have asserted that children themselves have rights in the circumstances of their procreation.[33] But even these are 'rights' which adults articulate on behalf of children, and, so far, little attention has been drawn to the children's rights implications of evidence that small and single-child families are beneficial to child welfare and development.

All such considerations can safely be left in the hands of women, according to several of the 'Fundamental ethical principles' issued under the title 'Women's Voices '94 – A Declaration on Population Policies' by the group of women's health advocates who met to lay the groundwork for the representation of women's interests in the 1994 Cairo conference:

> Women can and do make responsible decisions for themselves, their families, their communities, and, increasingly, for the state of the world .... Women have the individual right and social responsibility to decide whether, how and when to have children and how many to have; no woman can be compelled to bear a child or be prevented from doing so against her will .... The fundamental sexual and reproductive rights of women cannot be subordinated, against a woman's will, to the interests of partners, family members, ethnic groups, religious institutions, health providers, researchers, policy makers, the state or any other actors.[34]

This is a Utopian vision, which is still very far from the actual circumstances of most of the world's women. How is it to come about unless women's groups themselves make efforts to define 'social responsibility' and the benefits and drawbacks of childbearing for women, their children, their communities and 'the state of the world'?

The development of the principles of women's reproductive rights has been driven by the resurgence of the women's movement of the

---

cont.

    appeared in the institutionalized children as a result of transfusions with contaminated blood.

33) Indeed, David Heyd (in *Genethics*, Berkeley: University of California Press, 1992) argues that only those already born (or certain to be born) have rights; Heyd and others have developed into a 'generocentric' theory which assigns absolute rights over the (particular) unborn or unconceived child to its prospective parents. Nevertheless, since it is certain that *some* people will be born, there can be a generalized responsibility to save a liveable environment for future generations.

34) Documents, *Population and Development Review*, September, 1993, pp 638–9.

past decades. However, it is a long way from resolutions at international conferences to implementation in families. By the time the abstract resolutions on reproductive freedom become concrete and the technology of reproductive health becomes available, the pressure of the familiar old social and familial power structures may cruelly twist that freedom. Given freedom to abort, for example, should women be legally permitted selectively to abort their female foetuses? For feminists to accept this practice is to collude in the devaluing of girl children, but to prohibit it is to condemn many girls to lives of neglect and disdain within their own families, as well as to foresee large numbers of illegal and unsafe abortions. In campaigning for the prohibition of prenatal sex determination, moreover, many feminist groups violate their own principles of unfettered freedom for women's decisions.

Another inconsistency is that the demand for the availability of safe, cheap and convenient contraceptives and abortion is frequently coupled, not only with critiques of current methods, but with condemnation of the research and clinical trials necessary for the development of improved techniques and devices.[35] And, more generally, despite declarations of support for untrammelled female procreative decision-making, assumptions about the unquestioned and unquestionable nature of the desire to bear children are as entrenched in feminist discourse as anywhere else. For example, policies to encourage reproduction employed by some governments, in the form of child benefits, family allowances or privileged access to housing, have not received the opprobrium allotted to family planning programmes. In fact, some feminist organizations and individuals express views about motherhood and reproduction in terms even more romantic and antitechnological than those of spokesmen for the Catholic Church.[36]

---

35) The often-cited 1993 'Comilla Declaration' (issued by a conference of 65 women representing women's groups in 24 countries) advocates access to 'safe contraception and legal abortion' but also 'no to amniocentesis; no to sex predetermination; no to embryo biopsy and IVF', as well as condemning injectable contraceptives, hormonal implants, vaccines and RU-486.

36) FINRRAGE (Feminist International Network for Resistance to Reproductive and Genetic Engineering) takes a hostile position to every form of reproductive technology, including contraceptives and IVF, which are termed 'man-made' and juxtaposed against all that is female and 'natural'. In the words of one member, contraceptive technologies 'mutilate the human body, interfere with the biological processes, and build barriers with the reproductive organs, disrupting bodily functions' (Farida Akhter, 'The State of Contraceptive Technology in Bangladesh', *Issues in Reproductive and Genetic Engineering*, vol 1, no 2, 1988, p 153). To the argument that contraceptives, for all their side-effects, are safer than the perils of pregnancy and childbirth Betsy Hartmann and Hilary Standing respond that this stance penalizes the poor for their poverty (*The Poverty of Population Control*, London: Bangladesh International Action Group, 1989). The Marxist–feminist position that

Contraception in a man's world   The implementation of governmental birth control policies inevitably raises questions not only over the nature of the incentives and disincentives with which contraceptive methods and services are offered, but over the possibility of gender bias inherent in programmes planned and executed in male-dominant societies. This situation often leaves feminists inveighing against the government or the policies rather than against male dominance itself.[37]

Despite the greater ease and simplicity of vasectomies, the vast majority of sterilization operations performed in underdeveloped countries are on women, in an overall preponderance of approximately three to one. The issue of men's rights and responsibilities in procreation is occasionally discussed but never really clarified with respect to:

1)   the still generally predominant male power both within and outside of marriage, leaving women at a disadvantage in negotiating childbearing decisions;
2)   the general male disinclination to employ male methods of contraception such as vasectomy, condoms and coitus inter-ruptus; and
3)   the substantial evidence from many parts of the world of interest on the part of women in methods of contraception that could be concealed from male partners. (Should women be encouraged to deceive men over whether they are practising contraception, for example, by feigning headaches to avoid intercourse during their fertile periods, as some 'rhythm method' instructors advocate?)

The classic battles over women's reproductive rights have been over the right not to bear children when it did not suit them, and this should certainly be an absolute right. This right has still to be attained by a very large proportion of the world's female population, and is still occasionally under threat even where it has been legally accepted.

———————————————◇———————————————

cont.

motherhood should be considered an invaluable social contribution and recompensed accordingly was argued by Nicky Hart ('Procreation' *Contention*, Fall, 1991 and Winter, 1992) among others.

37)   For example, Zarina Geloo ('The darker side of choice', *ICPD Watch*, 8 September, 1994, p 3) reported on a public hearing of 'Crimes Against Women Related to Population Policies' conducted by Asian Women's Human Right Council (AWHRC) and UBINIG (Policy Research for Alternative Development, a radical feminist group). The article related the sad story of Bangladeshi villager who had a son and daughter and was then persuaded to be sterilized in exchange for wheat and money to build a house. Her husband was eventually persuaded to agree. There was no follow-up, she wasn't given the money and wheat coupons, is now often ill and always too weak to work. Her husband and his family have spurned her. She says she made a mistake. The women's groups blamed, not the medical workers, the programme administrator, the husband or his family, but the policy itself.

Moreover, an estimated half-million women now die each year from pregnancy-related causes, about one-third as a result of unsafe abortions. But, as the Women's Voices declaration implicitly acknowledges, childbearing cannot be considered an activity which affects only women, their rights and interests. The production of a child inevitably involves both a social dimension, relating it to its wider family and religious and national group, and, on the other hand, to the child's individual rights, separate from and sometimes possibly in conflict with those of its mother. Education in the benefits of lower fertility on all these counts should be included in the feminist and women's health agendas. In any case, there is evidence that lower fertility is welcome to women themselves, and that coerced childbearing, whether due to rape, to state laws against sterilization and abortion, to spousal veto over family planning services, to social and religious harassment, or to the inaccessibility of contraceptives, is more common than coerced birth control about which far more is heard.

FALLING FERTILITY

Despite continuing and even increasing inequality, death rates, including those of infants and children, have dropped and continue to drop in many parts of the world, and birth rates have already begun to follow suit. In Thailand, for example, fertility fell from 4.6 children per woman in 1975 to 2.3 in 1987; in Colombia, from 4.7 in 1976 to 2.8 in 1990; in Mexico, from over 6 in 1977 to 4 in 1987. In other countries the downward drift has been slower. In India, after 40 years of family planning programmes, the total fertility rate has dropped from slightly over 6 to 4 children per woman. But even in Africa, which for a long time seemed resistant to all attempts to lower the birth rates, and where women expressed wishes for the largest numbers of children, fertility has declined 26 per cent in Botswana, 35 per cent in Kenya, and 18 per cent in Zimbabwe.[38] Moreover, there is evidence of large still unmet demands for contraception. And all this has taken place in places where infant mortality is still five or more times what it now is in developed countries. Thus, the 'demographic transition' now taking place is unlike that experienced by the industrialized countries earlier in the century: it appears to be happening more rapidly and happening even without industrialization.

---

38) Fertility figures from Bryant Robey, Shea O Rutstein and Leo Morris, 'The Fertility Decline in Developing Countries', *Scientific American*, December, 1993, pp 31–7, except for India, which is discussed at length in Chapter 6.

The reasons for the accelerated pace of the demographic transition in developing countries have been a matter of speculation. The causes appear to be multiple, but, in addition to greater child survival, the factors often suggested include later marriage, better female education, and greater access to modern contraceptives and abortion services. All these factors are not only associated with each other, as well as with female earning power, but they are also associated with marriage to better educated men, who are likely to want fewer children, too.[39] Other observers, like John Caldwell, credit the modelling effect of western society working through 'improved communications'.[40] In his view, western values have been imposed upon or voluntarily adopted by other societies through such institutions as the UN, Christian missionaries and, with increasing importance, television. Along with ideas about desirable material possessions, diet and cultural productions, people all over the world have concluded that western-style prosperity may follow rather than precede western-sized families.

Some support for this reasoning emerges from an analysis of the 1981 census data in the south Indian state of Tamil Nadu which found fertility related more closely to lower child mortality and the accessibility of roads than to female literacy or affluence. Poverty was actually associated with fewer, not more children.[41] The author concluded that the opportunity for women to earn money by travelling to urban areas, and the rise of educational aspirations were more effective in lowering the desired family size than female literacy.

The extent to which a falling birth rate might reflect the preferences of women, coupled with increased power to exercise those preferences, rather than family or marital decisions, has caused some unease among governments and politicians who cannot manipulate female choices. The collapse of birth rates in eastern Europe following the collapse of welfare and job security there can be attributed to a 'birth strike' among hard-pressed women who refuse to bear and raise children under conditions of increased economic hardship. On the other hand, the sinking fertility rate in prosperous

39) See, for example, Thomas E Dow, Linda Archer, Shanyisa Khasiani and John Kekovole, 'Wealth Flow and Fertility Decline in Rural Kenya, 1981–92', *Population and Development Review*, June, 1994, pp 343–64.

40) John Caldwell, *Theory of Fertility Decline*, London: Academic Press, 1982, p 221.

41) R Savitri, 'Fertility Rate Decline in Tamil Nadu', *Economic and Political Weekly*, 16 July, 1994, pp 1850–2.

Japan is blamed on finicky feminine distaste for the social and housing arrangements that prevail there.[42]

What worries women's groups and other redistributionists, however, is that falling birth rates are considered evidence that contraception, rather than the relief of poverty, is the best contraceptive, which may be used to undermine the most effective argument in favour of the rich contributing to the relief of poverty in the countries from which they have profited so handsomely.[43] They fear that, since claims of justice and morality have been all too ineffective in the past, it would now be all too easy for the richer nations to conclude that any threat that growing populations may have posed to the sustainability of the world economy has now been averted, and to pursue business as usual.

IDEOLOGY AND POPULATION MEET

At the 1994 Cairo Population Conference, the confluence and conflicts of all the ideologies regarding sex, gender, population and development which had been gathering pace over the preceding 20 years put in yet another appearance. According to the draft programme of action, the conference was supposed to cover: the relationship between population, sustained economic growth and sustainable development; gender equality, equity and the empower-ment of women; the family; population growth and structure; reproductive rights, sexual and reproductive health; health, mortality and morbidity; population distribution, urbanization and internal migration; international migration; technology, and so forth – the entire range of topics implied by its title. In the event, however, the 'development' part of the conference title received relatively short shrift. In what was coming to be time-honoured fashion for UN World conferences, that part of the agenda – in particular a proposal that in future aid programmes, donor countries earmark 20 per cent of

42) Suvendrini Kakuchi, 'Japanese women want even fewer children', *Terra Viva*, Cairo, 8 September, 1994, p 12. The government predicts that last year's TFR of 1.8 will slide to 1.5 by the year 2000, leaving Japan with the largest ageing population in the world. The government has been trying to balance the situation through financial incentives and campaigns for more babies, but family planning experts say Japanese women will not give in: '… they feel the situation in Japan is not conducive to having big families.' Kyoko Ikegami (programme officer at the Japan International Family Planning Federation) says, 'Japan has empowered its women to decide whether or not to have children. But it has failed to give them rights such as better housing and working conditions which are the ultimate goals of population control.'

43) See Bryant Robey, Shea O Rutstein and Leo Morris, 'The Fertility Decline in Developing Countries', *Scientific American*, December, 1993, pp 30-7.

development aid for social programmes and developing countries set aside 20 per cent of their national budgets for such programmes – was postponed for consideration at yet another conference.[44]

The parts of the conference that caught world attention were less practical and more ideological in nature: clashes between feminist groups demanding reproductive rights and the religious right represented by various anti-abortion groups, the Holy See and some Islamists.In the weeks leading up to the conference it seemed as if the latter two had made common cause, but in the end it was obvious their preoccupations were quite different and reflected the differences in both their theological stances and political aims. On the Muslim side, points were made by denouncing the meeting. Four countries (Saudi Arabia, Lebanon, Iraq and Sudan) boycotted the conference altogether and two female prime ministers also stayed away, clearly from domestic political considerations; as women in positions where many religious fundamentalists claim women ought not to be, they found it prudent not to inflame further their difficulties by attending so controversial an event. The Prime Minister of Pakistan came but complained about the western bias in the draft statement that was supposed to emerge from the conference.

What really concerned the Islamists was the prospect of sex education for adolescent girls, and any language that might condone homosexuality. It was not reproductive control *per se* so much as any perceived threat to control over women and sexuality.[45] The Vatican

---

44) Jaya Dayal ('Cash crunch may bankrupt Cairo goals', *Terra Viva*, 9 September, 1994, p 1) reported that the 20/20 initiative was put off for consideration at the Copenhagen World Summit for Social Development in March, 1995 because of disagreements. There was more hope for the $17-billion-by-the-year-2000 goal for the funding of family planning programmes because it is more modest, and also more modest than the Agenda 21 target of $125 billion for environmental aid and development announced at the Rio conference. Moreover, it was supposed to come from a reallocation of existing money. The old 0.7 per cent of GDP which donor countries were supposed to contribute in aid, re-endorsed at Rio, had been ignored by all industrialized countries except Denmark, Norway, Sweden and the Netherlands. (Actually, the Women's Caucus have called the $17 billion into question as not being enough.)

45) In the end, it was the Islamic group that revealed itself both less monolithic and more flexible than the Vatican. Anita Anand, for example, reports ('The Pundits of Population', *ICPD Watch*, 6 September, 1994, p 1) that in Indonesia, the Ulema (religious scholars) were consulted in setting up the national family planning programme. At first they said that IUDs, vasectomy and tubectomy should not be used, as they were not certain if religion permitted such devices. Later they decided IUDs were acceptable if a female worker inserted them; then, as there were not enough female doctors, males were permitted to do insertions as long as the husband or another woman was present. A 1992 study by Abdel Omran, according to the Washington-based Population Reference Bureau, cites a number of justifications and restrictions for using contraceptives under 'Islamic theology'. Among the former are: protection of the mother's life and health; protection of children; 'avoiding embarrassment of having too many children'; 'to safeguard the wife's beauty and to keep her fit and in good form'. Restrictions include: permission of the spouse; the unacceptability of such motives as avoiding female children or 'shirking the maternal

representatives, however, focused their concern on abortion, not so much the prevalence of the actual practice of abortion – often more common in countries where it is forbidden than in some, such as Holland and Scandinavia, where it is not – as any possible implication that it was not condemned.[46]

It remains to be seen whether the results of this conference will be any more fruitful in human justice – as compared to gestures made with an eye on domestic politics – than those of previous world conferences have been.

POPULATION AND POLITICS, CHILDREN AND WOMEN

Given the rejection of any prospect of consumption reduction in the cause of environmental conservation by the élites and electorates of rich and poor countries, and the rejection of birth limiting policies by the governments of wealthy countries (for themselves), and by women's and other political groupings, and the overriding preoccupations of religious leaders with sexual and behavioural control, there still remain many reasons for supporting and encouraging the world-wide drift toward lower birth rates that is already taking place. The rest of this book is devoted to examining them by looking at a number of common beliefs about the nature and consequences of small families, on both national and personal levels, and the progress and problems of birth limiting policies,

The following chapters will take up and expand many of the points raised here in several different contexts. First of all, the over-whelmingly biased, non-neutral environment in which most women must make their reproductive decisions, in rich as well as poor countries, will be examined with respect to religious dogma, demographic competition, medical technology and parental power in law and custom. Chapter 3 then looks at children as economic assets, and the two following look at social attitudes, first from a consideration of the voluntarily childless and then of the single child family. In the final part, I look at the population policies in both North

---◇---

cont.

role' (*Terra Viva*, 6 September, 1994, p 10). There was also considerable disagreement among the Islamic delegations regarding the legality of abortion.

46) Another instance of doctrinaire disapproval of abortion with paradoxical implications is the recent refusal of a Catholic boys' public school in the UK to inject its pupils with a rubella vaccine developed on tissue taken from a foetus aborted for medical reasons in 1966. Rubella in pregnant women can cause foetal abnormalities – which can lead to more abortions. Use of the vaccine has already reduced the yearly toll of rubella-related abortions from 738 in 1971 to 10 in 1990 in the UK. Acknowledging this, the school authorities advised that parents of girls should have them vaccinated.

and South, first by studying the birth restricting policies of the most populous countries, India (Chapter 6) and China (Chapter 8), and the special cases that Kerala (Chapter 7) and Tibet (Chapter 9) constitute within them. Each of these four case studies, in addition to the generalities they exemplify and their specific conditions and histories, has received attention for a particular controversy that is of more general and increasing interest elsewhere as well. In China, it is the concern of its own government as well as that of outside observers with an increasingly distorted ratio of male to female children; in India, it is the long-running battle of feminists and radicals over the issue of contraceptive research, development and trials; in Kerala, the vexed question of fertility decline without economic development; and finally, in Tibet, the use of population policy in a nationalist movement. In Chapter 10, I look at the restrictive population policies of the developed countries, which are applied to immigration alone. The final chapter is an attempt to draw out explicitly the policy implications of the preceding arguments.

PART II
Pronatalism

Chapter 2

Background noises: ideology in religion, culture and nature

Over twenty years ago, Judith Blake published an essay which considered the components of 'voluntarism' and 'coercion' in childbearing as continua rather than an opposed pair. She pointed out that the 'free choices' that were then being made took place in what was in many societies a heavily pronatalist environment: 'People make their "voluntary" reproductive choices in an institutional context that severely constrains them not to choose non-marriage, not to choose childlessness, not to choose only one child, and even not to limit themselves solely to two children.'[1] Interestingly enough, the first two conditions apply even in so supposedly antinatal an 'institutional context' as that of China's one-child policy, which sternly enjoins marriage and birth of an heir as a guarantee of social stability and financial security.

But what are the 'institutions' that constrain free choice in a pronatal direction? The social institutions, including religion, 'ethnic' identity, the law, the media and medicine, whose influences are brought to bear on individuals and significant others in forming reproductive attitudes and decisions, are the subject matter of this chapter. The next chapter will explore the questions raised by children viewed as economic assets and address procreation from the

---

1) 'Judith Blake on Fertility Control and the Problem of Voluntarism', Archives, *Population and Development Review*, March, 1994, p 168.

child's side. The remaining two chapters in Part II of this book look at
families and individuals who seem to defy the pronatalist norm: those
with one child or none.

SCRIPTURAL INJUNCTIONS AND RELIGIOUS INDUCEMENTS

Every religious movement is also a political movement, and given
that birth constitutes the major form of religious recruitment, it is not at
all surprising that the *dirigiste* wings of all the world religions, those
whose concerns cover the most minute details of human behaviour,
unite in encouraging large families through both social and doctrinal
means. Although the views of the current head of the Roman Catholic
church spring readily to mind, he is not alone in opposing abortion
and birth control or giving general encouragement to large families.
Leaders of fundamentalist Jewish and Protestant groups, such as the
Mormons, the Hutterites, the Hasidic and Orthodox Jewry also
encourage many children among their followers, and often lead them
to believe that abortion or even deliberate family limitation is against
God's will, as do 'fundamentalist' Hindu and Muslim sects.[2]

Since every religion considers the spheres of ethics and morality as
peculiarly within its own authority, and since the area of sexual
behaviour is taken in both religious and common parlance as
specially subject to moral considerations, it is not surprising that
representatives of almost every religion have commented extensively
on every aspect of reproduction, not just for centuries, but for
millennia. Yet the current positions of spokespeople for the major
religions have developed out of very different historical climates and
scriptural stances.

Islamic tradition, for example, recounts the Prophet's explicit
acceptance of the practice of contraception in *hadith*, which is a body
of lore that has grown up to supplement the words of the Quran and
contains several references to *'azl*, a birth control technique identified
with coitus interruptus.[3] Many religious and legal authorities have built

---

2)   Although it originated as an appellation of Protestant sects that insisted on the literal truth
     of every word in the Bible, the word 'fundamentalist' will be used here in the current sense
     of denoting religious ideologies characterized by social conservatism, unshakable
     certainty regarding the roles of women and the will of God, and a general view
     of other belief systems as lacking in truth and morality. Although there are many shades of
     opinion among Roman Catholics, Catholicism is unusual among mainstream religions in
     that its highest conceded authority can be considered 'fundamentalist' in this sense.

3)   For example, 'Jabir said, "We used to resort to *'azl* in the time of the Prophet, and the
     Quran was then being revealed"' (al-Bukhari, *al-Sahih* [the major collection of *hadith*
     reports], 67 p 97).

upon and extended this basic acceptance of birth control during the succeeding centuries.[4] Within the past 20 years, the proceedings of Islamic conferences have repeatedly reiterated it, and the Ministry of Health of the Gambia has even co-sponsored an 'Imam project' to change the minds of local religious leaders who attempt to convince their followers that contraception is unhallowed.[5] The recommendations of the Arab Population Conference, which took place in Amman, Jordan in April, 1993, urged that population policies should be formulated with regard both to development and to the effect on the environment, saying 'the welfare of the present generations should not be based on additional economic and environmental loans to be repaid by future generations'. Sections on 'Women, population and development' and 'Maternal and child health and family planning' were formulated in feminist terms, urging 'the participation of women in public life at all levels, including decision making', 'acceptance of the question of family planning, in its broad sense, as a right of couples' and that '[t]he reproductive role of women should in no way be used as a reason for limiting women's right to work, education and participation in public life'.[6]

This is not to imply that the acceptance of contraception by Islam was formulated in circumstances that were anything other than patriarchal, or that male-dominant assumptions have not continued to influence even 'moderate' Muslim attitudes. Contraceptive practice was discussed by the revered 9th century historian al-Waqidi as follows: 'Abu Said al-Khudri said: We got female captives among the war booty. We were lusting after women and chastity had become too hard for us, but we wished to get the ransom for our prisoners [which could not be done if they were impregnated by their captors]. So we wanted to use the '*azl*. We asked the Prophet about it and he said, "You are not under any obligation to forbear from that." '[7]

———————————————◇———————————————

4)   See BF Musallam, *Sex and Society in Islam: Birth Control Before the Nineteenth Century*, Cambridge: Cambridge University Press, 1983.

5)   The 'Imam project' is also sponsored by Save the Children and the Population Council. See Caroline H Bledsoe, Allan G Hill, Umberto D'Alessandro and Patricia Langerock, 'Constructing Natural Fertility: The Use of Western Contraceptive Technologies in Rural Gambia', *Population and Development Review*, March, 1994, p 90.

6)   'Recommendations of the Arab Population Conference', *Population and Development Review*, September, 1993, pp 641 and 644. See also *Islam and Family Planning: A faithful translation of the Arabic edition of the proceedings of the International Islamic Conference held in Rabat (Morocco), December, 1971, vol II, Parts 3, 4, 5*, Beirut: IPPF, 1974, which contains many documents, including *fatwas* as well as discussions of the papers and of the draft report of the conference. There is also a listing of the *hadith* used in the discussions and papers. The general opinion of the participants was that contraception is clearly allowed for reasons of health, less so for social reasons (because of the implied doubt that God would provide). Sterilization was considered less acceptable than contraception and abortion was permitted within the first 120 days.

7)   Cited in Maxime Rodinson, *Muhammad*, New York: Pantheon, 1971, p 197.

This anecdote seems to pit the relaxed Islamic attitude to the use of contraceptives against the stricter prohibitions of Christianity and Judaism. But it is in Judaism, perhaps of all the world religions, that the theological position is most curious and paradoxical. It begins, of course, with the Biblical injunction: 'Be fruitful and multiply and fill the Earth and subdue it',[8] seemingly addressed to both Adam and Eve. Yet *halakha*, the religious law developed by generations of rabbis to explicate and supplement the written law contained in the books of Moses, holds otherwise. The Mishnah, a handbook of the law prepared under the supervision of Rabbi Judah the Prince about AD 200 and held to be the most authoritative of such compendia, states: 'A man is commanded concerning the duty of propagation but not a woman.'

Justifying this ruling requires a great deal of rabbinical discussion in the Talmud, the repository of oral law compiled between the 3rd and 6th centuries, where it is, as usual, embellished by apposite anecdote: 'Judith, the wife of Rabbi Hiyyah, suffered agonizing pains in childbirth. On recovery, she disguised herself and appeared before her husband to ask, "Is a woman commanded to propagate the race?" "No," he replied, and, relying on this decision, she drank a sterilizing potion.'[9]

Subsequent Jewish writings have built on these early rabbinical opinions right down to modern times. The reasoning which permits contraception to the woman is no less patriarchal than the Islamic tradition that permitted it to the male, for the rabbis argued: 'Scripture states, "Replenish the earth and subdue it"; it is the nature of man to subdue, but it is not the nature of woman to subdue.'[10] Abortion is now also held acceptable in Judaism for reasons of the life or health (or even the mental health!) of the mother or for foetal indications, but it was Biblically considered more a property crime against the

---

8)   Genesis 1:28.
9)   Babylonian Talmud, Yevamot 65b.
10)   David M Feldman (*Marital Relations, Birth Control and Abortion in Jewish Law*, New York: Shocken Books, 1974) includes rabbinical writings from ancient times to modern, all employing the same pattern of argument. He says the question of the inclusion of women in 'Increase and multiply' is answered in the negative 'for our purposes': 'It is interpreted to apply to one whose business it is to subdue rather than to be subdued.' Among modern writers, the former British Chief Rabbi, Lord Jacobovitz, 'advances the homiletic suggestion that the command need not be addressed to woman because her instinct for childbirth is already strong enough.' Not neglecting the more usual religious concerns for women, another writer felt that if the commandment were put to the woman to fulfil, 'it might inspire a kind of well-motivated promiscuity' (pp 53–4). For a rare and lucid feminist discussion of the same body of writings, see Rachel Biale, *Women and Jewish Law*, New York: Schocken Books, 1984. Biale points out, for example, that despite the Old Testament's thunderous strictures against male homosexuality, the writers seem as oblivious to the existence of lesbians as Queen Victoria was.

prospective father than a crime against the prospective child or its mother.[11]

The current pronatal stance of many Jewish leaders is based less upon scriptural prohibition of birth control measures than upon the recent history of traumatic loss of one-third of the world's Jewry, including most of that of eastern Europe, in the Nazi Holocaust. Summoning the memory of the Holocaust, many Jews all over the world see a duty to replace the numbers murdered by the Nazis as something of a posthumous victory over Hitler.

The involvement of Christianity with natality has a history that is even more convoluted. Originating in a climate in which many people expected the imminent end of the world, and reproduction seemed almost an irrelevance, Christian doctrine was formulated against the background of Jewish, Gnostic and pagan attitudes to sex, marriage and procreation, from which it was felt necessary to differentiate the new religion and resist their insidious influences. Christianity, though it viewed virginity as a superior state, therefore sought to justify marriage as an institution whose sole 'good' was the production of children, in contrast to Gnostic doctrine which viewed procreation as an evil that trapped the soul in the flesh.[12]

After early Christian expectations of an impending 'Redemption' died out, it was sometimes argued that procreation was good because it multiplied souls and (provided the children were baptized) increased the population of paradise, and repaired the shortfall occasioned by the fallen angels' long fall. Other writers stressed the virtues of virginity and the welfare of children, arguing against the production of numbers *per se*. In fact, from time to time fears about overpopulating the earth came to be expressed, even by revered church fathers. Thus many of the population arguments heard today have ancient pedigrees.

---

11) The Biblical text from which discussions of abortion generally start is Exodus 21:22. 'If, when men come to blows, they hurt a woman who is pregnant and she suffers a miscarriage, though she does not die of it, the man responsible must pay the compensation demanded of him by the woman's master.' The issue of elective abortion is first taken up in the Mishnah.

12) Nevertheless, celibacy, even within marriage, was approved. See John T Noonan, *Contraception: A history of its treatment by the Catholic theologians and canonists*, Cambridge, Mass: Harvard University Press, 1965, for an extraordinarily detailed treatment of the subject, limited by its publication date. It is amusing to read that the Romans attributed to the Christians what the Christians attributed to Gnostics: hypocritically advocating sexual abstinence while actually running riot with the help of birth control.

CHRISTIANITY AND CONTRACEPTION

Contraception was condemned throughout the middle ages as a 'sin against nature'. Such sins were held worse than adultery, seduction or rape, because while the latter were sins against reason, which proceeded from men, nature proceeded from God, and sins against nature offended God. Curiously enough, contraception was often considered worse than abortion, at least before quickening (the first movements of the foetus to be felt by the mother), because it was a peculiarly female practice, frequently involving the charms, spells and potions often equated with witchcraft. Consequently, according to John Riddle, contraceptive knowledge remained folklore and passed mainly by word of mouth. Christian disapproval meant that a good deal of ancient knowledge was lost as Europe became more completely Christianized, in contrast to the Islamic world, whose writings preserved many ancient Greek recipes. The inferiority of Renaissance contraceptive knowledge is also attributable to the campaign against witches. He points out that many of the accusations against witches had to do with fertility: they were accused of causing sterility, stillbirths, miscarriages and impotence.[13]

Riddle's work challenges the common belief that effective contraception began in the 18th century, and claims that even in the more distant past, family size and population were regulated less by famine, war and pestilence than by social norms. For example, he points out that population began to decrease in the 14th century before the impact of the black death appeared. He includes discussions of pessaries, as well as coitus interruptus, 'safe period' and infanticide, but claims that oral contraceptives were more popular and more effective than previously believed. For the purposes of current controversies, perhaps the two most important inferences to be drawn from his work on the chemical effects of folk medicine are:

1) the impossibility of drawing a clear-cut distinction between drugs and devices that are 'contraceptive' and those that are 'abortifacient' in their effects; and
2) objections to hormonal and chemical contraceptive research and implementation often ignore the popular use of substances, both in the past and present, which are also hormonal in their effect.

The 'sterile period' was spoken of by the Greeks and by the 2nd century Roman gynaecologist, Soranos. However, they thought the fertile period was right after the menses, not between them. The real

---

13) John M Riddle, *Contraception and Abortion from the Ancient World to the Renaissance*, Cambridge, Mass: Harvard University Press, 1992.

sterile period was not pinpointed until 1923. Prior to the mid-19th century, only abstinence was approved by the Catholic church as a method of birth control. At that point, 'sterile period' intercourse was declared licit, even though St Augustine had once denounced it. However, it remained more or less in limbo, tolerated but not recommended until 1951, when Pius XII gave it positive approval and even expressed the hope that science would render it more reliable. This step was a liberalization over his predecessor, Pius XI, who had been stung by the half-hearted acceptance of birth control by the Lambeth conference of 1930 into promulgating the encyclical *Casti Connubii*, which denounced attempts at family planning and advocated large families. The position of the current Pope is to advocate 'responsible parenthood' by periodic or sustained abstinence.

Much of the discussion of early scriptural views of contraception and abortion may seem to be of a rather recondite nature, if it were not the case that time and time again recent disputants have harked back to 'first principles' to strengthen their arguments. For example, in 1992 Malcolm Potts took issue with the Catholic ruling that the soul enters the body at conception by pointing out that in the case of identical twins, the division of the embryo into two individuals may not occur until three weeks after conception. Hence, he argued, if each twin is to possess an individual soul, 'ensoulment' cannot happen until then.[14] While early Protestant leaders, such as Luther and Calvin, modified the Catholic stand toward usury but did not relax prohibitions on contraception, birth control among most Protestant denominations has come to be considered a matter of individual conscience.

DEMOGRAPHIC COMPETITION

In November, 1991, the Pope addressed an international conference on resources and population expressing his concern about 'the relationship between the accelerated increase in world population and the availability of natural resources'. He was, until recently, said to be the leader of some four or five hundred million Catholics. More recently, the number has been quoted as eight to nine hundred million. Yet, still eager to enlarge his flock, in a letter to Archbishop Vinko Puljik of Sarajevo, concerning several hundred Croatian women who were raped and impregnated by non-Catholics,

---

14) Malcolm Potts, 'Abortion: a beneficial choice', *The World and I*, May, 1992, p 533.

he recommended that the women ' "accept the enemy" into them, and to make him "the flesh of their own flesh" '.[15] In other words, have the children and raise them as Catholics.

The war in former Yugoslavia is among the most violent of the current instances of demographic competition, where the contending groups are identified by nationality, and where nationality is conflated with religion. As in other violent religious conflicts, rape is an instrument both of injuring the adversary and of denying him recruits, whether or not the rape results in recruitment to the rapists' side. In the Bosnian case, when Muslim women were raped by Christians and impregnated, they were often reported to have been detained until it was too late to obtain an abortion, in the belief that the resulting babies would be stamped by the rapists' religion.

Muslim authorities concurred. The Imam of the Islamic centre in Zagreb's view of the plight of Muslim women in this situation was: ' "We need to change our mentality when confronted by these women and cannot consider them in the light of our ancient customs." '[16] In contrast to the Catholic women, they are permitted to abort rather than bear children whose fathers are not Muslim. In Kosovo, abortion is freely available to (Muslim) Albanian women, but forbidden to the ruling (Orthodox Christian) Serbs.[17] At the same time, under conditions of extreme deprivation and the threat of violence, Croatian women are being exhorted to have more babies.

India affords another current example where religious difference is used as the primary distinction between two groups occupying the same territory and often otherwise difficult to distinguish. The controversy over the site of a mosque in north India has widely publicized this aspect of Hindu fundamentalist politics.[18] Claiming that excessive Muslim fertility will soon reverse Hindu numerical dominance (which now stands at about 85 per cent of the Indian population), in the riots following the destruction of the Ayodhya mosque in December, 1992, Muslim women were raped and mutilated

---

15) E Vulliamy, 'Pope warns raped women on abortion', *Guardian*, 1 March, 1993, p 1.
16) E Vulliamy, ibid.
17) Sheena McDonald, 'The World this Week', Saturday, 21 August, 1993.
18) Compared to traditional Islam and Judaism, which consider the use of contraceptives in social and medical contexts, early Hindu objections to birth avoidance seem to stem directly from pronatal enthusiasm. By the time of the writing of the Dharmashastras (600–300 BC), still taken as the authoritative texts, child marriage – which is only with difficulty being stamped out in the 20th century – was justified by the ruling: 'Let him not keep a daughter in his house after she has reached the age of puberty. He who does not give away a marriageable daughter during three years doubtless contracts the guilt of destroying an embryo.' (Baudhayana, iv, 1, 11–12.) Yet the adoption of contraception by modern Hindus has been almost completely unopposed by religious leaders of this most complex and all-inclusive religious movement.

'so they would no longer bear Muslim babies'. Hindu communalist organizations parody the 'We Two, Our Two' family planning slogan of the Government of India by putting up posters saying, 'We Five, Our 25', depicting a supposedly polygamous Muslim man with his legally permitted four wives: 'By the logic of this demographic argument that ... Muslims multiply in geometrical progression, the Muslims are perceived as a threat to India's population problem and thereby to the country's economic progress.'[19] In fact, the same fears of Muslim numerical competition in adding to what is frankly referred to as its communal 'vote bank' have been expressed among Indian Hindus for several decades.[20]

Encouraging women to procreate as a form of patriotism by demographic competition was prominent in the Nazi programme, but did not stop with the demise of Hitler. Nor is the wish to replenish lost membership as quickly as possible now peculiar to Jewish sensibilities: it occurs as well in the many and increasing numbers of survivors of conflict and massacre in which contending social groups, however they identify themselves, play out their political aspirations. It is an irony of the Jewish situation, however, that the State of Israel now faces a dilemma over its continuing occupation of a large and growing Palestinian population, which it sees as involving a choice between retaining a democratic state or a Jewish state. Israeli population policy, as a consequence, is explicitly driven by the 'demographic race' with the Palestinians, whose leaders often respond in kind.[21] Similarly, Tibetan nationalists, despite their far higher birth rates, claim genocide through birth control is being forced upon them by the Han Chinese majority. In Egypt accusations have been made against Christian doctors who supposedly wish 'to reduce the Muslim population through contraception'.[22] Many Protestants in Northern Ireland, a territorial unit devised originally to ensure a Protestant majority, gloomily foresee the coming of Catholic numerical superiority in the higher Catholic birth rate, and the list

19)   Vibhuti Patel, 'Gender Implications of Communalisation of Socio-political Life of India', unpublished paper, March, 1993.
20)   See, for example, Dharma Kumar, 'The Sex of One's Child', in RF Chadwick, ed., *Ethics, Reproduction and Genetic Control*, London: Routledge, 1987, 1992, p 175.
21)   See Nira Yuval-Davis, 'National Reproduction and "the Demographic Race" in Israel', in Nira Yuval-Davis and Floya Anthias, eds, *Woman–Nation–State*, London: Macmillan, 1989.
22)   D Hirst, 'Nervous Egypt awaits the fundamentalist explosion', *Guardian*, 25 July, 1992. The accusation of attempted 'genocide by birth control' is very frequently made by people who purport to speak for groups with high birth rates and/or large numbers. The charge that population programmes were plots to wipe out Muslims was made at the Cairo conference. More recently, Ruth Chinamano, a Zimbabwean MP, stated that campaigns urging the use of condoms or other contraceptives were a plot to wipe out Africans (*Guardian*, 17 December, 1994, p 10).

goes on through Croatia and Iraq, whose governments urge women to bear children under conditions extremely adverse to the health and well-being of both groups.

Religion is but one way in which ethnic or nationalist groups differentiate themselves in order to engage in a demographic conflict which is at base driven by competition over land or other forms of economic advantage. Demographic competition can occur where groups are marked off from each other by almost any real or imagined characteristic. One example of this is that of the Welsh Nationalists, who have recently launched a campaign to encourage Welsh speakers to '... increase their families up to the limit they could afford – possibly four children – and rear their offspring in a wholly Welsh atmosphere'.[23] At the other end of the scale of demographic competition is the horror of Rwanda, where what was originally more of a class difference has been used to mark for genocide a minority indistinguishable from the majority by race, religion, language or even, despite attempts at stereotype, appearance.

Attempts to increase or maintain the ethnic or national proportion of an increasing world population have also been expressed by governments of the affluent industrialized countries whose native-born fertility rates have, within the last 40 years, all fallen to near or even below replacement. Although, as a whole, this part of the world will contribute about 8 per cent of the planetary growth over the next 30 years, some countries – Sweden and France – have been worrying about depopulation for a long time. Even Japan, overcrowded as it is, has recently calculated anxiously that if things keep up as they are going, there will be only 400 Japanese left in 700 years![24]

There have been more general fears expressed over the impending change in the proportions of European-descended people, yet this change will simply restore the proportions that existed before the industrial revolution,[25] and European governments have been generally unable to implement successful birth-stimulating policies.[26] This has not deterred the government of Singapore from instituting a

---

23) *Guardian*, 15 November, 1990.

24) P McGill, 'Women ordered to lie back and raise workforce', Observer, 24 June, 1990, p 11.

25) See Amartya Sen, 'Population: Delusion and Reality', *The New York Review of Books*, 22 September, 1994, p 63. Sen quotes the combined Asian and African share of world numbers in 1650 as 78 per cent, where it remained for the next hundred years. During the following demographic transition, the European-descended population grew much faster than the rest, and even now is about 29 per cent. At about 2050, when the population of the world will hopefully have stabilized, Asia and Africa are predicted to return to their combined 18th-century share. See also Lincoln H Day, *The Future of Low-Birthrate Populations*, London: Routledge, 1992, p 1.

26) See Paul Demeny, 'Pronatalist Policies in Low Fertility Countries', in K Davis, MS Bernstam, and R Ricardo-Campbell, eds, *Below Replacement Fertility in Industrialized Societies*, Cambridge: Cambridge University Press, 1987.

population policy that attempts to encourage 'educated' women to have more children, while offering inducements for the 'less educated' to be sterilized after bearing no more than two.[27] The rationale for the policy is unashamedly based on work done on IQ and inheritance in the United States and Great Britain and now largely discredited. Moreover, educational opportunities in Singapore seem to be largely a matter of ethnicity, with the result that the policy may be more concerned with increasing the Chinese proportion of the population over the Malay than with increasing its academic bent. In the event, the resentment on the part of 'educated women' caused a rephrasing of the policy to seem to encourage fertility among all, while the incentive for sterilization remained on the books – and had a surprising number of takers.

THE MEDICAL IMPERATIVE

It may strike some as strange to examine the medical profession, supposedly rooted in scientific neutrality, for its contribution to the pervasive pronatal ideology that informs all debates about politics, human welfare and population in any quarter of the world. Yet medical and health considerations have contributed to pronatalism in at least two major ways: the first by understatement, and the second by a kind of hype or overselling of certain technical developments.

Medical qualifications are no more a guarantee of objectivity in social issues than a degree in any other subject, but in many cases the statements of medical workers have been distorted or misused in addition. Perhaps the media, if not reporters then sub-editors, should receive more blame for unbalanced and selective reporting of medical matters than the medical profession. To take one example, an article on the findings of a 'privately-funded commission ... involving 25 prominent anti-abortionists' was captioned 'Abortion on demand seems easy, but, says Lois Rogers, a new study highlights the trauma suffered by the "mothers" '.[28] What the article actually said, however, is that the Royal College of Psychiatrists had objected to the report's claim that 'there is no psychiatric justification for abortion'. Dr Margaret Oates is then quoted as saying, 'What I actually told them is that having an unwanted baby is the biggest tragedy in the world, but you couldn't *guarantee* that a psychiatric condition would deteriorate

27) See CK Chan, 'Genetics on the Rise: A Report from Singapore', in R Chadwick, ed., *Ethics, Reproduction and Genetic Control*, London: Routledge, 1992.

28) Lois Rogers, 'Living with choice', *Sunday Times*, 7 August, 1994.

if a woman didn't get an abortion.' The article then went on to quote several other medical experts who delivered differing statements about the frequency of post-abortion psychiatric sequelae. It was then rounded off with the usual selection of potted case histories. No mention was made of the well-confirmed findings that serious mental illness is far more common after (welcome or unwelcome) childbirth than after abortion.[29]

Moral objections to abortion, as seen above, derive largely from fundamentalist religious dogma, that of Christianity in particular. The abject respect for religion that pervades almost all cultures has succeeded in making most speakers or writers on the topic very defensive. It has not succeeded in changing public support for legalized abortion or in making abortion less frequent, though it has often made it more dangerous. Having lost the legal battle in many countries, anti-abortionists have attempted to reinforce their moral armoury with medical arguments, particularly of a psychological nature. Among the more bizarre attempts to provoke guilt in women seeking abortions has been the use of the unsurprising finding that the foetus may feel pain. This has been said to imply that foetuses are 'human' (as if animals do not feel pain), and that carrying the pregnancy to term would spare it future pain. What is surprising, given the bias displayed by almost all public and professional figures on the subject, is how meagre the results have been, to the point where a number of women have expressed guilt over their lack of guilt.[30] Yet

---

29)	In one of the few studies to compare the aftermaths of abortion and childbirth, R Kumar ('Neurotic Disorders in Childbearing Women', in IF Brockington and R Kumar, eds, *Motherhood and Mental Illness*, Cambridge: Butterworth, 1988, p 87) notes that 'Severe mental illness, compared to "puerperal psychosis", after abortion is virtually unknown, and most investigators have found that states of depression and anxiety lift once pregnancy has been terminated.' Kumar also points out that early research on the connection between abortion and psychiatric illness is suspect, because many women felt they had to present as insane in order to be aborted (p 88).

30)	See Angella Johnson, 'Aftermath of an abortion', *Guardian*, 18 September, 1992, p 29; and Suzanne Moore, 'Unwanted pain of an unwanted pregnancy', *Guardian*, 8 October, 1992, p 32. Even Moore, however, states that 'Abortion is not an experience any woman would put herself through lightly.' Mirjana Morokvasic ('Sexuality and Control of Procreation', in Kate Young, Carol Wolkowitz and Roslyn McCullagh, eds, *Of Marriage and the Market*, London: CSE Books, 1981), however, examines the rationales of women who, despite the availability of modern contraceptives, choose abortion as a preferred method of birth control.

31)	The need to justify an abortion became a distraction at the inquest of the death of a woman from a massive internal haemorrhage and heart failure following an ineptly performed and monitored abortion. (According to IF Brockington, G Winokur and C Dean ['Puerperal Psychosis', in IF Brockington and R Kumar, eds, *Motherhood and Mental Illness*, Cambridge: Butterworth, 1988, p 39], heart failure is a well-recognized complication of childbearing.) The woman had three daughters and wanted the abortion because she had discovered her expected baby was another girl. Since this reason is illegal in Britain, she

women who have decided upon abortion must undergo counselling, and justify their decision, which is never required of women who decide to become pregnant (unless they have intractable fertility problems and an unconventional marital status).[31]

In contrast to abortion, the process of gestating and delivering a baby is almost invariably depicted as a 'natural' one and therefore not a medical condition at all. A rare exception was an article by Andre Picard, who cited research done at McGill University which shows that the pain of childbirth ranks well above that of chronic back pain or cancer, and is about the equivalent of the amputation of a finger. Although there are wide variations among women, 60 per cent of them described the pain as horrendous. The author of these findings added that being psychologically unprepared made the pain worse, and urged that women should be told the truth, confirming that they seldom are.[32]

Expectant mothers are repeatedly told they are not ill. Therefore, some of the difficulties, discomforts and symptoms often come as a shock. This was illustrated in an article by Joanna Trevelyan, who was by profession an editor of publications on midwifery. In her own case, a failure to turn the badly positioned baby resulted in a lengthy, painful labour, a forceps delivery, haemorrhage and back pain that can continue for up to three years afterwards. Her complaints to a gynaecologist were treated as psychosomatic, and none of the books on childbirth she consulted mentioned the kinds of problems she faced.[33] Yet her experience has been documented as not uncommon in a study conducted by a group at the University of Birmingham on 11,701 women who delivered babies in a Birmingham maternity hospital between 1978 and 1985.[34] They found that 14 per cent of their sample reported backache as a newly occurring symptom after the birth, and that two-thirds of them had not yet recovered when the women answered their questionnaires several years later. Backache was not the only lingering health problem. Other aches, pains and long lasting weakness were reported by 8 per cent. Bladder problems

---

◇

cont.

    had presented a more acceptable financial motive (Sally Weale, 'Asian woman died after abortion to avoid birth of fourth daughter', *Guardian*, 4 March, 1994, p 3) The story implied that a non-Asian woman would not be eager for a son after three daughters, and she was labelled devious and criminal. Adjacent to the report of the inquest, in the same issue, was a light-hearted story reporting on a group of women who decided to have more children in order to keep the village school open. No disapproval was implied. (James Meikle, 'Parents conceive idea of baby boom to keep village school from closing'.)

32) Andre Picard, 'Doctors urged to be candid about the pain of childbirth', *The Washington Times*, 5 September, 1993, p D8.

33) Joanna Trevelyan, *Guardian*, 21 June, 1994, p 19.

34) C MacArthur, M Lewis and EG Knox, *Health after Childbirth*, London: HMSO, 1991.

afflicted one in ten, haemorrhoids one in 20. New, but lasting, depression and anxiety were the lot of 9 per cent, and one in eight experienced extreme fatigue. (That this last had physical as well as social roots was indicated because it was more common after first births. Breast feeding was also related to fatigue and depression, as was the unmarried state.) Altogether, almost half of their sample reported one or more long-term symptoms.

If these findings indicate the health conditions of new mothers in a developed and relatively wealthy society, the situation of mothers in poor countries is far worse. Of the half a million or so women who die every year from pregnancy-related causes (an estimated one-quarter to one-third of them from unsafe abortions), 90 per cent live in the Third World, where one woman dies in every 220 births. This figure does not, of course, include the much greater numbers who do not die but are left weakened or disabled or infertile, or who simply undergo prolonged suffering, not only of a physical but of a social nature. Women who are left sterile or incontinent as a result of obstetric procedures, difficult labour or infection, whether or not as a complication of 'female circumcision' (female genital mutilation or FGM), are often stigmatized and rejected. Those who are simply left weakened or ill are frequently harassed by their in-laws for neglecting their work. Nor does it include the excess infant or child mortality associated with adolescent maternity or too short spacing between births.[35] All in all, it is hard to disagree with the comment of James Grant (significantly in the yearly Unicef Report):

> Family planning could bring more benefits to more people at less cost than any other single 'technology' now available to the human race. But it is not appreciated widely enough that this would still be true even if there were no such thing as a population problem.[36]

---◇---

35) See Mahmoud Fathalla, 'Family Planning and Reproductive Health – a Global Overview', in Francis Graham-Smith, ed., *Population – the complex reality*, London: The Royal Society, 1994. Birth spacing of more than two years has been found to reduce infant mortality by between 10 and 20 per cent. In a paper given to the British Society for Population Studies, 1 September, 1994, on 'Birth Spacing and Child Survival in Rural Senegal', Carine Ronsmans found that the effect on the older child of too short birth spacing is even stronger: mortality in the second year of life is four times higher than when the next birth is delayed for two years or more.

36) James Grant, *The state of the world's children 1992*, New York: Oxford University Press, 1992. 'Family planning' as a euphemism for birth control or contraception (which may imply too much devolving on individuals, particularly women) has become, as all euphemisms do, merely another synonym and will be used here as such.

INFERTILITY AND ITS DISCONTENTS

In wealthier countries (and among wealthier people in poorer countries), much more attention is currently given to a much more expensive set of technologies, those of infertility treatments.[37] The case for such treatments, and the belief that involuntary sterility is a kind of illness, reached a sort of apotheosis when a professor of obstetrics and gynaecology declared:

> Those suffering from sub-fertility should have one of the highest priorities for NHS treatment, and should come before chemotherapy for advanced cancers, before hip replacements and before cataract surgery. If someone were to ask me whether I would rather have a few more years of life, or have my own children, I would have no hesitation in saying that children were more important.[38]

Despite criticism, the extremity of his view has since been reflected in numerous testimonies concerning the sorrow and devastation felt by women unable to have children, some of whom claim they find no other point in living.[39]

———————————◇———————————

37) In Britain, fertility treatment if obtained through the NHS is sometimes free. Changes in the Health Service have led to some health authorities either charging relatively moderate amounts or not offering it at all. Obtained through private medical organizations, the most expensive sort, IVF (*In Vitro* ['test tube'] Fertilization) has been variously estimated at about £1400 to £2000 for each attempt. In the United States, a review of the charges made at six major centres found a single attempt typically cost $8000. Since the chances of pregnancy resulting from any one attempt typically average only one in six, the average costs came out at about $70,000 ('Cost of Test Tube Babies Averages £72,000', *The New York Times*, 28 July, 1994, p A16).

38) 'Infertility help "more urgent than cancer therapy" ', *Guardian*, 11 May, 1993, p 2. The issue is so emotional that, in the furore that followed, no one remarked that Professor Lilford, in seeking to promote his own funding over that of his colleagues in other specialties, had accepted government claims that the distribution of the meagre resources allotted to what is acknowledged to be the most efficient health service in Europe must be a zero sum game.

39) The idea that children are the meaning of life is also embedded in the frequent stories of maternal triumph over difficulty whose final flourish is the acquisition of 'delightful grandchildren'. The extreme depth of feeling expressed by those who want children and those who speak for them is intended to convey the idea that the desire is instinctual and inborn, a medical condition rather than social in origin. See, for example, Katherine Whitehorn ('The foetal attraction', *Observer*, 10 July, 1994, p 23) who quotes Irma Kurtz as saying 'wanting a baby ... it's primitive, it's tigerish, it grips you like hunger', and then goes on to list among 'sensible reasons': 'enjoying their company', 'wanting someone to help when you're old' and 'feeling dynastic about who inherits the farm or the family silver'. Social reasons are assumed to be 'sensible', while irrational ones are 'natural'. Other media treatments include articles titled, 'The urge that's stronger than sex', and 'I want a baby and I want it now'. Another presumed indication that the desire for children is medical is its connection with 'the biological clock', whose stoppage is now being challenged by combinations of expensive techniques.

Although never explicitly pointed out, it is assumed in most western discussions that only women could have a direct claim to a 'right' to have a baby: a man's right is contingent on his obtaining a willing female collaborator. But the view of the former Chief Rabbi that while men must be enjoined to increase and multiply, women's instincts for motherhood are naturally strong enough, is a widely shared one. So much so that cudgels have been taken up on behalf of such groups as lesbians, the disabled, and women who already have numerous children, for whom the voices urging them to bear children are heard to be less than enthusiastic, or even mixed. Such groups often see these ambivalent messages as discriminatory.[40] So in fact do many infertile couples I have interviewed. Not having children is, they feel, viewed as an abnormality which somehow entitles others to look down on them.

Despite claims that rates of infertility are rising, only about one couple in six seek medical help with fertility problems. Those who do are often disappointed, or, if successful, seldom have the resources to repeat very often what is at best a very unpleasant process.[41] From a population point of view, therefore, the treatment of fertility is irrelevant; what is relevant is the attention it has received and what it reveals about general social attitudes to procreation, for it is in this area that attitudes toward blood, birth and nature are at their most confused; equally significant though, it is only the new medical techniques and their implications that have finally commenced a public debate over just why women want children. Unfortunately, the crux of the debate has been over whether certain classes of women, those who are single, or lesbians or beyond some arbitrary age, should be legally permitted to receive medical treatment, even though if they were not sterile or unwilling to resort to self-insemination with possibly infected semen, no law would withhold from them the full powers and status of parenthood. That a good part of current concerns over childbearing is really over the control of women appears from the fact that while a lot of the feeling against abortion stems from the view that unmarried women should be punished for their 'sin' by being forced to bear their unwanted children; in the area of sterility treatment, babies should be granted only to the married.

---

40) See, for example, Maggie Davis, 'When push comes to shove', *Guardian*, 5 August, 1992. Objections have sometimes been raised to the 'right' to have a baby of those with inheritable genetic conditions of a debilitating nature, such as brittle bones, or a transmissible infectious condition, such as HIV, which could result in the early death of the parent or child.

41) It is true that some fertility treatments result in multiple births, but this is rightly considered a medical hazard with significant dangers to the children so produced, and efforts are made to avoid this effect.

Since the little evidence that exists indicates that the children of unconventional mothers are no worse, and possibly better than the usual kind, a variety of more tenuous religious, philosophical and psychological arguments have been brought into play in an attempt to limit treatment to them.[42]

In the past, those who had need of, or desires for, children but were unable to implement them in the conventional manner had recourse to adoption. This possibility has become more complicated and difficult recently, even as the numbers of children orphaned in disasters, wars and epidemics all over the world have proliferated. At the same time, changes in social attitudes have diminished the traditional supplies of adoptable babies: abortion has been legalized, the consensus against unmarried motherhood has weakened, and the importance of blood and 'background' has increased. Most daunting of all, adoption, from the point of view of officials who control the legal procedures, is now seen as a service to children, not to parental candidates. The detailed questions now being asked about the ages, income, resources and lifestyle of applicants are received as another humiliating sign of discrimination.[43] Even the possession of money may be deemed a dubious qualification if the possessors are suspected of attempting to use it to buy a child; hence, a fine distinction between 'expenses', 'administrative costs' and purchase price is often made. In addition, the legal safeguards which used to transfer parental rights over children to their adopters are now under review. Not only do children, once they are of age, now have the 'right' to trace their original parents, but suggestions have been made which will give the 'first' parents (usually the mother) the same right to recontact a child even after adoption.[44]

Transnational adoptions are increasingly running into the same obstacles that are put in the way of transracial adoptions at home: children are held to belong rightfully to their ethnic or national group, failing the claims of their biological parents. And, finally, people

---

42) A study done by psychologists at City University, London, compared families with IVF, DI (Donor Insemination), adopted and normally conceived children. They found 'parents with IVF, DI or adopted children displayed more warmth, emotional involvement and "interaction" than parents with normally conceived children.' On the other hand, they were no more 'clinging, anxious or neurotic' about the children. Other studies had found no psychological problems for children resulting from donor insemination (Chris Milhill, 'IVF couples "better parents"', *Guardian*, 10 January, 1994, p 8). Similar reports have appeared concerning the performance of lesbian (though not gay male) parents.

43) The accepted medical risks to young children of passive smoking has resulted in guidelines being issued by the health department recommending that children under two should not be placed with smokers (Louise Jury, 'Smokers "not suitable to adopt babies"', *Guardian*, 25 March, 1993).

44) Meg Henderson, 'Keep your hands off my children', *Guardian*, 13 September, 1994, pp 8–9.

having fertility difficulties often resent suggestions that they should adopt older, difficult, disabled or otherwise 'hard to place' children as yet another indication that they themselves are considered inferior to the fertile; to be accepted as 'normal', one must be given a 'normal' child.

Against all of these hurdles to child acquisition, the only and best answer seems to be the hopefully unquestionable and unanalysable claim that the aspirant to parenthood is 'loving and caring'. While it is obvious that children (like adults) should be treated with kindness and affection (and respect?), parental love and care seems to embody much else both qualitatively and quantitatively: control, training, and discipline on the one hand, and, on the other, unconditionality. It is not surprising that some would-be adoptive parents (like some natural ones) have found that demands for 'loving and caring' can indeed exceed personal capacity.[45]

Faced with such social and psychological obstacles, the best hope for women who find themselves involuntarily childless is increasingly to turn to medical interventions, whose very existence encourages the belief that sterility is a disease which should be cured. If conventional childbearing is, according to the UN Convention on Human Rights, an absolute right, at least of women, and adoption may be hedged around with a variety of conditions supposedly in the child's interest, the right to children conceived as a result of medical assistance occupies a contested point on the spectrum in between. Strangely little concern has been aired over the long-term health effects of these procedures on both women and children, despite some evidence that, even in the short term, rates of congenital defects are increased, and the known dangers of multiple births.[46] Instead, a variety of philosophical and psychological dangers are posited to be set against the otherwise unquestioned power of love and care. Most of the psychological dangers, like those imputed to children raised by parents of different race or cultural background, have to do with

---

45) The most succinct formulation of this position among a large number that I have come across was that of newspaper letter writer Liz Finney: 'As a woman who has been trying to conceive for a number of years, I simply want to produce, out of me and my partner's love, a human being to love and care for. I challenge anyone to find fault with that wish.' (*Guardian*, 20 August, 1993, p 15, section 2.) Another newspaper story detailed the plight of a woman who adopted a pair of abused young children who proved uncontrollable: 'We were told "keep loving him, the breakthrough is just around the corner".' (*Guardian*, 26 August, 1994.)

46) One doctor who attempted a long-term project monitoring the health and development of IVF children found that they were significantly smaller and more likely to be premature at birth. She was forced to abandon her study by the children's doctors' charges of invasion of privacy (see Robin McKie, 'Dangers to test-tube babies totally ignored', *Observer*, 9 January, 1994, p 8).

'identity', the confusion that a child may feel if told of the unnatural route through which it entered the world, as if the natural one were not confusing enough.

In the philosophical debate, the Catholic Church on one side is adamant that all types of medical treatments that involve either masturbation (for DI or IVF) or abortion are illicit, although, curiously, the use of hormones such as birth control pills to stabilize and regulate the menstrual cycle to assist conception may be acceptable. Uncertainly in the middle, the British Government has not been slow to appoint commissions to consider the questions raised, and then to pre-empt their reports by hedging the newer technologies around with restrictions and 'ethical' considerations; while the Human Fertilization and Embryology Authority was still holding consultations over the possible use of eggs from aborted foetuses, the Conservative MP Jill Knight entered an amendment forbidding such use in the Criminal Justice Bill of 1994, which just happened to be under consideration at the time. On the other side, a recent survey of Scottish women of childbearing age indicates that most women do not share the qualms being aired by a variety of professional moralists and public figures.[47] It seems that large numbers of women stand ready to approve almost any procedure that produces motherhood.

PARENT POWER

The debates surrounding such disparate phenomena as illegitimacy, adoption and medically assisted pregnancies are not important here for their impact on fertility and the environment – they affect only a small minority – but for what they reveal about the usually obscured and romanticized motives impelling the majority of women to motherhood. Beyond the promptings of nature on the one hand, and the general climate of pronatalist opinion on the other, there are real, tangible rewards, at least in prospect, which make childbearing a perfectly rational choice. The rest of this chapter will explore the political and psychological rewards of parenthood, and motherhood in particular, while the next chapter will concentrate on the economic aspects.

---

47) Bob Wylie, 'Women back embryo research', *Scotland on Sunday*, 17 July, 1994. A survey of 1200 Edinburgh women either seeking contraception, infertility treatment or the termination of a pregnancy (admittedly a selected sample which excluded those who were too old or uninvolved in reproductive decisions for some other reason) found 90 per cent in favour of research using live egg donors and two-thirds in favour of research using tissue from the dead. Similar proportions favoured the use of such tissues. A majority also favoured using foetal material to produce babies.

To call the desire of the majority of the world's women for children a 'need' is not necessarily to agree that it springs from female nature. In many societies bearing children, even multiple children or children of the preferred sex or birth interval, makes the difference between social acceptance and rejection, and even between economic security and destitution.[48] In many cases, of course, the hope of obtaining the future good will and devotion of a son is even more powerful than the forces for compliance with husband's or in-laws' wishes.[49] But where women have the power and relative freedom to choose, and current and future economic security does not depend upon it, their choices may be no less rationally grounded.

The recent discussion of 'designer babies' is particularly revealing in this regard. The realization that medical technology now holds out not only the possibility of choosing the sex of one's child, but, potentially at least, many other attributes, such as intelligence, freedom from hereditary disabilities and disease, and even race, has focused attention on the limits of parental power, but has not brought about any reconsideration of its traditionally enormous scope.[50]

That the prospect of power and control over one's children is an important motivation for childbearing has already been noted in a number of places. For example, Paul Demeny, reviewing the ineffectiveness of pronatalist policies in the West, urged governments to place greater stress on increasing individual parental power.[51] His recommendations include: earmarking adult children's earnings

---

48) See Caroline H Bledsoe, Allan G Hill, Umberto D'Alessandro, and Patricia Langerock, 'Constructing Natural Fertility: The Use of Western Contraceptive Technologies in Rural Gambia', *Population and Development Review*, March, 1994, for a study of a society where birth intervals as well as numbers are controlled by social pressures. Many traditional African societies are aware that birth intervals of two years or more brings health benefits to the children on both sides of the interval.

49) As an example of this widespread attitude, explicitly compared to the findings among Chinese mothers by Margery Wolf in Taiwan, Ellen Lewin ('By Design: Reproductive Strategies and the Meaning of Motherhood', in Hilary Homans, ed., *The Sexual Politics of Reproduction*, Aldershot, Hants: Gower, 1985, p 126) quotes one of her Latina informants saying, 'If your children know what you've given up for them, they'll always do what you ask'.

50) See Lawrence Donegan, '"Designer" baby sparks race choice row', *Guardian*, 31 January, 1993, p 1. The story described the case of a black woman who requested the egg of a white woman donor in order to spare her child future racial discrimination. There is a tendency to consider ethically problematic the ability to achieve quickly by technology effects which usually take place naturally over much longer periods of time. Such judgements are really more aesthetic and ideological than anything moral. In fact, much of the animal and plant kingdoms have been 'designing' offspring for many millions of years, often by using the opportunities for female choice of mates now largely denied to women in so many human societies.

51) Paul Demeny, 'Pronatalist Policies in Low Fertility Countries', in K Davis, MS Bernstam, and R Ricardo-Campbell, eds, *Below Replacement Fertility in Industrialized Societies*, Cambridge: Cambridge University Press, 1987.

specifically to their retired parents; strengthening the general political power of parents by permitting them to vote in the names of their underage children as well as in their own (reminiscent of some Muslim countries in which men are permitted to vote in the names of 'their' women); and increasing direct parental power over children's education by weakening the state school system and placing educational choice completely in parental hands.

The Conservative British Government has already taken at least the last recommendation to heart, more as a vote-getter than a population-builder, by purporting to offer parents almost unlimited choice in the schools that their children will attend. The controversy over this policy has been more about the Government's inability to deliver on this promise to large numbers of people, rather than over any doubts about the ability of parents, the vast majority of whom know little about child development, education or the subject matter to be taught, to choose the 'best' schools for their particular children. (From the information supplied, however, it is clear that parents are being directed to consider as the best schools those in which discipline is strictest and examination results, even if obtained by pupil selection, are highest.) Moreover, when the leader of the opposition party chose to send his son to a school eight miles from home, the one element in the choice that was not raised for discussion by any party was that in so doing he promised the boy would remain there until he was 18 years of age. It never occurred to anyone that this promise on behalf of an 11-year-old might constitute an infringement of the boy's rights similar to the forced marriage of underage girls.

Apart from the important (and assumed) right to compel affection, the unquestioned powers of parents have always been to a great extent formalized in law as well as custom. The Roman paterfamilias, for example, had chattel rights over his children extending to the power of life and death, and before the Conquest, English fathers could sell a child under seven into slavery.

Some of the standard categories of parental power include the right to name children, to control their actions and whereabouts, to claim their services and earnings, to determine their religion and education and to discipline and punish, notably for disobedience.[52] Historically such laws have often been justified as beneficial either to the state or to the children because they enabled parents, especially fathers, to carry out their customary duties and obligations. For example, the duty of support and care is held to imply the power to determine

---

52) Some American fundamentalists, seeking a return to Biblical sanctions, point out that in those good old days, crimes punishable by death included not only murder, adultery, incest, sodomy, rape, witchcraft and blasphemy, but also filial disobedience.

where the child will live, and what it will eat and wear, as well as the medical care it receives. The duty to provide a favourable moral environment is held to imply the rights to punish and to censor almost any experience to which the child may be exposed, as well as far-reaching rights over the manner and extent of a child's education, limited only by the sometimes countervailing interests of the state. In practice, in the words of one American legal authority, 'The scope of effective parental power in a particular household probably is restrained more by the imagination of the parents and the efficiency of the available sanctions [at their command] than by law.'[53]

Several recent trends have begun to modify the child's legal position somewhat. The first is the gradual limiting of the patriarchal power of husbands over their wives, which has sometimes been followed by limiting the analogous power of parents over children. For example, in American law, the demise of 'parental immunity' in civil courts followed the disappearance of husband's immunity in cases of wife battering.[54] The second, and more important aspect of the weakening of patriarchy is the devolution of family power, which was vested entirely in the male head, increasingly upon adult women, especially in their maternal roles. For example, in Britain child benefit is now paid exclusively and unaccountably to mothers in the first instance. This trend, somewhat paradoxically, is partly a manifestation of the conventional belief in the sacred nature of the maternal-child bond, and partly an outgrowth of the newer development of feminism. The next step is to consider the question of family power from the point of view of children, and their need for rights of their own.

---

53) Andrew Jay Kleinfeld, 'The Balance of Power Among Infants, Their Parents and The State', *Family Law Quarterly*, 1972, p 413.
54) Andrew Jay Kleinfeld, 'The Balance of Power Among Infants, Their Parents and The State', *Family Law Quarterly*, 1972, p 427. Kleinfeld also points out that in civil law, children have long been able to sue their parents in property matters, but for many years after an 1891 decision American courts held parents immune from actions involving physical assault or cruelty, including rape. The rationale given was the importance of the preservation of harmony in the home, and this is still a consideration in the prosecution of child abuse cases. Even after the end of 'parental immunity' in civil law, it became clear that the problem of child abuse could really be tackled only through the criminal law (where the state is a party to the action). Laws against cruelty to children, in both Britain and the United States, however, lagged far behind those against cruelty to animals. Indeed, in New York City in 1874, when no public authority would act against the parents of a child who was chained to her bed, beaten daily and fed only bread and water, the American Society for the Prevention of Cruelty to Animals successfully prosecuted the case on the grounds that children were members of the animal kingdom. It was in the aftermath of this case that New York State passed its first child abuse legislation.

Chapter 3
Children: value added

Discussions about childbearing all too often stop at the 'take home baby' point, when, natural or assisted, the project is declared a success. The media, and even women themselves, all too often do not imagine the child development process as extending much beyond the baby or toddler stage. But what should parents do with children once they have them? What activities should children be put to that would maximize their human potential throughout life? Or, as the question is more frequently posed, to what extent does the actual or potential income or labour to be derived from children influence the decision to become parents or state policies to encourage child-bearing? And what are children's own rights in the process? To what extent should children belong to their families, their national or cultural affiliation, and to themselves?

THE CULT OF THE CHILD

Most discussions of attitudes to children begin with the work of Philippe Aries, who argued that 'childhood', as a special period of human life such that those passing through it require special types of care and experience, was a discovery, or invention, of the early modern period in the west. Before then, those who could not participate in adult work and leisure simply did not count.[1] More

---

1)   Philippe Aries, *Centuries of Childhood*, New York: Alfred Knopf, 1962.

recent work focuses attention on the late 19th century as a critical period following the industrial revolution, in the early phase of which it was not unusual for mills or plants to hire the labour of entire families. The participation of children and their mothers in industrial work became a contentious issue for its implications both for the health and fitness of future adults and for the adult male wage.[2] In the work of Viviana Zelizer, however, the changing attitude to child labour is located in a set of cultural forces – most notably the Victorian sentimentalization of the family – that led to the dominant present view of children as emotionally gratifying rather than economically useful beings. To exemplify her argument, Zelizer traced developments in the legal and financial valuations put on children in the late 19th and early 20th centuries in a number of specific contexts.[3] Since this is the model of childhood that is the basis of charitable fundraising, legislation and UN declarations for application all over the world, it is worth looking at her argument in some detail.

One of her most telling examples is the course of awards to parents in 'wrongful death' actions, when parents sue employers or others who had accidentally or negligently been responsible for a child's death. Courts at one time evaluated children on the basis of their potential earnings and economic contributions to their families, and the compensation awarded to parents reflected the income they would be deprived of. Accordingly, the death of a girl was valued at half the death of a boy. But as large numbers of children were withdrawn from the market by child labour and compulsory schooling legislation, that is, as they became economically unprofitable to their parents, they became invested with sentimental, emotional and spiritual value, hence 'priceless' – and 'wrongful death' awards,

---

2)   Concern over the health effects of early labour on the part of governments was often pragmatic in nature. For example, Myron Weiner (*The Child and the State in India: Child Labor and Education Policy in Comparative Perspective*, Princeton: Princeton University Press, 1991, p 129) points out that earliest official qualms about child labour in Prussia was in 1817, when the chancellor, von Hardenberg, sent a message to 'high presidents', worried that children would be chained to their particular factory and lessen the supply of labour for other purposes. He also 'expressed his concern that the hard labour done by working children would make them unfit to defend their country ....' Shock over the unfitness of military conscripts attended preparations for many wars, including the two World Wars, and gave rise to campaigns aimed at getting women to stay home and care for their babies, as well as movements against child labour. A notable victory of the labour movement was its success in establishing the principle that a man's wages should be enough for a family to live on.

3)   Viviana Zelizer, *Pricing the Priceless Child*, New York: Basic Books, 1985. Although based on American sources, most of her discussion is equally applicable to western Europe.

disconnected from calculations of current and future earnings, shot up.[4]

Another area in which the changing value of children could be traced was that of adoption. In the 19th century, families sometimes took in sturdy older children and put them to work. In 1854, the New York Children's Aid Society could place three times as many boys as girls, and those between seven and eleven years old were the most popular. After the 1860s, however, as abortion became increasingly illegal and expensive, many women were forced to divest themselves of unwanted babies by 'baby farming': paying a fee (usually $50) to a woman who agreed to keep it and find it a home. The few adopters that could be found paid only a pittance to the baby farmer, whose profit came mostly from the mother's side. In practice, abandoned children had an infant mortality of 80 to 90 per cent, and even foundling hospitals had rates almost as high as baby farms.

The development of the sentimental cult of the child changed all that. Sentimental adoptions made babies and toddlers more desirable, and girls were favoured over boys: ideally, blue-eyed, golden-haired, angelic-appearing two year olds.[5] But the increasing emotional value of children meant that the needs of children began to be considered more important than the wants of adopting parents. Parents on their part were now expected to provide children with 'loving homes', and adoption procedures entailed the specification of exactly what a loving home consisted in. Adopting parents themselves began to be screened for suitability, and, if denied, were willing to make payments of tens of thousands of dollars in fees, bribes or outright purchases for foreign or private adoptions.

In the late 19th and early 20th century there was a craze for child actors to play the newly sentimentalized child on stage. These children were few, but so highly paid and prominent, that their exploitation by parents and employers, and the distortion in their education and development, was publicly debated. The same debate is currently being echoed in the case of child models and sports stars. In 1939, as a result of a law case in which a former child star sued his

---

4) On the other hand, the development of the medical techniques of contraception and sterilization meant that in litigious America wrongful death suits were paralleled by 'wrongful birth', when sterilization failed due to medical incompetence. Until 1967, an accidental child was deemed a blessing (at least at law); since then, surprised parents could claim compensation for the ever-rising costs of childrearing. Children were now 'priceless' if wanted, but otherwise merely expensive.

5) Viviana Zelizer, *Pricing the Priceless Child*, Basic Books, 1985, p 193. Although parents said girls were easier to rear and gave more companionship, polls showed they still preferred their own children to be boys. Possibly middle-class adopters felt they could not expect the same standards of achievement from adopted children that they would have from their own; sex-role stereotyping meant that less would be expected of girls.

own parents, a Child Actors' Bill was passed which required half a child's earnings to be put in trust: a public admission that parents could exploit their own children, and that the law could protect them – at least if they were rich.

The removal of the majority of children from the labour market between 1870 and 1930 created a new range of economic opportunities for adults. Mass schooling provided jobs for teachers and other educators. Specialized products to educate and entertain children were developed, and, in addition to the purchases by parents, relatives and friends, children increasingly spent their allowances and earnings from part-time jobs and chores on them. In Zelizer's words: 'As children became increasingly defined as exclusively emotional and moral assets, their economic roles were not eliminated, but transformed.'[6]

Although he concurs that the sentimental model of childhood has become universalized, Alec Fyfe takes a slightly different view of its development, when he says: 'Out of the moral crisis presented by child labour [in Britain in the 1830s and 1840s, which was often more concerned about the sexual danger to women and children than their physical safety in such industries as mining] emerged the view of the 'innocent child' (but also of the savage child) whose rightful place was in the schoolroom.'[7] He believes that the notion of childhood that 'has now become a pervasive one through cultural transfer to the developing world' is a peculiarly western one which sometimes has economic self-interest and cultural imperialism in it.

In fact, closer examination reveals the notion to have more class than geographic origins.[8] The ideal of the child whose role was not earning but costing, whose occupation was in school rather than in the field or workshop, whose function was that of a consumer rather than a provider is neither new nor western, but a spread of middle- and upper-class views about the nature of their own children, to become a democratized, or at least mass marketed, cultural ideal.

Yet it cannot be argued that the change has been one of unqualified improvement in the condition of even those children for whom it has actually occurred. Parents of the precious child can insist on more

---

6)   Viviana Zelizer, ibid, p 112.
7)   Alec Fyfe, *Child Labour*, Cambridge: Polity Press, 1989, p 2. In England, children began to be withdrawn from the factories in favour of schooling after 1850. See Harold Perkin, *The Origins of Modern English Society 1780–1880*, London: Routledge & Kegan Paul, 1969, pp 149–56.
8)   Nancy Sheper-Hughes (*Death Without Weeping*, Berkeley: University of California Press, 1994) notes that while middle-class Brazilian mothers lavish almost hysterical affection on their children, the poverty-stricken mothers of the *favela*, which is the focus of her research, seem unmoved by deaths of young babies, and even select those among their too numerous offspring whom they do not care to see survive.

complete control of the minds and bodies of their children than parents of breadwinners. And the increasing physical danger to children in the streets (from traffic or abduction by strangers) has led to their progressive confinement in the home or in restricted play areas. While 90 per cent of children walked or rode bicycles to school 20 years ago in Britain, only 9 per cent do so now; the majority are now driven by their parents.[9] Paradoxically, the withdrawal of children from the streets for the purposes of playing and getting to school now contrasts with the growing numbers of young beggars, runaways and prostitutes who live there continuously, increasingly as a result of violence and abuse in the home.[10]

The danger of abduction, assault or molestation of children by strangers has been exaggerated out of all proportion by the huge amounts of publicity given to the few children who are kidnapped in public places (itself a manifestation of the sentimental cult of the child, which expresses itself in emotional outpourings over individual children, but indifference or insensitivity to arrangements that would safeguard or benefit children as a class). British government neglect of child welfare has been documented and condemned by UN monitors concerned over such matters as the increasing numbers of children in poverty and child refugees held in detention in violation of UN conventions on children's rights.

The real danger of attack and abuse, sexual or otherwise, is far greater within the home and at the hands of relatives or family friends; well-publicized court cases and government-issued guidelines have reinforced the rights of parents to assault their own children, and even to designate others to do so, despite the fact that such powers inevitably result in a proportion of badly injured children and are connected with no demonstrated developmental benefit.[11]

---

9) The extent of middle-class children's exclusion from public spaces is shown by protests on the part of residents in an exclusive housing development in Dorset that some of the tenants permit their children to play in the street (Edward Pilkington, 'Tenants' bathtime provokes discord', *Guardian*, 13 July, 1994, p 3). The problem of increasing traffic, which has both environmental and health effects in the increasing number of children with asthma and other respiratory problems, could have been dealt with by stringent traffic calming devices and the improvement of public transportation. Instead, parents have opted for an individualistic 'solution' which involves creating more traffic – and lead emissions – and disadvantages the children of the carless classes. Environment *Guardian*, 18 February, 1994, G2, pp 14–15 coincidentally juxtaposed both these aspects of traffic increase.

10) Large numbers of teenagers living on the streets began to appear after 1988, when the Government denied unemployment benefit to school leavers under 18. More recently, many of the street children are even younger, often well below 16, who are there for less directly economic reasons.

11) Additional evidence, should it be needed, comes from children themselves over a telephone 'helpline' set up and maintained by a charity. It has the capacity to answer only 30 per cent of the 10,000 children who try to call every day. One in eight complain of

CHILD LABOUR

Meanwhile, the proportions as well as the numbers of child workers in many parts of the world are actually on the increase. China, since the 'reforms', has seen more parents take their offspring (especially girls) out of school to begin earning. The proportion of children between 10 and 14 at work in Nepal has risen from 28 per cent in 1952 to 58 per cent in 1981. Nor has the effective removal of children from factories and other workplaces even in wealthy countries really occurred in practice. Indeed, as Alec Fyfe points out:

> Despite official disinterest in the subject, children, particularly of ethnic minority groups, like gypsies, do engage in illegal work and are exposed to unhealthy and unsafe working conditions. When it comes to child prostitution and pornography some industrial countries are world leaders. The fact that millions of children work, most of them illegally and some of them to the detriment of their health and development, contradicts the popular mythology that child labour is a thing of the past.[12]

But do people have children in order to exploit their labour? Who benefits from child labour, and why is it on the increase?

It is still a widespread belief that children are profitable to Third World parents and that the poor there insist on having large numbers of children because they are essential to 'family survival'. This argument has been received with surprisingly few questions by women's groups and many western liberals who would not recommend having children in order to supplement the family budget to their friends and neighbours – even to those who are fairly hard up. For example, the Women's Environmental Network puts out a leaflet called 'Population: An Ecofeminist Perspective'. In it no mention was made of child welfare or development, except for the suggestion, under 'What you can do': 'Celebrate children: think about your family as valued members of society who enrich the whole world, not simply as "family property"'. Under 'Power for the Poor', however, a much longer statement explained how much economic value even young children can contribute to their families.

———————————————————◇———————————————————

cont.

sexual abuse and the same proportion of physical abuse and other family problems. Four times more girls than boys call. Contrary to conventional belief, fathers are cited in one-third of sexual abuse charges, stepfathers in only one in 12, 'boyfriends', including mother's boyfriends, in one case in 25 (James Meikle, 'Thousands "live as child drudges"', *Guardian*, 2 December, 1994, p 6).

12)   Alec Fyfe, *Child Labour*, Cambridge: Polity Press, 1989, pp 2–3.

This is not to say that child labour is not an important concern in Britain and throughout Europe and the United States as well as in the Third World, or that it should not be examined in contexts besides those of household economics and fertility control. For example, one should look at possible trade-offs between current and future earnings, between adult and child wages, between child benefit and child management, that is, between what is best for a child to be doing at a particular stage in his or her development, and what is safest or most convenient for his or her adult carer.

Investigating the child labour hypothesis   The classic terms in which the argument about poverty and fertility has been pursued have centred around the economic opportunities perceived by heads of families for the deployment of family labour, on one side, and 'population controllers', national or international, who see a high rate of population growth working against economic growth, on the other. From one side, poor villagers are seen as pitted against an international cabal of western governments concerned about immigration or communism, NGOs concerned about their funding, academics seeking career advancement, pharmaceutical companies seeking profits, national governments concerned about social unrest, and native 'modernizing élites' of 'neo-Malthusian' persuasion. Alternatively, from the standpoint of policy-makers, the rural or urban underclass is studied and probed for those conditions and incentives which will manipulate their birth rates in such a way as to increase national productivity and extractable hard currency surpluses. Only recently have the assumptions about the relationship between fertility and child labour been questioned. A large amount of this work has been done in India, in which one-third of the total child labour population in the world is said to be found.

The current cycle of this argument may be said to have begun with the publication in 1972 of Mahmood Mamdani's *The Myth of Population Control*.[13] The attention it received was at least partly due to its provocative and misleading major title. Not really about population control, the book was actually a critique of 'the Khanna study', which was an early (1950s) attempt by a group of scientists from the Harvard School of Public Health both to study population dynamics from an epidemiological point of view, and also to modify birth rates by offering contraceptives to a group of villages in the Punjab. In the site chosen, the population density was 75 per cent

---

13)   Mahmood Mamdani, *The Myth of Population Control: Family, Caste and Class in an Indian Village*, New York and London: Monthly Review Press, 1972.

higher than the all-India average, but the birth rate was about the same (40 per 1000, at the time).[14] In any case, not much happened, either in comparison with the control villages or as a function of the time over which the study took place (1955 to 1959, with a follow-up ten years later). Birth rates remained high, even though, according to the authors, the villagers were not opposed to birth control *per se*. They simply didn't see the need for it.

The 'myth' Mamdani sought to nail was that population growth, the result of falling death rates and stationary birth rates, resulted in poverty due to the fragmentation of land among increasing numbers of surviving heirs. This, Mamdani maintained, was a worry only for the wealthy classes, who could afford mechanization to increase productivity. For the poor, more surviving children meant more family labour, who could farm land more intensively, could be hired out, or could migrate and send back remittances.

The Khanna study failed, said Mamdani, because the villagers not only wanted but *needed* more surviving children. Since then, Mamdani's book has been used triumphantly as an argument, first against the attempt to introduce contraception before development, and more recently as an argument *against* attempts to aid the Third World poor to improve their standards of living. For example, Virginia Abernethy argues that an improved standard of living and opportunities to migrate only stimulates the poor to maintain a high birth rate, using the Khanna study as a case in point: 'The Khanna people *liked* large families. Khannaians were delighted that now, with lower infant mortality, they could have the six surviving children they had always wanted.'[15] She contends that if the hungry and crowded are left to their misery, despair will inspire them to lower their birth rates.

Mamdani's critique has many flaws, among them the failure to note (as the authors of the Khanna study did) that the period and place of the study were exceptional in that technology, in the form of mechanization and irrigation, and later new varieties of grain, was raising productivity while there was still land to be bought and leased, and when there were opportunities for emigration. Unemployment does not seem to have been a problem. Another point made by the authors and overlooked by Mamdani is that during the study period, although general rates of mortality in the district had fallen considerably, infant and early child mortality was still high. For every 1000 deliveries, 36 were stillborn, and 53 died in the following

---

14) John B Wyon and John E Gordon, *The Khanna Study*, Cambridge, Mass: Harvard University Press, 1971.

15) Virginia Abernethy, *Population Politics*, New York: Plenum Press, 1963, pp 77–8.

week. In the first five years, children, who constituted 15 per cent of the population under study, had 55 per cent of the total mortality. A follow-up to the Khanna study found that some of the most vehement respondents in denouncing contraception on economic grounds had later had themselves sterilized. Since then, birth rates have fallen there and elsewhere in a trend which is proceeding more rapidly in the Third World than it did in Europe. More generally, Bryant Robey *et al* have claimed that, even without development, 'access to contraceptives is the best contraceptive'.[16]

What has been little challenged about Mamdani's thesis are the assumptions that children cost less than they contribute, and that they are entirely under parental control at least until they marry. In particular, he gives no more than cursory consideration to the separate costs of children to women and to men, and then only to point out that the stigma attached to barrenness (which includes sonlessness) and the veneration of motherhood is such as to overbalance any such disparity.

Mamdani's assumptions still form part of the conventional wisdom regarding child labour. Furthermore, he said, unlike other possible investments, the return grows as they get older. Sons constitute financial security in old age, and physical security in youth. Another issue lightly touched on is the difference between the perceived costs of sons and daughters versus their economic contributions. The birth of a girl is mourned, said Mamdani, but she too can be set to work, and can even earn much of her own dowry. (Nevertheless, the common sentiment that 'caring for a daughter is like watering a tree for your neighbour' was endorsed among his informants, and in fact the preponderance of males over females among farmers in the Khanna study was 123:100 – long before the days of ultrasound and the abortion of female foetuses.)

The underlying assumption in all this is that the family is a sort of miniature socialist society, in which each contributes according to his or her ability, and all benefit according to the resources available. More recent work, such as that of John Caldwell, Naila Kabeer and Olga Nieuwenhuys has pictured the family as more of a feudal despotism, in which the more powerful members, usually older and male, benefit disproportionately at the expense of the younger and female.

---

16) Bryant Robey, Shea O Rutstein and Leo Morris, 'The fertility decline in developing countries', *Scientific American*, December, 1993, pp 60–66. Recently, Lant Pritchett ('Desired fertility and the impact of population policies', *Population and Development Review*, March, 1994, pp 1–56) claimed that it is the changing wishes of parents, particularly women, 'within the social economic and cultural environment' that accounts for falling fertility, not contraceptive availability. But what it is that has changed wishes over so widespread an area is not specified.

Household economics   In 1982, Caldwell published an influential book called *Theory of Fertility Decline*, in which he basically argued that large families were desired as long as the overall intergenerational flow of wealth was upward, from child to parent, and small ones when, after various economic and social changes took place, the overall flow was reversed. Moreover, investment in children is socially unexceptionable, while, should hard times come, there would be pressure to cash in any other form of investment to tide the family over. Where the investment has been made in children, the whole family must simply tighten their belts. Caldwell did, however, recognize that not only was the cost of childbearing and rearing unequally distributed within the household – with the most influential decision-makers, the husband or his family, often the most lightly charged, but also that the contribution of girls – and women – to the household economy was usually undervalued. In this he anticipated Naila Kabeer's recent book, *Reversed Realities*.[17] He also points out that in places where there are extended families and children may eat out of more than one household pot, it is difficult to decide just what they cost. Nevertheless, most fertility studies of what he calls pre-transitional societies, in places as far flung as Ghana, India, Kenya, Turkey, Tunisia and Sri Lanka, find wives less likely to favour high fertility than husbands. (The exceptions include Taiwan, Malaysia and currently industrialized countries, that is, post-transition.) And Kabeer points out that pregnancy, childbirth and even breast feeding (let alone childcare) are not costless with respect to women's health, energy and nutritional reserves.

The overall argument, however, assumes that peasants (or at least fathers) know whether or not their investments in each additional child are likely to be returned with interest by that child's labour. So the two questions to be asked on this point are: are such calculations made correctly and are they made at all? Do children on balance contribute more than they cost, and is that why poor parents want so many?

In the 1970s and 1980s several anthropologists attempted to quantify the costs and contributions of children to agricultural households in a number of societies, and these attempts were assessed and compared by Tim Dyson and Michael Vlassoff.[18] One study, for example, calculated that in an agricultural village in Bangladesh, a boy's contributions reach the breakeven point at age

17)   See John C Caldwell, *Theory of Fertility Decline*, London: Academic Press, 1982; and Naila Kabeer, *Reversed Realities*, London: Verso, 1994.

18)   Tim Dyson, 'Child Labour and Fertility', and Michael Vlassoff, 'An assessment of Studies Linking Child Labour and Fertility Behaviour in Less Developed Countries', both in Ramesh Kanbargi, ed., *Child Labour in the Indian Subcontinent*, New Delhi: Sage Publications, 1991.

12, at least with respect to calorie equivalents; by 15 he has cleared his parents' food investment, and by age 22 compensated for a sister's cumulative consumption as well. Between 22 and 39 years, a man is assumed to produce twice as much as he consumes (by which time much of his contribution may be directed to his children rather his parents).[19] Another study concluded on the basis of several alternative models that on balance children are a negative economic investment for peasant agriculturalists: 'Up to the time that they become parents themselves, children consume more than they produce.'[20]

In the end, despite the difficulties of making this sort of calculation, both Dyson and Vlassoff concluded that although, once born, children are put to work, and do make important contributions to the family budget, there is no real empirical evidence that poor rural families need child labour to survive, and Vlassoff found no reason to believe that the prospect of child labour motivates fertility behaviour. A number of other studies bear this out.

Their conclusions agree with those of Robert Cassen. He did some elaborate calculations and estimated the probability of a son surviving and contributing to parental income was 0.3, while that of a daughter is 0.225. His calculations were sensitive to the age at which children begin to work: if children are given a 'malnutritional' diet and start work at age seven, 'the parents investing in a child are in the black only after waiting about 30 years. If a child starts at age five, however, with the same support costs, it pays off as an investment by age fifteen, even earning 20 per cent above costs.'[21] (Interestingly, the most common age at which children are said to be put to work in much of the developing world is six years.) Nevertheless, after having calculated costs and possible returns under a variety of assumptions – whether diets were adequate, poor or 'malnutritional'; whether children were male or female; whether they began work at five or seven, and so on – he admitted that such calculations are probably very distant from what really went on in the mind of an Indian villager, and finally concluded that investment in children actually makes economic sense only as a sort of life or disaster insurance.

---

19) Mead Cain, 'The Economic Activities of Children in a Village in Bangladesh', *Population and Development Review*, September, 1977, pp 201–27.

20) Eva Mueller, 'The economic value of children in peasant agriculture', in Ronald G Ridker, *Population and Development*, Baltimore: Johns Hopkins University Press, 1976, p 145.

21) RH Cassen, *India: Population, Economy, Society*, London: Macmillan, 1978, pp 66 and 71. However, he gives the probability of survival of both sexes as 0.75, whereas the death rates for girls in south Asia are higher than those of boys. On the other hand, all surveys show that the nutritional status of females is poorer than that of males at all ages, so that the investment of parents in girls (outside of marriage costs, which are held to overwhelm all other considerations) is lower for girls.

Another point often neglected in this sort of calculation, is that the costs and value of each child to its parents are often considered regardless of family size. Yet not only do the psychological and social values of children inhere predominantly in the first few survivors, but the likelihood of illness and death, and hence cost per surviving child, increases as family size increases. In fact, the idea that a desired family size may be decided upon and achieved is a relatively new one, and the adoption of contraception in underdeveloped countries seems to be fuelled, at least at first, more by a rising 'concern over a growing supply of surviving children' than a downward revision in the number of children desired.[22]

Calculations of food costs also tend to neglect other factors which can affect the future income of the household or the child itself, and ways in which current income is offset against future earning power. For example, Myron Weiner claims that children who have had several years of schooling are more productive in agricultural labour as adults, regardless of what they have or have not learned in school, simply because of the health benefits of having been spared much of the dangers and damages of work at an early age, and a host of studies have added specificity to this general observation.[23] Normal growth spurts during puberty and adolescence are adversely affected by poor nutrient intake and increased manual work. Employed children are more likely to be undernourished children as well, and hence more susceptible to infectious diseases, anaemia and inadequate sleep, bone lesions and postural deformities from working doubled up – as they must in carpet factories – and from lifting heavy weights. Other health hazards of the carpet industry include allergic asthma, and nasal fungus infections caused by wool and cotton dust, tuberculosis and dermatitis.

There are health hazards in modern as well as traditional industries. In high-tech electronic assembly plants, as in the handicraft industries of *zari* work, embroidery and gem cutting, the eye-sight of young girls working for 12 to 14 hours a day is damaged within a period of 5 to 8 years. The glass industry threatens asthma, bronchitis, tuberculosis and eye problems, as well as burns. Rag picking produces tetanus and skin diseases; stone and slate quarries, silicosis.[24]

22) G Narayana and John F Kantner, *Doing the Needful: the Dilemma of India's Population Policy*, Boulder, Col.: Westview Press, 1992, p 42. See also Patricia Jeffery, *Frogs in a Well*, London: Zed Press, 1979, pp 137–42. This suggests that parents initially concerned about growing numbers of surviving children will opt for sterilization, while those who are accustomed to the idea of 'planning a family' will find non-terminal methods more suitable.
23) Myron Weiner, 25 January, 1990, personal communication.
24) See Nazir Ahmad Shah, *Child Labour in India*, New Delhi: Anmol Publications, 1992, pp 40–7; SK Tripathy, *Child Labour in India*, New Delhi: Discovery Publishing, 1989, p 103.

CHILD LABOUR, FAMILY SIZE AND MOTIVATION

So, with all the costs and risks attached, if families actually do not profit from child labour and do not have large numbers of children in order to put them to work, is there nevertheless a relationship between family size and child labour? Nazir Shah did a survey of the reasons given by children and their parents for their employment in four types of industry in Kashmir. He found the most usual reason given by both was the inadequacy of parental income for the support of 'large families'.[25] A study in the Delhi area by Parveen Nangia found a significant association between family size and the type if not the probability of child employment. Children from large families (nine or more members) were more likely to seek wage labour; those from medium-sized families (six to eight) tended to self-employment; and those from smaller families tended to work for family members.[26] Interestingly, BR Patil, who denies any relationship between family size and child labour, also found that, although working boys outnumbered girls, the percentages of working girls were larger at the earlier ages: girls were 41 per cent of those below 10, but only 16 per cent of those between 13 and 15. In other words, girls are put out to work earlier than boys (presumably because boys remain longer at school) but are withdrawn at puberty. Furthermore, the proportions of girls from smaller families were larger, implying that only when family size causes more desperate poverty are boys sent out. Hence these studies also support the view that families send out children to work because they must, but do not have them in order to put them to work.

So much for the motives of parents. What about employers? Shah's study included a survey of carpet-making, papier-mâché, hotel and teashop, and domestic service employers in Kashmir. He found that the most common reason given for employing children in all four sectors (30–38 per cent) was the frank admission that 'child labour is cheaper and helps in bargaining with adult workers'. In the handicraft industries of carpet-making and papier-mâché, the need for a long apprenticeship and maintenance of craft traditions ran a distant second (at around 10 per cent).[27] This echoes a 1980 report of the Committee on Child Labour of the Government of India, which listed employer motivations as, among others:

---

25)   Nazir Ahmad Shah, *Child Labour in India*, New Delhi: Anmol Publications, 1992, pp 80–3. Unfortunately, the data he provides are inadequate. He found 70 per cent of child workers came from families of more than five members (averaging between six and seven), but the family size distribution of non-working children (with income controlled) is not known.
26)   Parveen Nangia, *Child Labour: Cause–effect Syndrome*, New Delhi: Janak Publishers, 1987, p 188. BR Patil, Working Children in Urban India, Bangalore: DB Publishers, 1988, p 30.
27)   Nazir Ahmad Shah, *Child Labour in India*, New Delhi: Anmol Publications, 1992, p 91.

children had less developed ego and status consciousness'; were 'less afflicted by feelings of guilt and shame'; had 'no hesitation [about] non-status, even demanding, jobs'; had 'greater discipline and control'; were 'less expensive to maintain' [fewer fringe benefits?]; 'lack of [union?] organization'; greater stamina; and, finally there was a 'moral consideration ... to help and to provide succour to the destitute or forsaken children.[28]

For employers, then, the employment of children has several attractions, very like the advantages of female, immigrant and illegal labour. Children are relatively docile, not unionized and undemanding of benefits such as paid holidays, medical care and pensions; they are often innocent of the safety implications of their jobs. Thus, the employment of children seems to be pitted against the general interests of adults, viewed as workers rather than employers, parents or consumers. However, there is another alternative increasingly open to employers. When Mrs Girija Eswaran (the Labour Minister in charge of child labour laws), was asked whether the enforcement of child labour laws would lead to the shut-down of match factories in India or to the hiring of adults, she replied, '[The employers] said that if the government ended child labour they would cut costs by mechanizing rather than hire more adults.'[29]

Children versus automation   The match-making business in India offers a clear illustration of how near the labour of children can be to that of machinery in cost. In 1922, two Indian businessmen imported machinery from Germany and set up a factory in Sivakasi in South India. Because child labour was so cheap, they soon switched to hand production, and Sivakasi has become the most notorious centre of child work in India. Up to 200 children, some as young as three, are packed into each van or bus between 3 and 5 a.m. to get them from their villages to the factories and workshops up to 20 miles away by 6 or 7 a.m. There they work a 12-hour day for between 6 and 15 rupees (18 to 45 pence), depending on the child's age. Forty-five thousand are under 15. Three-fourths of them are girls. They do almost all the operations in match manufacture, including mixing the

---

28)   Report of the Committee on Child Labour, Government of India, 1980, pp 11–12. Parveen Nangia (*Child Labour: Cause-Effect Syndrome*, New Delhi: Janak Publishers, 1987, p 259) in a survey of employers of children in 17 industries in the Delhi area, reports that 42 per cent claimed a child worker was just as productive as an adult and 30 per cent found them between half and equally productive. Overall, Nangia estimated that 1.65 children did the work of one adult.
29)   Myron Weiner, *The Child and the State in India*, Princeton: Princeton University Press, 1991, p 48.

chemicals and dipping the match frames into the mixture.[30] Parents are given an advance of 200 rupees when the child is enrolled. Hence, this is really a form of bonded labour, which is supposedly illegal.

The chief competition for the child-staffed manufactures is WIMCO, a Swedish-owned mechanized company founded in India, in 1927. WIMCO produces 30 per cent of Sivakasi matches with 6000 workers and at lower unit cost than the unmechanized industry, which has 250,000 workers. In 1988, the government started a programme in Sivakasi that supplied non-formal education, free lunches and free health care. The costs were met by the government from excises imposed on WIMCO. They are effectively a subsidy for the child-employers and ensure the children's attendance.

According to Indian law, children younger than 14 are not permitted to work in factories, which are subject to at least some inspection, but may work in cottage industries, family households, restaurants and agriculture, paid or unpaid, where conditions are often worse than in the factories. But while in some industries, the employment of children seems to be a step on the road toward automation, in others, such as carpet-making, cigarette rolling, the harvesting of delicate crops such as jasmine, and more recently, electronic assembly, the opposite reason is given: children are said to be more suited or even not replaceable with larger, harder-handed, less diligent and nimble-fingered adults (including women, about whom many of the same stereotypes are invoked).

It is also claimed that without children many industries would have to close, and developing national economies would suffer. A cautionary tale, often cited, is the fate of the carpet industry in Iran. In the mid-1970s India was able to expand its carpet exports after the Shah banned the employment of children in Iran. Carpet prices rose as Iranian exports dropped. India and other countries, such as Morocco, Turkey, Pakistan and Nepal also took advantage of the opportunity. There are now 300,000 children working illegally in the Indian carpet industry, 500,000 in Pakistan and 200,000 in Nepal. With that kind of competition, according to Mrs Eswaran, 'the Commerce Ministry says we must look at the economics of it.'[31]

These considerations look like becoming even stronger under the recently agreed GATT (General Agreement on Tariffs and Trade) conventions, where low labour costs will be the main competitive advantage that the poor developing world's manufacturers can set

---

◇

30) Weiner, ibid, p 24; see also Russell Miller, 'Pity the Child', *Sunday Times Magazine*, 30 September, 1990, p 30 (box by Jonathan Bastable).
31) Myron Weiner, *The Child and the State in India*, Princeton: Princeton University Press, 1991, p 49; numbers of children in the carpet industry from *Friend*, 13 May, 1994, pp 589–90.

against the highly mechanized competition of the industrialized rich. Thus child labour can pit the interests of 'free market' competition, Third World governments and small businesses against those of labour unions, large mechanized firms, and adult workers.[32] In any case, a recent Indian Labour Ministry report estimated that the number of working children had risen to 17.02 million from 13.6 million in 1981.[33] And this is certainly an underestimate, since illegal and household child labour is by its nature almost invisible.

SCHOOL AND WORK

On the moral and political plane, 'parents' rights' can also be pitted against children's human rights and child development. According to UN convention, school is a child's proper place, and a child has a right to education. School is a kind of work, not necessarily tailored to the particular stage of child development at which it is administered, and not necessarily preferred by children themselves, but having health and development advantages over dangerous, prolonged or unhealthy employment, at least when school and work are substituted rather than added. But what is the actual effect of schooling on child labour, and on the labouring child?

In order to establish basic literacy and numeracy, it is generally agreed that more than four or five years of schooling are necessary. (Of course, much more than basic academic skills can be taught in that time, such as the elements of health education.) It is also important to remember that primary schooling, which is basically what is at issue in the discussion of mass education in the developing world, has a significance there that is more equivalent to tertiary education in the West – something considered universally desirable but by no means universally necessary. While in the western world the skills learned in primary school are simply part of shared culture, which do not equip the child for any particular occupation, in the underdeveloped world, parents (and children) view them as education, and education as something that equips a child to pursue

---

32) Actually, there are even instances where unions have argued against eliminating child labour. In the tea plantations, for example, labour unions objected to raising the wages paid to the children, arguing that if the wages were raised the employers wouldn't hire children (usually the children of adult workers), but hire adults from outside the plantations and when the children grew up they would not be given jobs (Myron Weiner, *The Child and the State in India*, Princeton: Princeton University Press, 1991, p 50).

33) SWB (Summary of World Broadcasts monitored by the BBC), Part 3, Weekly Economic Report, 27 April, 1994, p 1. This does not include part-time, domestic or other family work. Other estimates put the number at 44 million.

a trade different from that of his or her parents: a better-paid, higher status trade, or at least one that substitutes for rapidly disappearing traditional handicrafts or industries. Schooling that does not achieve that is often considered by parents at best a waste of time, at worst an interference with the acquisition of traditional skills, and actually contributing to their loss.

Although mass schooling by no means eliminates child labour, the most general finding is that there is a negative correlation between the two. But schooling is also strongly associated with smaller family sizes, so that the direction of the influence of these three factors upon each other is somewhat unclear. Sending children to school, even when ostensibly free, increases the economic burdens on families, and lessens the income from children in the short term. Decreasing the employment opportunities for children, whether by decline or mechanization in the industries in which they are employed, increases the time available for children to attend school. On the other hand, smaller family sizes make the training and the expected future income of offspring a more affordable proposition for parents. As old-age security, schooling a small number of children may be a trade-off for having a large number.

Girls are less likely to be sent to school and, even when not in waged labour, are more likely to be employed in the 'non-productive' work of housework, childcare, and 'helping' parents generally.[34] But with the increasing recognition that female education is closely associated with falling birth rates, education, especially for girls, would seem to be an ideal way of relieving the economic pressures of high fertility on developing countries, as well as eradicating the evils of child labour. The logic of these arguments makes it somewhat surprising to learn how very uneven progress in mass literacy has been in many underdeveloped countries. Among countries with substantial populations but per capita incomes below $500, many, such as Sri Lanka, Tanzania, China, Zaire, Ghana, Burundi and Kenya have achieved rates of school retention to the sixth grade and beyond of 70 per cent or more, while India, Pakistan, Bangladesh, Nepal, Sudan and Ethiopia have literacy rates of 40 per cent or less.[35] Some countries with higher literacy rates and a higher proportion of school

---

34) See Ramesh Kanbargi and PN Kulkarni, 'Child Work, Schooling and Fertility in Rural Karnataka', and Abusaleh Shariff, 'The Family Economy in South India', both in Ramesh Kanbargi, ed., *Child Labour in the Indian Subcontinent*, New Delhi: Sage Publications, 1991.

35) See Myron Weiner, *The Child and the State in India*, Princeton: Princeton University Press, 1991, pp 157–61. The data Weiner uses are from UN sources, the World Bank, and the *Britannica Book of the Year 1990*. It should be noted, however, that despite their higher rates of schooling and literacy, African and Latin American countries too have numerous child labourers.

children actually spend less per capita than India, which has developed its facilities for higher education instead. Less than half of the country's 82 million youngsters between 6 and 14 are in school, and the high primary school drop-out rate makes the achievement of each case of literacy that much more expensive.

The critics of schooling In many countries, the middle classes, whose children benefit from the opportunities in higher education, fear competition and dissatisfaction from an educated working class. But in India resistance has come also from parents and social reformers, including the revered Mahatma Gandhi, who complained that schooling imparts nothing of use, and the mere acquisition of literacy disqualifies children from menial work. Another social reformer, Ela Bhatt, the founder and organizer of the Self-Employed Women's Association which has improved the lot of many poor women peddlers and other petty traders by helping them obtain loans and protecting them against police harassment, concurs: 'The children work with their mothers. That is how they learn their trade …. These are precious years for learning their trade and these preparatory years would be gone if they went to school.'[36] The 'trade' referred to in this case was 'the recycling trade, sorting scrap and junk', in other words, rag-picking.

Work on top of school Even where children attend school in developing countries, education may compound rather than displace other work. This is the case in Kerala, where 86 per cent of the population between 10 and 14 are still in school. Hence, a study by Olga Nieuwenhuys of several aspects of the economics of survival among the poor (and chronically hungry) children in a Keralan fishing village is of special interest.[37] In the village studied, the land is highly fragmented due to high levels of population growth in the past, and the economy now revolves around fishing and the manufacture of coir (coconut fibre). It is predominantly boys, both paid and unpaid, who work in the fishing industry, while girls help their mothers' coir work by relieving them of a variety of household tasks, or by supplementing

---

36)   Myron Weiner, ibid, p 60.
37)   Olga Nieuwenhuys, *Children's Lifeworlds: Gender, welfare and labour in the developing world*, London: Routledge, 1994. The children studied belong either to the Muslim community or to the Ezhava, a low-ranked Hindu caste. The population of the latter is growing more slowly, with one-third under age 15, while the Muslims have 44 per cent under that age. This difference seems mainly due to the later age at which Ezhava girls are married: 57 per cent are single at age 20, while only 11 per cent of the Muslim girls are. Contraception rates, except for abstention and lactation, are low in both communities, 5 per cent for the Muslims and 19 per cent for the Ezhavas. The infant and child death rates are over three times as high among the Muslims.

their work with their own. Girls may also be hired out to help neighbours or wealthier members of the community to whom the family may be indebted. In most cases, when girls work for pay their wages are collected by their mothers and added to the pool of family income. In this way, it may be denied that girls are economically active at all. By custom, men are fed first, so many women and children, especially girls, eat poorly. But while boys may keep part of earnings to buy food or schooling needs, girls' earnings in cash or kind belong to the family.

The expansion of foreign markets for fish has increased the demand for child labour. The unpaid activities of children often enable them to obtain free fish or other food for the family, but even this little compensation has had an depressing effect on the wages of adult fishermen, which must be supplemented by the women's coir-making to make ends meet. The activities related to the fishing industry in which children engage include line-fishing, foraging for seaweed or shellfish, small-scale fish selling, helping the boat-owner and his crew on the beach, and working with a seine-crew. But only the foraging is open to the young of both sexes. At menarche, girls are withdrawn into the home and neighbourhood, while boys may proceed through the other activities until accepted as full-scale fishermen.

Coir-making is carried on in the household. It is now an industry in decline, due to a sequence of world-wide depression and war, followed by the rise of low-priced synthetic floor coverings, which has reduced it to the production of fibre from coconut husks. That it survives at all is thanks to the unpaid work of girls. By the time a girl is ten, she can usually substitute for a grown woman in many of the operations. In addition, she is expected to be able to do all types of housework: sweeping, washing, cooking, fetching water and fuel, and caring for the younger children and seeing they don't interfere with the mother's work. Consequently, girls and boys are channelled early into gender-specific occupations that have implications for the rest of their lives.

Nieuwenhuys argues that much of children's work is underpaid and devalued, and that this is especially true for girls. Children's unpaid work, she says, especially that of girl children, is 'irrationalized': it is assumed, and they are socialized to believe, that their contribution is given as a duty of 'love' and they should be happy to receive only love in return. Yet, she maintains, the Keralan economy needs the children's work, the real costs of which are borne by the women and children themselves.

Nieuwenhuys' study is unusual in a number of ways. First of all, it is done in the Indian state where school rates are highest and child labour rates are lowest. Second, it takes the children's point of view seriously. Third, it is acutely aware of the gender effects of parental exploitation even among the very poor. Fourth, it shows that schooling may not displace child drudgery, but merely add to it. Fifth, it examines work within the home as well as external employment, and argues that the unpaid domestic labour of children is no less exploitative. It is not that work at home (or foraging on the beach), if done in a sociable atmosphere and at an unstressful pace (a big if), may not be at least as harmless a way for children to pass time and stay safe and out of trouble as spending hours in front of a television set; the damage to child potential and development lies elsewhere.

CHILD LABOUR IN THE DEVELOPED WORLD

The combination of school and work that Nieuwenhuys studied is common in the developed world. In the United States, illegal child labour is concentrated in agriculture, and mainly involves migrant, immigrant and refugee children, often said to number 800,000 and to constitute 25 per cent of the paid labour force in this sector. They are exposed to pesticides, and in the height of the summer season work in temperatures that may go up to 100 degrees fahrenheit. In addition to the hazards listed above, their work often involves heavy lifting and carrying and proximity to dangerous machinery. Many are well below ten years old. At first even Cesar Chavez, the organizer of the United Farm Workers who won a famous victory for the grape workers, accepted their presence 'because otherwise our families couldn't survive'. Later, he changed his policy.[38]

In Britain children can legally work on farms from the age of 13. Nevertheless, younger children are recruited to top carrots or do other piece-work. The sheds in which they work are called 'factories' and therefore outside the reach of the farmworkers' union. Illegal child labour in factories and delivering milk is also rife. The children work with their parents' approval and co-operation.[39] Delivering papers (and collecting for them) is still permissible. Recently some newspapers have become so heavy with advertising that the weight of paper deliverers' packs sometimes exceeds the allowable postal

---

38) He is also on record opposing the use of contraceptives, 'so as to increase the number of the poor'. Perhaps he has also changed his mind on this issue.

39) Milk rounds can start as early as 4 a.m., and a five-year-old was recently killed falling off a milk float ('Look who's working', TV documentary, Channel 4, 28 September, 1994). Many employers claim to be doing the children a service by keeping them out of trouble. Parents tend to concur.

worker's maximum. According to Ruth Fisher, head of the British Child Poverty Action Group:

> When an 18-year-old went into hospital for an operation on a protruding disc in his back he was told the injury was due to the three years he had spent as a paper boy .... Newspapers for a Sunday round can weigh anything up to five stone [70 pounds], but post office workers are not allowed to carry bags weighing more than two.[40]

On the continent, child labour is particularly prevalent in southern and eastern Europe, and has been the subject of numerous studies. Portugal is notorious for the children in its shoe factories, where they are exposed to toxic fumes from the glue that can cause 'glue polyneuritis' which leads to paralysis of the limbs and deformity in future offspring.[41] A similar situation prevails in Italy, which is estimated to have the largest number of working children in western Europe. Since the state-run education there takes only four hours a day, a full day's work can easily be fitted around it, even for those who do not truant or drop out entirely. (The rate of truancy in Naples is said to run at 64 per cent.)

Italy is also next door to eastern Europe, where many of the child workers are of the Roma (gypsy) community, who have very high birth rates, live in great poverty and were subjected to discrimination and isolation even under socialist rulers who in theory had policies of improving their condition. At present, not only do large numbers of Roma children work illegally, but many have been kidnapped or sold to criminal gangs. Some are smuggled into western European countries and there trained to operate as thieves and pickpockets by adults who thereby take advantage of laws which do not subject young children to prosecution.[42]

---

40) 'Growing up', *Life* (magazine section of the Observer, 600 grammes), 15 May, 1994, p 69. A recent survey by Ann Clwyd, Labour's employment spokeswoman, turned up children working at night, and from the age of eight. Previous studies show up to three-quarters of the 2 million working school-age children 'are likely to be employed illegally' (Stephen Bates, 'Illegal child labour widespread', *Guardian*, 29 August, 1994, p 2). Children are much less likely to be issued with protective clothing and equipment, especially if they are illegal, as it helps to conceal what they are doing if they are without it.

41) Jonathan Bastable, 'Pity the child', *Sunday Times Magazine*, 30 September, 1990, p 30.

42) According to Alec Fyfe (*Child Labour*, Cambridge: Polity Press, 1989, p 55), in 1985 the price for a trained child varied from £2500 to £3000. Tim Tate ('Trafficking in children', in C Moorehead, ed., *Betrayal: Child exploitation in today's world*, London: Barrie and Jenkins, 1989, p 116) citing the files of Defence for Children International, concludes that the average price paid to their impoverished parents in Yugoslavia in 1986 was $150. They could clear up to $200 a day begging. Thieves probably garner quite a bit more.

In actuality, conditions for children are similar on both sides of the development divide, with only the larger numbers of the poor making the problem of child labour and exploitation seem peculiar to the developing world.

CHILD WORK AND PARENT POWER

At a UN Seminar held in 1985, the representatives of a number of countries, including Bangladesh, Ivory Coast, Colombia, Egypt, Algeria and Syria, among others, opined that child work, within the family at least, was a duty or honour and an expression of family solidarity. This is a view also held in many European countries (Italy for example) as well, especially among the peasantry. But, as Alec Fyfe says: 'We should be sceptical of such ingrained assumptions. Many children make a deliberate choice in favour of "exploitation outside the home" and control of their own earnings, often in the face of parental opposition, rather than endure the "eternal apprentice-ship" of long hours without remuneration under the control of parents.'[43]

Fyfe's sentiments find some support in a survey by Parveen Nanjia of children in 17 industries in the Delhi area, which found them more ready to complain of ill treatment by parents or guardians (7.4 per cent) than employers (1.7 per cent) or co-workers (1.7 per cent).[44] Further evidence that the 'irrationalizing' of children's work for love or family solidarity which Nieuwenhuys referred to is not always convincing, is found in the study of young rural Indonesian workers by Benjamin White and Indrasari Tjandraningsih, who concluded that children prefer waged to family labour and see the former as an escape from the latter.[45] They found that older children who work in family enterprises did so willingly only to learn a trade, and demanded payment for it. (In contrast to child workers in India, the young Indonesian workers generally receive and control their own wages.)

None of respondents here was in school; most had voluntarily left education because they saw no benefit from it. (However, many had

43) Alec Fyfe, *Child Labour*, Cambridge: Polity Press, 1989, p 73.
44) Parveen Nangia, *Child Labour: Cause–Effect Syndrome*, New Delhi: Janak Publishers, 1987, p 259.
45) Benjamin White and Indrasari Tjandraningsih, *Rural Children in the Industrialisation Process: Child and Youth Labour in 'Traditional' and 'Modern' Industries in West Java, Indonesia*, The Hague: Institute of Social Studies, 1992. In this investigation of 'child and juvenile workers', 'children' meant below 14, and juvenile 14 to 19. There are some indications that children as young as seven are involved, but for the most part ages are not too well specified.

already completed six years.) Like Weiner, the authors think school content should be reviewed, to be more relevant, also that it should be made easier to combine school and work, but they also point out that children are becoming more eager to have their own money, thanks to media encouragement of consumerism, so that the employment of children is becoming a matter of relative rather than absolute poverty.

Parental power, 'more absolute than that of an employer or the state', also presents a constant temptation for abuse. Children working for or with the consent of their parents, especially when they also go to school, often end up working longer hours than adults. This is particularly true for girls, whose domestic tasks are not limited in any way. There are opportunities for abuse in other ways as well. Parents can appropriate children's income as it is paid, or agree an advance sum with the employer, or simply settle for a lump sum payment. And they may sell their children for almost any purpose.

Children are used as bonded labour to pay off parental debts, however incurred, or sometimes just the interest. In this, India represents the worst case.[46] Although the system of indenture, whereby adults contract their own labour for a specified period, was prohibited, the practice of parents pledging the labour of their children was not. If this seems strange, it must be recalled that the widespread practice of arranging the marriages of children, especially girl children, has often been a form of sale or bonding. In the traditional Chinese minor marriage custom, for example, poor families would sell very small girls to parents of boys for a small sum. The relationship was a quasi-adoptive one: the purchasing family had rights to the girl's labour for life, and married her to their son when the children came of age. In India and elsewhere, those groups that practised brideprice conceived of it in a similar fashion: the groom's family purchased the bride's labour and fertility for life; sometimes the brideprice was considered compensation for the investment the bride's family had made in feeding and caring for her before marriage.[47]

---

46) Once more, we are faced with numbers that are so difficult to assess that vastly different estimates can appear in the same source. For example, Fyfe (*Child Labour*, Cambridge, Polity Press, 1989, p 17) says: 'As many as 100,000 bonded labourers exist in India, despite attempts to outlaw it'. On p 75, he says: 'In contemporary India, where conservative estimates of bonded labourers start at 3 million ....'

47) The dowry paid to the groom's family by the bride's family among upper-caste Indians – now become customary among almost all castes – has sometimes been termed 'groom price', but the position of the groom, who remains within his own family, is in no way comparable.

Sexual slavery   However acquired, parents have almost unrestricted discretion over the use of the child's revenue, extending to the finance of large purchases, or the support of a drug habit. Such abuses exist in practice in many places, including Thailand, for example, whose government is only slowly coming to grips with the scale of the problem of its million working children and the open market in their recruitment. Still far more embarrassed by the sale of children into prostitution than into sweatshops, the looming scale of the AIDS problem has played a role in jolting Thai officials out of complacency.[48]

Even children's rights organizations may blame parents (and western capitalism) more for selling children into sexual than industrial slavery. Citing the testimony of a child prostitute whose parents had sold her to a brothel when she was 13, Peter Lee-Wright observed:

> She was proud that it had enabled her to help her family back home, and she announced that she had been able to buy them a colour television set, a refrigerator and two motorbikes. These hardly seemed the needs of poor peasants facing famine .... but Mr Samphasit [Co-ordinator of the Centre for Protection of Child Rights] makes that a point of distinction between those who send their children to the sweatshops and those who celebrate their birth as a prelude to sending them to the brothel. The latter are more motivated by material desires .... It is a poignant image of the corrupting influence of western capitalism, that so many are willing to sell their daughters into sexual bondage for a fridge.[49]

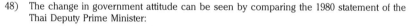

48) The change in government attitude can be seen by comparing the 1980 statement of the Thai Deputy Prime Minister:

   I ask all governors to consider the natural scenery of your provinces, together with some forms of entertainment that some of you might consider disgusting and shameful because they are forms of sexual entertainment that attract tourists .... We must do this because we have to consider the jobs that will be created for the people (J Ennew, *The Sexual Exploitation of Children*, Cambridge: Polity Press, 1986, p 99);

   with the recent letter to the *Guardian* from a London Thai Embassy secretary:

   Anyone caught sexually exploiting children, whether Thai or foreign, will be met with the full force of the law. We must destroy the myth that Thailand is a country where immoral, exploitative behaviour is somehow permissible (Atchara Shayakul, Second Secretary, The Royal Thai Embassy, Letter to the *Guardian*, 16 July, 1944, p 28).

49) Peter Lee-Wright, *Child Slaves*, London: Earthscan, 1990, p 149. See also Russell Miller, ('Pity the Child', *Sunday Times Magazine*, 30 September, 1990, pp 24–32), who says parents are given £12 to £14 by a recruiter, called a 'fisherwoman' who tours the villages. 'Fisherwomen' charge buyers £135 for a twelve year old girl. The youngest on offer are seven. Anyone can buy them, including brothel keepers. The practice is so well established it is impossible to believe that a significant number of parents are being hoodwinked.

Sex tourism (involving boys as well as girls) has certainly become part of the flow of tourists from rich to poor countries, including Turkey, Sri Lanka and Southeast Asia. Although Americans are blamed for having turned many places in Vietnam, Thailand, the Philippines, Korea and Taiwan into 'rest and recreation' (R&R) centres during the Korean and Vietnam wars, the Japanese now provide most of the demand in the area, supplemented by the continuing American military presence. The American bases in Subic Bay and the R&R centre in Olangapo remain the largest centres of prostitution in Asia. Since 1980, and local protests in the Philippines, many young girls have been imported from the Philippines into Japan. Recruiters from Manila tour the provinces using various pretexts, but the lure of quick cash earnings from child prostitution is often enough to convince parents to encourage their children to take the work, as in Thailand. At the other end, the Japanese Mafia Yakuza is involved in a business that grosses about $1.5 million per day and imports about 8,000 to 10,000 girls per year.[50]

Street children   Whether or not children are initially viewed by their parents as economic assets, there is a sizeable and growing number who, gradually or abruptly, refuse that role. Some, but not all, urban street children are in this category. In some cases they have run away from abusive homes. In others, they are thrown out, either by their natural or step-parents, or by other adult household members. In still others, having found they can support themselves, however precariously, they gradually repudiate the duty to contribute all or part of their earnings or takings to the household, in much the same manner as migrant workers may drift away from sending home remittances.

Street children have drawn a good deal of attention because they are the most visible part of the phenomenon of child labour. In fact, the early 19th-century reformers, including Lord Shaftesbury, were worried about them as a social problem more than about the less visible children working in factories and on farms. Almost two centuries on, they are a growing presence, not only in the older industrialized countries, but even in parts of the world where they had traditionally not been observed. So far, the largest numbers have been in Latin America, but there are growing bands in Africa and Asia, as these continents become increasingly urbanized. On the other hand, according to Judith Ennew, 'Cuba used to have an enormous street child population which has now disappeared, despite the fact that the

---

50)   Tim Tate, 'Trafficking in children', in C Moorehead, ed., *Betrayal: Child exploitation in today's world*, London: Barrie and Jenkins, 1989, p 116.

country is not much wealthier now than it was before the revolution.'[51]

The total number of street children is hard to estimate. In world-wide terms, the conventional figure, 100 million (the same as the estimate of the number of labouring children) is often quoted.[52] Some estimates for Latin America alone are so high they amount to a third of the total number of children, or 50 million.[53] Since they represent so peculiar a manifestation of the economic connections between children and their families, street children are often classified according to how much family contact they retain. (In some places, such as India, however, whole families often live together on the streets, so it is particularly difficult to categorize them in this way.) In 1986, Unicef estimated that 75 per cent of them maintained continuous contact, 20 per cent had fitful contact, and 5 per cent none at all. These are the 'abandoned children', whom in 1985 the Anti-slavery Society estimated at 7.7 million (excluding the socialist countries and runaways in the developed countries). Street children are predomi-nantly boys, and the presence of girls is particularly embarrassing for officialdom, since child prostitution, although it affects both sexes, is more salient among them.

Piled on top of the hazards of the poverty-stricken urban life that they are exposed to, including drug trafficking and sexual exploitation, street children are also sometimes murdered by agents of the state and respectable society, in operations known as 'social cleansing', most notably in Colombia and Brazil.[54] Projects to help them have attained world-wide publicity. There are an estimated 300 such projects for them in Brazil alone, which usually include a step-by-step programme of offering food, washing facilities, followed by education and counselling, as well as sheltered workshops.

The most difficult children to help are said to be those who have lost all contact with their families, but the assumption that the return of a child to its family is a measure of success may have something to do

51) Judith Ennew, *New Internationalist*, 'Children of the street', October, 1986.
52) Russell Miller, 'Pity the Child', *Sunday Times Magazine*, 30 September, 1990, pp 24–32. p 30: Jonathan Bastable estimates there are more than 100 million child slaves; the Report of the Conference 'Amnesty Working for Children', Session on Street Children, cites 'an estimated 100 million children living on the streets', of whom between one-fifth and one-third have no adult support.
53) Judith Ennew, *New Internationalist*, 'Children of the street', October, 1986. Ennew believes a more realistic number is 8 million.
54) Amnesty International has documented the killing of thousands of 'street children' between 1990 and 1994. The killings are often carried out by the police, but with the approval and assistance of local industrialists, shopkeepers and business groups, who consider them 'social undesirables' and petty criminals, harmful to business. Groups or persons who have tried to help the children have also been threatened. None of those responsible has been punished. See, for example, *Focus*, Amnesty International, January, 1994.

with this finding. In fact, street life often has a structure and organization of its own, and, particularly in Latin America, some street children have formed groups that seem very like trade unions, and even hold conferences.[55]

Constructing kinship   The inverse of the street child problem is that of domestic labour, mostly of girls, which is almost invisible. Frequently little girls are given by their parents to wealthier households for fictive 'adoption' or fostering which is really household slavery. The practice is particularly rife in Latin America, where both relations of patronage and sentimentality over family ties are ingrained.[56] In Brazil nearly one-third of the domestic workers are children, who may be farmed out as 'kin' when as young as three or four years old. They are usually unpaid, but are sometimes working off parental debts. Because of the fictive relationship, if they run away their 'guardians' can take legal steps to get them back. Frequently children from the countryside are taken into domestic service in the towns and cities, so that they would not know where to run to in any case. In domestic service, they are isolated but traditionally sexually available to the household males. If pregnancy results, they can be turned out.

Children are sometimes trafficked between countries as well as within the countries in which they are born. The smuggling of children from Yugoslavia to Italy is only one example; children are taken from one country to another under many circumstances.[57] They are taken in various ways, often kidnapped, sometimes by tricking their parents into thinking they are being taken for one purpose and then using them for another; and sometimes they are knowingly sold. But in most cases, money is passed from one adult to another in the process. None of this is new, but, according to Tim Tate:

---

55) Alec Fyfe, *Child Labour*, Cambridge: Polity Press, 1989, p 112.
56) See, for example, Nancy Sheper-Hughes, *Death Without Weeping*, Berkeley: University of California Press, 1994. The phenomenon of fictive kinship is not confined to Latin American countries, however. Benjamin White and Indrasari Tjandraningsih (*Rural Children in the Industrialisation Process: Child and Youth Labour in 'Traditional' and 'Modern' Industries in West Java, Indonesia*, The Hague: Institute of Social Studies, 1992) also point out that fictive kin relations in the employment of children in Indonesia weaken the children's bargaining powers.
57) The crisis of Rwanda has already produced evidence of child use, kidnapping and trafficking. Chris McGreal ('Aid with biblical strings attached', *Guardian*, 17 December, 1994, p 11) cites cases of opportunistic 'charities' fundraising by starting 'children's centres' which are stocked by taking children from their villages. He also says, 'The Catholic agency Caritas has been criticised for giving children into adoption into Zairean families without keeping tabs on their fate. A UN source reported Zaireans trafficking in Rwandan children through Burundi.' An American organization was also accused of child-stealing for international adoption.

What has transformed trafficking from an occasional bit of business to an international trade, which – according to some of its participants – rivals cocaine smuggling in scale and value, is air travel. The comparison with cocaine is an apt one. Child trafficking is at heart no different from any other form of illicit trade ... [such as] drugs or pornography .... Frequently the same people are involved in all three trades, and use the same shipment routes .... Drugs ... are a common feature in most forms of trafficking, and the trade in children is no exception.[58]

This sounds a bit melodramatic. However, there have been documented cases of babies being kidnapped or sold, allegedly for adoption, but then killed, their stomachs opened and filled with drugs, and transported across borders as if asleep. Another horrific practice is the traffic in kidnapped or 'adopted' children to be used for organ transplants, and there are also claims that Third World children are sold to wealthy American or European paedophiles for sexual abuse or pornography.

Tate cites allegations by the Secretary General of the National Council on Social Welfare, Leonardo Villeda Bermudez:

'Many families came forward to adopt children with physical defects. At first we thought they were decent people who loved children, but in time it was discovered that they wanted to sell them for body parts ....' Villeda Bermudez [also] referred to previous reports suggesting that children had been used by foreigners for sexual abuse and as couriers in drug trafficking. Various branches of the Honduran government subsequently disowned Bermudez' allegations. Nonetheless, the trafficking of children for spare-part surgery is known to occur in other Central and South American countries. California officials have confirmed several cases of Mexican children being sold to American paedophiles for prostitution and child pornography, and Justice Department officials in California have confirmed several cases.[59]

During the recent controversy over the red tape now involved in the adoption of Romanian children by Britons, Jonathan Edwards of the Christian Children's Fund of Great Britain alleged that the use of 'adopted' children for illegal organ banks is a danger in transnational adoptions from eastern European countries as well.[60]

58) Tim Tate, 'Trafficking in children', in C Moorehead, ed., *Betrayal: Child exploitation in today's world*, London: Barrie and Jenkins, 1989, p 115.
59) Tim Tate, ibid, pp 116–7.
60) Jonathan Edwards, 'Romanian children are not there for the taking', *Guardian*, 1 August, 1994, p 19.

INTERNATIONAL ADOPTION

Yet most inter-country adoptions are quite genuine in intent. That is, they are like other adoptions in which the adults aim at all the rights, powers, status and roles accorded unquestioningly to biological parents. But they are usually resorted to after attempts at adoption within their own country are unsuccessful. Would-be adoptive parents find that while natural parents are subjected to no institutional or social assessment, they not only suffer the stigma of infertility but must pass every detail of their lives under the judgemental eyes of a social worker. Frequently they are considered 'too old' at ages at which coevals are still reproducing. Adoption, they are told, is a service to children, not adults.

Turning to transnational adoption, they are constrained to justify their purpose as need meeting need, not simply the unquestioned right to parenthood. And not just another piece of imperialism, or, as Tate puts it:

> At the heart of the trade is a simple economic equation: the First World is rich but has a low birthrate. In Third World countries the position is exactly the opposite . . . . Some countries have grown tired of what they see as a new brand of colonial exploitation – the stripping of a nation's greatest potential asset, its children.[61]

It is also partly a matter of the same pride and sensitivity to suggestions that they cannot take care of their own which has convinced many adoption services within Britain and the United States that it is in the interests of children to be adopted only within their own racial group. Here two strands of the mystique of parenthood are pitted against each other: the 'loving home' against 'culture', the belief that, lacking biological parents, a child belongs to the race, religion and nationality of its birth.

Need meets need in Brazil   With a rapidly expanding child population of over 63 million, half of whom are in poverty and 9 per cent registered abandoned, Brazil is currently the largest exporter of

———————————————————◇———————————————————

61) Tim Tate, 'Trafficking in children', in C Moorehead, ed., *Betrayal: Child exploitation in today's world*, London: Barrie and Jenkins, 1989, pp 115–8. The novelist Mary McCarthy expressed the same sentiments when plane-loads of orphans were air-lifted to the United States for adoptions at the chaotic end of the Vietnam war. 'These children', she protested, 'are part of the patrimony of Vietnam.' The migration of children with their parents (including those among the 'boat people' in all the years since then) have drawn no such protests, demonstrating that nationality (or 'background' or 'culture') is a residual category of ownership, exercised only in the absence of parental claims.

babies. Yet, for some, Brazilian adoptions, in common with others between the poor and powerless and the rich and powerful nations, have been tainted with the racial and political overtones of two notorious historical examples of the taking of children from their parents by powerful oppressors: the Nazi example of stealing children who had 'desirable' racial characteristics from conquered countries and taking them to Germany for adoption and 'Germanification'; and more recently, the example of Argentina under dictatorship, where the children of arrested dissidents were taken for adoption by government and army officers.

In addition to Europeans and Americans, a surprising number of the adoption-bound who travel to Brazil are from Israel. The majority of the children they adopt come from the southern states, like Parana. Ironically, the state of Parana has many fair-skinned children because of a history of several attempts by German migrants to set up 'racially pure' white settlements in the mosquito-ridden jungles where their impoverished descendants still reside. The Swiss charity Terre des Hommes, which runs an official, rule-bound, bureaucratically hamstrung and slow-moving adoption programme, and tries to place handicapped and older children, has complained that, on the open market, the going rate for an 'easy to place baby' – a white, blond, blue-eyed male under three months – is $25,000.[62] Older children, and the female or dark-skinned cost less.[63]

Romanian babies for adoption   The idea that adopters actually pay for a child, as if it were just another commodity, rather than simply for 'administrative costs', as others might pay medical expenses, is peculiarly emotionally fraught. The arguments over the attempts of British couples to adopt Romanian babies over the past several years have followed a similar course, with the added suggestion that the British government might view these adoptions as a form of devious immigration. Romanian and British governments have jointly collaborated in the last few years to apply the same stringent criteria to Romanian adoptions as to domestic ones, drastically changing what was previously an almost unhindered procedure. The anguished outcry of those who see Romanian

---

62)   The price quoted relates to the 1980s, and has probably risen. The development of high-tech fertility treatments have probably not caused much downward pressure, since such treatments are also expensive. In the United States, in vitro fertilization has been estimated at upwards of $60,000 for each successful pregnancy. For older women and men with low sperm counts, if the couple is willing to soldier on to up to six tries, the cost can escalate to $800,000 ('Cost of Test Tube Babies Averages $72,000', *New York Times National*, 28 July, 1994, p A16).

63)   Claudia Cabral, quoted in Tim Tate, 'Trafficking in children', in C Moorehead, ed., *Betrayal: Child exploitation in today's world*, London: Barrie and Jenkins, 1989, pp 119–20.

adoptions as rescuing the children from squalid orphanages has encountered, in addition to the spectre of organ trafficking and reproaches to adoptive parents who reject damaged children, the overriding principle of blood and culture within races that was formerly applied between them.[64]

CHILDREN'S RIGHTS

The question of the proper treatment of children is a complex and difficult one in which their disposition is disputed by groups and individual adults who see them as treasure, commodity, instrument and symbol, and only fitfully as human beings with rights, interests and preferences of their own.

In a sense, all children have the status of slaves, since others exercise for them the civil rights that are accorded to adults; others have the power to determine their place of residence, and even their whereabouts from hour to hour; others determine what their occupations shall be, from hour to hour; others can command their companionship and wages. Students of the condition of children have been forced to the admission that families can and do exploit children as well, but the concurrent movement with respect to children has been to transfer rights and powers over them from father to mother, and only gradually to recognize the rights of children over themselves.

The idea that children have any rights that could conflict with the rights of their parents is a relatively new one. A final version of the UN Convention on the Rights of the Child was formulated in 1989, in recognition that

> it had become obvious that the position of the child, vis-à-vis its parents and the state, needed reformulating, and also that in the modern world increasing numbers of parents are no longer able or willing to feed, house and protect their own children . . .. Early agreements about children were about duties. The Convention is about rights.[65]

---

64) See, for example, Jonathan Edwards, 'Romanian children are not there for the taking', *Guardian*, 1 August, 1994, p 19. The controversy reached a climax when a British couple was arrested trying to smuggle a Romanian baby over the border, having paid its parents as well as the middlemen. Another twist in the case was the suggestion that the baby would have to remain in an orphanage because it was of Gypsy stock, against which other Romanians are prejudiced. Since then, there have been reports that some Romanian prostitutes sell their babies to Turkish middlemen for about £3000 (Reuter, 'Baby trade', *Guardian*, 13 December, 1994, p 14).

65) Caroline Moorehead, in *Betrayal: Child exploitation in today's world*, London: Barrie and Jenkins, 1989, p 13.

Although still not accepted by a number of nations, and still far from noticeable implementation in many who have, the Convention is based on four principles, including the primacy of the child's best interests, the duty of the state to insure his or her development, and the right to be respected: to express freely his or her views, and to have due weight given to these views.

Strengthening children's rights could have practical advantages, too. If children were accorded more respect and consideration of their interests and optimal development – in contrast to the mixture of brutality and suffocating sentiment with which they are currently regarded – they themselves might feel less need to escape control through paid labour and school avoidance, and their parents less reason to collude in the employment of their children. But just how these lofty principles can be implemented within such closed and private structures as the family is not altogether clear. One can only suggest programmes and campaigns similar to the education and communication processes that are slowly acclimatizing large portions of the globe to the moral principles and practical advantages of women's rights.

Chapter 4
The zero option

Despite the arguments already adduced that the prospects of parental power constitute an important motivation for childbearing, it is likely that the weakening of these powers through a strengthening of children's rights would have no more influence over birth rates than women's rights have had over marriage rates. The latter may be falling where women have achieved the most independence, yet marriage still represents not only the fate but the desire of the overwhelming majority of women. Similarly, there has always been a proportion of women for whom all the inducements to motherhood have seemed inadequate, and their numbers may increase, but they are still a small minority and are likely always to remain so.

CHILDLESSNESS AND THE MEDIA

Almost all discussions of voluntary childlessness include something of a media sampling on the issue. For the most part, these survey the American scene; so here is a dilatory sample taken from British media over a period of about a year:

April 1993 Several programmes on the same night. 'The Snapper', BBC2, 10 pm: Daughter in large Irish family becomes pregnant; family welcomes new baby as romantic and badge of potency. 'You Me and It', BBC1, 9:10 pm: Couple having difficulty in conceiving. Unpleasant friend who hates children falls pregnant to despair of wife (whose fecund relatives are avoiding her because they think their children and conversation are causing pain). Couple is shown going through unpleasant, painful, inconvenient and humiliating fertility tests and procedures, feeling inadequate when they fail. Equation made of people who don't want children hating them, while people who do are loving, sensible and kind.

Spring, 1993   Revival of Lorca's *Yerma* by a Punjabi troupe. The original play was Spanish and concerns a woman who has not been able to conceive in five years of marriage and is finally driven to kill her husband in despair. It seems to travel well across cultures.

9–16 May, 1993   National Fertility Week began with an allegation that infertility is a disability in more urgent need of medical care than cancer, hip replacement, and so on and controversy that followed. A number of articles and a TV programme on donor insemination (DI). *Observer Magazine* (9 May, Gill Gorell Barnes) and *Guardian* Women's page (10 May) also have short pieces on DI (in both cases about the shame the husband with a DI child may feel, and the possible resultant hostility). *Guardian* also features one on fertility screening, with advice on how to be maximally fertile, plus one on egg donors (the latter also notes the obstruction egg donors may have from their husbands, who don't like the idea of wives having babies by other men). There is no mention of other possibilities, or discussions of the childbearing enterprise in general.

The theatre, at least since Shaw and Wilde, who seemed to take childless couples more or less for granted, has become a rich mine of marriages and lives twisted by childlessness, regardless of class or circumstance, from Edward Albee's *Who's Afraid of Virginia Woolf?* to Terence Rattigan's, *The Deep Blue Sea*.

Headline in *Daily Mail*, 10 June, 1993, three inch letters   'My husband's infertility drove me to despair.'

3 January, 1994   *Nativity*, BBC Radio 4 Monday play by Nigel Williams concerns dirt-poor couple who find an abandoned baby. Couple had been unable to have own child, and man at first rejects child who isn't his. Wife (age 20) takes view, which eventually prevails, that having a baby – who needs nothing but love – is having something, and an achievement in life. Arguments about family cruelty and children not being property (propounded by bureaucratic social workers) are invalidated before the all-conquering power of love. Then wicked landlord and his even wickeder wife (who turn out later also to have been sterile, having adopted children who disappointed them and were sent away to school) try to trick the couple out of the child. Eventually, child's natural mother gives it to them with her blessing after they try to get her to take it.

15 June 1994 ITV police detective programme 'A Touch of Frost', in which detective 'Jack' Frost goes about solving a child disappearance and an old murder while his wife lies dying of cancer. When she dies he confesses to sympathetic nurse that their marriage had been bad since she discovered she was infertile. She changed, became house-proud, insisted that he strive for promotion in his job, 'make her proud' as a substitute for children.

Almost any of the more popular detective series has featured, in the last few years, more than one murder where the villain is a man of character so mean that he forced his wife to remain childless, or of character so weak that his wife's inability to produce children drove him to crime. Alternatively, a woman's childlessness drives her to drink, crime or other manifestations of a twisted psyche. These themes have so long a history in literature they are considered motivations plausible enough to be produced as solutions without need of further clues or evidence in the windup to the mystery.

Until recently, childlessness was always assumed to be an involuntary condition, caused by infertility within marriage or celibacy without. Yet, despite the current drumbeat of cultural outpourings, there is evidence that there has always been a proportion of the population whose lack of offspring was intentional, and as more countries approach average fertility rates of two children or fewer, many more men and women will end up, intentionally or otherwise, among the childless. The most recent spate of publications on voluntary childlessness began to appear in the 1970s, as the post-war baby boom receded. But whereas the previous bout of low fertility had been attributed to the Great Depression of the 1930s and the exigencies of the World War that followed, the present increase seems to have more complex origins.

NAMES AND NUMBERS

It is one sign of a stigmatized group that even the term by which they wish to be known is a matter of sensitivity and debate. Some prefer to be called 'childfree'; however, one wonders whether the very rejection of the term 'childless' is an not acceptance of the assumption that more of anything is better. Perhaps the provisional last word is that of Root Cartwright, Chair of BON (British Association of Non-parents), who comments:

> It's hard to know which usage colludes more with pronatalist
> prejudice. Whereas 'childless' implies a deficiency (moral,
> perhaps, as well as physical), 'childfree' does suggest both an
> unnecessarily negative view of the 'with child' state, and that kind
> of self-centred consumerism which surfaces in the press all too
> often.

He goes on to say that even

> alternatives, such as 'elective non-parent' are clumsy in some
> ways and seem more about distinguishing ourselves from those
> who can't than defining a neutral status 'other than parenthood'
> .... Ultimately, only history and numbers can solve the problem!

In the discussion that follows here, all such terms will be used interchangeably.[1]

The question of numbers is at least as fraught as that of nomenclature. Surveys of the childless, such as those taken from census data, do not query the cause of the respondents' status (though nearly everyone else does), while investigations of causes make no attempt to calculate numbers. An early report using (American) census data claimed that the proportions of ever-married women who remained childless throughout life (in addition to the 5 to 10 per cent who never married) rose from 8 per cent in the mid-19th century to 20 per cent in the 1930s, and then fell to below 10 per cent during the post-war baby boom.[2]

But how can you know what proportion of any age cohort of women will actually end up childless? The authors of the above report found that women at ages 70 to 74 reported having had fewer children than the same group did at 40 to 44, largely, they believed, because women with small numbers of children (and none) survive in greater numbers than women with larger families. Looking at younger women produces a different result. Jean Veevers noted that at 1978 rates, 30 per cent of women then in the childbearing years would end up without children.[3] This did not happen: the numbers had reflected a trend toward postponed reproduction.

When it comes to the proportion of those who are childless by intent, the numbers are even more uncertain. Studies of Mormons and

1)   Root Cartwright, personal communication.
2)   WH Grabill and PC Glick, 'Demographic and social aspects of childlessness', *Milbank Memorial Fund Quarterly*, 1959, vol 37, pp 60–86.
3)   Jean E Veevers, *Childless by Choice*, Toronto: Butterworth, 1980, p 157.

other high-fertility and relatively healthy populations indicate that the proportion of physically infertile women is probably less than 5 per cent and may be as low as 3 per cent. A recent British report compared the proportions of women born between 1945 and 1965 who remain childless.[4] For each succeeding group, the proportions of the childless were greater at the same ages. Of those born in 1950, 42 per cent were childless (from all causes) at age 25, and 15 per cent at age 40; of those born in 1960, 60 per cent were childless at 25. The authors concluded that involuntary infertility now affects less than 2 per cent of their practice, while voluntary childlessness was about 11 per cent. Since average age of first-time mothers in Britain is now 27, this casts doubt on the findings of several of the main studies, which tend to concentrate on younger women.

INVESTIGATING THE CHILDFREE

Wherever a trend is spotted, explanations and investigations are not far behind. The increasing use and reliability of contraceptives on the one hand, and the increasing effectiveness of fertility treatments on the other have forced both experts and the general public to recognize that some childlessness is actually planned and intended.[5] Still, voluntary childlessness goes so much against the grain of normative belief that it is perhaps the most under-researched phenomenon, not only in population studies, but in studies of women, employment, the family, economics and the environment, to name only a few of the areas it affects and is affected by. Like most research on unconventional 'lifestyles' the bulk of what there is has been done in the United States. A search for the British Library's list of books about childlessness, brings up ten titles, of which only two are positive: Ellen Mara Nason and Margaret M Poloma, *Voluntarily Childless Couples* (see note 10), and Jean Veevers, *Childless by Choice*, 1980 (see note 3). The rest tend to bear titles like: 'Coping with Childlessness', 'Never to be a Mother', 'Unfocused Grief' and so forth.

The overwhelming influence of conventional wisdom with respect to the voluntarily childless, so much in evidence in media treatments of the phenomenon, is scarcely absent from scholarly ones, most strikingly because it is precisely the stereotypes which are at once the

---

4)   Gina Johnson, for the South Bedfordshire Practitioners' Group, *British Medical Journal*, 30 October, 1993, p 1116.
5)   See Nathan Keyfitz, 'The family that does not reproduce itself', in K Davis, MS Bernstam, R Ricardo-Campbell, eds, *Below Replacement Fertility in Industrialized Societies*, Cambridge: Cambridge University Press, 1987, pp 139–54. Keyfitz discusses low fertility in a variety of economic and political explanatory frameworks.

most puzzling and least explored aspects. The usual method, in books and articles, is to round up a sample who exhibit the 'disorder' and question them about how and why they made their decision, and about their childhood experiences, where the investigator is sure the root causes of aberrance actually lie.

In an early investigation, the distinguished sociologist Paul Popenoe concluded that 'most of the cases are purely neurotic'.[6] That little has changed in 60 years, at least among those favouring psychological explanations, is illustrated in a recent newspaper article by Angela Phillips, who, alongside testimony by three cases in point that she had garnered, commented, 'Among the women I have spoken to, the decision to say no to motherhood was often tied to unhappy memories of childhood'.[7]

In common with such stigmatized groups as, for example, people with facial disfigurements, the childless (both voluntary and involuntary) complain that perfect strangers feel justified in asking them to account for their condition. But unlike other stigmatized groups, including the reluctantly barren, the childfree do not invite pity but rather seem to inspire hostility. In the 1960s, the sociologist Lee Rainwater found that the childless are thought maladjusted, emotionally immature, immoral, selfish, lonely, unhappily married, and prone to divorce. Some of his respondents even questioned whether adults who intended no children should marry at all; most of them thought you should have as many children as you could afford. Since then, the conventional wisdom has remained more or less intact.

What is at least as striking about these stereotypes as their lack of any kind of objective evidence (in fact, there exists much evidence to the contrary), and the firmness with which they are held, is the resentment almost universally directed towards the childfree, despite the view that the condition has its roots in dysfunctional childhood, which one would think would elicit compassion.[8] Optional parenthood seems to call into question not only the usually unquestioned reasons for childbearing, but even the politically sensitive institution of the family itself.[9] Indeed, the first question raised in their classic study

---

6) Paul Popenoe, 'Motivation of childless marriages', *Journal of Heredity*, 1936, 469–72.
7) Angela Phillips, 'Will you be mother?', *Guardian*, G2, 30 May, 1994, p 6.
8) That there is some malice in these opinions is suggested by Jean E Veevers (*Childless by Choice*, Toronto: Butterworth, 1980), who found that the happy childless couples in her study were subjected to more hostility than those who are clearly unhappily married.
9) During the 1992 presidential campaign, many Americans, upon hearing that Hillary Clinton was a prominent lawyer, apparently got the idea that the Clintons were childless, which forced them to bring out and expose their daughter to photographers. Reservations roused by their having only one child were only partially assuaged by the publicity given to their cat.

by Ellen Nason and Margaret Poloma is whether a couple without children can be called a 'family' at all, noting an expert opinion that 'Having children, not simply being married, becomes the significant criterion for qualifying a family'.[10]

Overall responsibility for 'qualifying as a family' rests, as usual, largely upon women. Overwhelmingly, they are the suspects called in for questioning in investigations of childlessness. Part of the reason is that, until recently, only the married had to account for the fact that they were childless and wives were more available, more co-operative and generally proved more articulate when it came to self-explanation. But there was also an assumption that the having or not having of children would affect the lives of women more, and that the practice of childlessness would depend upon the woman's decision and determination to a greater extent.

This assumption actually received some support in the small sample of 30 couples studied by Nason and Poloma, who, unusually, interviewed both members.[11] Nevertheless, the general tendency to neglect the study of childless men is rather a pity, since when they are questioned they often reveal themselves as a particularly interesting, thoughtful group (to the extent that they can be said to form a group). For example, some men felt childlessness left them free to take risks or lower-paying jobs or to concentrate on interests other than work; their marriages tended to be more egalitarian than those with children; they greeted the slurs on their masculinity which they encountered from friends and colleagues with amusement rather then resentment; and they were even relaxed about the possibility of their wives earning more than they did.[12]

For the women, childlessness often had the complementary attraction, that of allowing them greater freedom to concentrate on careers or other serious interests. In fact, the most robust finding with respect to childfree women (as compared to mothers) has been their higher career achievements, although this effect has been attenuated

---

10) Ellen Mara Nason and Margaret M Poloma, *Voluntarily Childless Couples: The Emergence of a Variant Lifestyle*, London: Sage Publications, 1976, p 5.

11) Ellen Mara Nason and Margaret M Poloma, ibid. Women's choice was particularly notable among those couples who were characterized as 'strongly committed' (though not 'irrevocably committed', which would have been signalled by one or both having been sterilized, according to the authors) (p 27).

12) See also Jean E Veevers, *Childless by Choice*, Toronto: Butterworth, 1980, p 99. Veevers interviewed 120 wives and 36 unrelated husbands in 1972–78. As to the egalitarian tendencies of childless marriages, Veevers found husbands were often the instigators here. In any case, family studies show that the addition of children almost inevitably generates pressures for more conventional sex roles, if only because of the effects on male and female incomes. The disparity in income among childfree couples has been found to be less than that for parents, in the proportions 55 per cent to 45 per cent for the childfree, and 66 per cent to 33 per cent for couples with children.

over time as working mothers have become more common and accepted. Between 1926 and 1970, for example, the proportion of childless women in *Who's Who* declined from 54 per cent to 24 per cent. But even in 1982 (in the United States), while 18.6 per cent of college-educated women aged 35 to 44 were childless, the proportion was only 9.7 per cent of high school graduates.

In both Nason and Poloma's study and that of Jean Veevers, the educational level of both male and female non-parents tended to be above average.[13] For women at least, cause and effect are reciprocal. In the physical sciences, having a child tends to decrease a man's chances of getting a degree by 1 per cent, but a woman's by 31 per cent; in the humanities, the figures were 2 per cent and 13 per cent; in the social science, 3 per cent and 11 per cent, respectively. Once the degree is obtained, however, childless men's chances of a successful career were slightly below average, while those of childless women were above the women's average. Some of the women in Veevers' study confessed that the only times they considered having babies were in response to a career setback: failing an important examination, or not getting a good job, or when a crucial experiment failed.[14]

Like Nason and Poloma's subjects, the average age of the wives in Veevers' study was 27, but, unusually, she compared her interview group, for background and social data at least, with a parent group of the same ages and lengths of marriage. She found the childfree were more likely to be urban in residence than the parent group, and tended to come from more middle- and upper-class backgrounds: only 15 per cent were working-class in contrast to 50 per cent of the parents. Unsurprisingly, they were more likely to have no religion, 74 per cent versus 7 per cent, and more unlikely to be Catholic than Protestant. The childless are more likely to have been only children (or first-born) than the reference population: 21 per cent versus 7 per cent, were onlies, while 50 per cent versus 33 per cent were first-borns.[15]

A Dutch study is among the few that included older couples and made use of a large sample, supposedly representative of the general

13) Jean E Veevers, ibid. Twenty-five per cent had advanced degrees in Veevers' childless group versus 6 per cent of a parent group.

14) Jean E Veevers, ibid, p 80. This finding stands in interesting contrast to the image, still common today, that ambitious young women must make an agonizing decision at the start of their careers and in the abstract. A letter from a Dr PG Baddeley regarding the career risks of highly trained and placed whistle-blowers in the Health Service remarks, 'A high proportion at risk are women who may have sacrificed marriage or motherhood to care for others.' (*Observer*, 19 June, 1994, p 22.)

15) Jean E Veevers, ibid, p 152, Table 4.

population, to ask 'Is there an innate need for children?'[16] While the outcome (and even the measures used) cannot really be said to answer the question posed, his comparison of parents and non-parents on a number of measures of physical and mental well-being at various ages produced some interesting results. Although very few of the differences reached statistical significance – for example, there were no significant differences in marital or social adjustment – the interesting finding to emerge was that, on all the questions, the tendency was for non-parents to feel happier and healthier. In fact, for couples between ages 55 and 65, the differences actually reached significance; and between ages 55 and 59, the parents were found to feel significantly more anxiety than the childless. Nor are these findings isolated ones. While some researchers have found marital happiness greatest for those with between one and three children, others have actually found it greatest among childless couples.

The more general and reliable finding is that 'happiness' decreases as family size increases. In one study the clearest finding was that marital happiness was most strongly connected with successful fertility control (but which is cause and which effect is not so clear).[17] For parents, marital happiness is known to be connected with stages in the childrearing cycle. The birth of the first child is notorious in the sociological literature as a difficult time, and one at which divorce rates soar. Another dip in happiness occurs when the children reach adolescence, but it rises when they leave home. (Recent research has also confirmed that, far from feeling depressed and lonely when children fly the coop, women's confidence, contentment and self-esteem improve.[18]) Divorce rates are highest for couples with children under 16, next for childfree couples, and lowest for those with children over 16. Many other factors, such as age and selectivity – grossly incompatible couples probably divorce early in marriage – may influence these findings, but they do cast doubt on the popular conviction that children stabilize a marriage and increase domestic bliss by giving a couples a common interest they might have lacked.

---

16) R Veenhoven, 'Is there an innate need for children?' *European Journal of Social Psychology*, 1974, vol 4, pp 485–91.

17) See Robert Reed, 'Interrelationship of marital adjustment, fertility control and size of family', *Milbank Memorial Fund Quarterly*, October, 1947, pp 383–425. Reed's experimental sample was 860 native-born white Protestant Americans.

18) Norval Glenn and Sarah McLanahan, 'The Effects of Offspring on the Psychological Well-being of Older Adults', *Journal of Marriage and the Family*, 1981, 409–21; also, Harkan Slatter and Gunnar Klackenberg, 'Discordant Family Relations in Intact Families', *Journal of Marriage and the Family*, 1992, 940–56.

THE MAKING OF A NON-PARENT

What is usually of most interest in quizzing the intentionally childless is how did they, in a climate that takes motherhood for granted, come to think so differently from everyone else? The question is of great interest to the childless themselves, and makes of them a notably self-conscious and articulate group to interview. In the books and articles that examine them, in addition to speculating about what in their experience influenced their decision, they also take up the various charges that have been levelled against them.

In many cases, childlessness may be seen more as an evolving state than a sudden decision. Only one-third of Veevers' sample had made the decision before marriage; those who did often felt strongly and chose their mates accordingly. The other two-thirds arrived at their choice by a series of stages, beginning with several successive postponements of intended parenthood. But they were more effective contraceptors (than the parent sample) from the start. After successive postponement came a period of explicit consideration of pros and cons. In half the cases one partner convinced the more reluctant or dubious other, and in the remainder the decision was mutual.

The stages of development in the commitment to childlessness are reportedly matched by a progression in the pressures experienced from friends and relations to become parents. A newly married couple is accorded a 'honeymoon' or grace period of about two years during which their failure to produce offspring is not subjected to comment or disapproval. Pressures begin to build in the third year, reaching a peak during fourth and fifth years, after which the issue is gradually resolved, either by fiat on the part of the targeted couple, by acceptance of whatever excuse they eventually settle on, or else well-wishers simply give up in despair, and hope that future regrets will vindicate their rejected advice.[19]

Both Veevers' and Bartlett's studies elicited a variety of both short- and long-term reasons for refusing parenthood, and some of both samples had not absolutely ruled children out. Closely related to motivation are the perceived advantages and disadvantages of the childfree state, which the childless are routinely questioned about. Uniformly, freedom is cited as the overriding advantage, which seems to take in freedom at many levels and in diverse areas: not only freedom to spend or allocate money without regard for current or future descendants' claims, neither current demands for toys nor

---

19)   Jean E Veevers, *Childless by Choice*, Toronto: Butterworth, 1980, p 134.

future financing of education and housing, but also freedom to arrange time, activities, and even relationships at will.[20] In fact, Veevers was somewhat taken aback by the difficulty many of her subjects had in naming disadvantages.

The popular view that childless women had a morbid fear of childbirth was not generally borne out. Many were interested in the childbirth experience, and while some expressed revulsion, others actually said they would have wanted to go through process except for the prospect of being stuck with a child afterwards![21] Do childless women, then, dislike children? Some of those interviewed revealed having thought long and deeply about the matter of childrearing in all its aspects, and some of them had concluded that they would not be good parents because of failings of temper or patience or a lack of interest in teaching.[22] Some had had experience with disabled siblings that put them off. Some thought they themselves were of poor eugenic stock. Others rejected the view that children confer eternal life, preferring to find their immortality through achievement or good works.[23]

Many looked to the older rather than the younger generation for their decision. Many of the childless women interviewed saw their parents, particularly their mothers, as unhappy, either incompetent or unfulfilled. Some had had role models of glamorous successful childless women to emulate. But overall only half reported that they actually did not like children. Some indeed had special relationships with small relatives to whom they act as godmothers or favourite aunts. Others were teachers, nurses or volunteers with extensive professional or quasi-professional involvement with children, sometimes difficult children with special needs. Surprisingly, a few of those interviewed expressed willingness to adopt or quasi-adopt children in need. Like parents, some think babies are particularly appealing, while others think children become more interesting as they get older. Still others (again like some parents) frankly admit that they find the

---

20) Bartlett points out that Veevers tends to underestimate the real freedom that the childless enjoy when she (Veevers) notes that 'Like their more conventional counterparts, most are bound by the constraints of a monogamous marriage, a nine to five job, and a limited amount of time, money and imagination'. In fact, despite the general contentment of the marriages among the research samples, many expressed satisfaction in knowing they could leave whatever relationship they were in without the damage to children and finances that divorce among parents engenders.

21) Jane Bartlett, *Will you be mother?*, London: Virago, 1994, is a British study of 50 childfree women ranging in age from 22 to 75. In Chapter 2, she says that even among women who did mention fear of childbirth, none listed fear or revulsion from the physical aspects of childbearing as her only reason.

22) Jane Bartlett, ibid, pp 66–74.

23) This group includes the actress, Julie Christie, who told an interviewer (Jill Parsons), 'I don't need to perpetuate myself through a child.' *Daily Mail*, 4 December, 1992.

company of the young boring or unrewarding, if not actually
disagreeable.

People without children of their own, whatever their observations
of friends and relatives, are often unaware of or at least unread in the
considerable literature by and about the difficulties even advantaged
middle-class parents face. In addition to testimony by parents who
have physically abused their children, there are several categories of
confessional writing by authors who admit their inadequacy in
meeting the prescribed demands of parenthood, among them many
female journalists. For the most part, such writing tries to give the
impression that the writer (deep down) actually enjoys the cheerful
anarchy in which the family lives, and is unaware that the account
could convey a less inviting picture. An example of this type is an
article by Sue Arnold, a well-paid columnist for the London *Observer*
who lives in a high-income household with six planned children.
Before explaining why she had them all – 'just that I like having
children' – she mentions the day when one of her daughters had to go
to school in bedroom slippers because no one could find her shoes.[24]

Another common genre is one that admits grimness, gives advice
on management skills, and pleads for the help and support mothers
no longer receive (if they ever did).[25] Rarest and most painful is the
literature of regret, exemplified by Shirley Radl's *Mother's Day is Over*.
The writer is American, but the book bears a foreword by Joan
Bakewell acknowledging its equal relevance in Britain. Based on her
own experience and interviews with 200 mothers, Radl says: 'My aim
is to show that it is not enough for every child to be a wanted child, as
Planned Parenthood advocates. The planned and wanted children of
the world often wind up unwanted after they've been around
awhile.'[26] Admitting that she hesitated to write her book because of
the likelihood of family members taking the general argument
personally and being hurt, she asserts that having children caused
serious disturbance in her marriage through no fault of the children
themselves.[27]

---

24) Sue Arnold, 'Now we are six ...', *Observer*, 21 January, 1990, p 52.

25) Examples of this are Brigid McConville, *Mad to be a Mother*, London: Century, 1987; and
Jane Price, *Motherhood, what it does to your mind*, London: Pandora, 1988.

26) Shirley Radl, *Mother's Day is Over*, London: Abelard-Schumann Ltd, 1974, p xi.

27) That hers was not a lone sentiment, was indicated by the famous result got by Ann Landers
when she asked her readers if they thought being a parent was worth it: 80 per cent of the
10,000 parents who bothered to write in said 'no', and 70 per cent of the responses were
from women (*Denver Post*, 23 January, 1976, p 62).

MANAGING THE OPPOSITION

Even without the back-up of parenting literature, most of the childfree have had considerable practice in suiting their reasons to their audience, giving one justification out of a complex of reasons to parents or grandparents, another to colleagues and friends. Concern about overpopulation is increasingly mentioned, but many audiences (including the researchers) tend to consider it merely a pretext not to be taken seriously. As Nason and Poloma put it:

> Some couples tend to 'use' this particular reason for maintaining their childless status when they interact with some friends and acquaintances on a social basis. Most of these couples were not environmental crusaders; rather they simply used a socially acceptable reason (and one that was less 'selfish') for not having children.[28]

Other couples try to deflect criticism by announcing an intention to adopt, and some, stricken with guilt at their ease and affluence in a world of deprivation, have actually considered trying to adopt a needy child, in a half-hearted sort of way.

The most frequent accusation flung at the childfree is undoubtedly that of 'selfishness'. It is a curious charge, when those who make it simultaneously believe that the childless are deprived of the 'deepest', if not the greatest, joys known to humanity, and that their lives are significantly if not totally bereft of meaning. It is even more curious that the epithet is never (and never required to be) spelled out precisely. It may refer to the fact that the childless have more money to spend on their own rather than on childish pleasures, or may also be a coded allusion to the (actual or imagined) enhanced sexual activity the childless are thought to enjoy.[29] Or it may refer more generally to the freer and less stressed lives they seem to lead. In any

---------------------◇---------------------

28) Ellen Mara Nason and Margaret M Poloma, *Voluntarily Childless Couples: The Emergence of a Variant Lifestyle*, London: Sage Publications, 1976, p 38. In a study by Susan O Gustavus and James R Heley ('Correlates of voluntary childlessness ...', *Social Biology*, September, 1971, pp 277–84) of 72 childless couples, population concern was mentioned most frequently. Bartlett too reported that all of her group claimed to be greatly concerned about overpopulation.

29) Jean E Veevers (*Childless by Choice*, Toronto: Butterworth, 1980, p 99) finds that childlessness in the popular imagination is equated with both sexual inadequacy and sexual promiscuity or other forms of deviance. While few or no probing questions about sexual adjustment were asked in this (or any other) study, and she did find suggestions that an uninhibited sex life was seen as one of the benefits by at least some of her respondents, most researchers have concluded that the sex lives of the childfree are generally unremarkable.

case, the term seems to have both a social and a moral dimension, and is most disapproving when aimed at women, whose highest calling is still thought to reside in sacrifice for the benefit of family members. Thus it is particularly difficult for a childfree woman to justify her state to her mother, since the mother may take her decision, sometimes correctly, as a judgement on herself as a woman as well as all her efforts.[30]

The childfree respond to criticism in various ways, ranging from cheerful acceptance to guilty defensiveness, from thoughtful discussion to boomeranging return of the insult. Men tend to defend themselves primarily by appealing to the compensatory social aspects of their behaviour. They point to the fact that they unprotestingly pay taxes that go towards the care, welfare and education of other people's children, that they contribute more lavishly to charity than their colleagues, that they volunteer time coaching or as 'Big Brothers', or other types of community work.[31]

The women's responses are sometimes more diffident. Some agree readily (if facetiously) that 'I indulge myself disgracefully', while others retort somewhat confusedly: 'What's wrong with being selfish? The world would be a better place if all women were a bit more selfish and chose what is right for them.' Still others hit back resentfully:

> Women with children are selfish in overpopulating the world and always expecting other people to cope with their children and overlook their bad behaviour . . .. Also they expect their children to look after them in old age: they are selfishly too dependent on their own children.[32]

Although many of the subjects of these studies are comfortably off and travel extensively or take other forms of elaborate holidays, money was seldom given as a reason for refusing the responsibilities of parenthood (although Veevers claims that her childless group had an exaggerated fear of debt). In Bartlett's study, too, if money was an issue, it centred primarily on the fear of poverty rather than the desire for wealth. Overall, it was time and energy they valued more than a high-consumption lifestyle.[33]

---

30) Jane Bartlett (*Will you be mother?*, London: Virago, 1994, p 27) points out that, in spite of all the sentiment and lip-service devoted to motherhood around the world, mothers are despised as sources of unpaid labour, untrained and often credited with having no more intellect than the children they are raising.

31) Jean E Veevers, *Childless by Choice*, Toronto: Butterworth, 1980, Chapter 6.

32) First statement by Liz Lowen quoted by Angela Phillips, *Guardian*, 30 May, 1994, p 6; second attributed to 'Jo' and third to 'Rose' by Bartlett, pp 205–6.

33) Jane Bartlett, *Will you be mother?*, London: Virago, 1994, pp 207–9.

Broadening the outlook on the childless   Bartlett's study is an improvement over previous books about childlessness because she acknowledges so many more dimensions and aspects of the subject, pointing the way to future serious studies. She even includes a section on the infertile, recognizing continuities as well as the differences between the two groups. At least one of her subjects had had a still birth, though no deaths of older children are reported. Unusually, she takes account of the trend over the past several decades toward the separation of motherhood and marriage – which has previously been noticed only with respect to rising non-marital fertility – by interviewing unmarried women and lesbians living in various types of relationships, including quasi-marriage, as well as alone. She also included respondents from other black and minority ethnic backgrounds, for example, Asian, Jain and Greek–Cypriot, where marriage and childbearing within marriage are even more exigent than within the usual white Protestant or middle-class milieu.

Besides recognizing the diversity of the intentionally childless, her findings indicate that, in addition to their rising numbers, their class distribution is becoming more even, in contrast to the isolation expressed by her oldest subject: 'Other women who decided not to have children were not in my class. I'm sorry to use that word, but it does come down to that. They would have been upper middle-class women, well educated, and I was working class ... but they were not the women with whom my income allowed me to live.'[34]

OLD AGE AND SOCIAL SECURITY

Even in comparatively wealthy industrialized economies, with well-developed pension systems, the majority of people tend to think of offspring and old age very much in the way members of more traditional peasant societies do. In all of the debates that I myself have witnessed, the childfree participants are invariably warned that they face a lonely if not impoverished old age without the support and companionship of children. In the studies reviewed here, surprisingly little of the expected fear of old age and loneliness surfaced. Instead, a typical comment was that of a man who said:

> I can remember times of being frightened of getting old without having children to make me feel good. But recently I have been thinking that, if I have to become 80 years old and have to

---

34)   Jane Bartlett, *Will you be mother?*, London: Virago, 1994, p 24.

> depend on my children for whatever they want to give me, then
> my life won't be worth a whole lot.[35]

This comment relates to the emotional support that people expect from children in their declining years. The citizens of wealthy countries have become accustomed to the idea that even if their own efforts to cushion themselves financially fall short, they will have some measure of social security to fall back on. The governments of these 'advanced' countries, however, are becoming more and more concerned about the coming effects of low fertility on the social security systems installed only a few decades ago, but now almost taken for granted. The most frequent fear expressed is that the age structure of a stagnant or declining population will eventually contain one-quarter or more who are over 65.[36] How will such numbers of supposedly dependent and increasingly long-lived people be supported financially and cared for physically? This is an increasing worry not only for industrial societies but also for many developing countries, as their life expectancies rapidly lengthen even before mass pension systems are developed.

In countries with well-developed social security systems, there are reasons to believe that fears have been exaggerated for political reasons. First, the rise in the numbers, or even the proportion of the elderly does not mean that pension, medical and social service expenditures need go up proportionately, since many of the costs of establishing and administering services change little as the numbers served increase, and the statistical effects of fluctuations in need over time and space are diminished.[37]

Second, many of the economic benefits of growing populations, if they ever had validity, are actually extremely dubious in modern industrial societies, rapidly automating and connected as they are to world markets.[38] Such societies are characterized, not by a shortage

---

35) Ellen Mara Nason and Margaret M Poloma, *Voluntarily Childless Couples: The Emergence of a Variant Lifestyle*, London: Sage Publications, 1976, p 39.

36) See, for example, David Brindle, 'Not as young as we were', *Guardian*, 5 March, 1993, p 13, for a typically alarmist popular treatment of the subject. Lincoln H Day (*The Future of Low-Birthrate Populations*, London: Routledge, 1992) gives a far more optimistic assessment. Day also believes that the current generation of old people may actually live longer than future ones, because they haven't been exposed to as many pollutants as future generation will have been. They also may be the greatest gainers financially, because they have put in relatively little and future pensions may be reduced (p 32).

37) These effects are called 'economies of scale' which make the cost per unit smaller as the numbers of clients (or products) increase. See V Fry, S Smith, and S White, *Pensioners and the Public Purse*, Institute for Fiscal Studies Report No 36, 1990.

38) See Geoffrey McNicoll, 'Economic growth with low fertility', in *Below Replacement Fertility in Industrialized Societies*, K Davis, MS Bernstam and R Ricardo-Campbell, eds, Cambridge

of youthful labour, but rather by growing numbers of the unemployed, no longer associated with the classical business cycle but now a seemingly permanent feature of the economy. Recent surveys by several international agencies indicate that unemployment rates run to 33 million workers in the OECD (Organization for Economic Co-operation and Development) countries alone. If discouraged job-seekers and the part-time employed (who constitute much of recent 'job creation') are included, the number runs as high as 50 million, or one-eighth of the available workforce. In Spain, one-quarter of the workforce is admittedly out of work. Moreover, the numbers of the long-term unemployed are increasing, and in Europe and the United States, racial minorities have several times the rates of unemployment as those of the 'native' white population.

Whenever labour shortages in particular areas developed in the past, governments often resorted to encouraging immigration to redress it, a solution at present politically unpopular.[39] In any case, there is still some slack available for female employment, and of course technology can to a certain extent offset labour shortages; however, to the extent that industrial societies are able to substitute automation for cheap labour, the developing countries that now attempt to compete with the older industrial countries on the basis of their lower wage bill will eventually have to automate as well, which will exacerbate their own unemployment rates.

With such considerations in mind, the absence of an increasing proportion of the population from the job market, the so-called dependent elderly, may actually be seen as economically benign, particularly if environmental considerations are added. If, for example, the increasing numbers of the elderly require a greater proportion of services than goods compared to a younger population, as they are said to, and engage in fewer environmentally damaging activities, the long-term economic effects may well be beneficial on balance.[40]

---------------------------------◇---------------------------------

cont.
  University Press, 1987, for an interesting discussion of the social conventions that influence economic accounting.
39) Although it is still broached from time to time, even in a Germany newly determined to stem the flow of asylum seekers and other 'foreigners', some of whom have lived in the country for over 20 years. See, for example, David Gow, 'Old Germans need young migrants pay', *Guardian*, 1 September, 1993, p 9. Gow pointed out that about 2 million (out of a population of over 80 million) non-German workers produce about 10 per cent of national output.
40) Lincoln H Day (*The Future of Low-Birthrate Populations*, London: Routledge, 1992) claims the elderly engage in more swimming, walking, bicycling and dancing, but supplies no evidence. In any case, he does not mention drinking and driving. David Gow ('Old Germans need young migrants pay', *Guardian*, 1 September, 1993, p 9) asserts, on the contrary that, 'the increase in pensioners is threatening to overload German roads ..... More elderly people are buying, retaining and driving cars ...'.

But are those over 65 really as 'dependent' as they are assumed to be? And, in particular, are they dependent on their children? In fact, most of the care and help given to the old is actually rendered by other old people. Day argues that (like those of women and children) their non-market services are seriously undervalued. Private house-holds supply much transportation, food and laundry services, as well as nursing, and these, in developed as well as undeveloped societies are frequently supplied by the old. More generally, he points out that, although the increasingly elderly age structure has been looked at mostly in economic terms, the problem is more social and philosophical than economic; the basic meaning of life, which has too long centred on procreation, should include guaranteeing a dignified old age, made as comfortable as technology permits. And finally, most of the publicly financed arrangements that would help the elderly would also help other segments of the population, such as women, the young, the disabled, in fact just about everyone. Among these are public transportation; and neighbourhoods on a human scale with good public amenities, such as clean rest rooms, libraries, parks and other facilities for walking, swimming, and cycling.[41]

But even the flow of financial support is not as one-way as is usually supposed. In a study of over 11,000 Americans taken over a decade, Pat Keith found that at least through their 60s, older people were generally at least as likely to be helping their children financially as vice versa (for example, helping to pay for a house or a grandchild's education).[42] In Keith's study, the childless were more likely to live alone. But

> those living alone were not disproportionately deprived of social
> ties with others, and in instances, they were advantaged and
> were able to secure the most contact with neighbors, friends and
> relatives .... The health of those living alone tended to be at least
> marginally better than those who were non-heads of households
> and this may have fostered a more active social life ....[43]

Her overall results agreed with other findings that childlessness was a benign condition as far as the elderly were concerned. Glenn and

---

41)   Lincoln H Day, *The Future of Low-Birthrate Populations*, London: Routledge, 1992, p 156.
42)   Pat Keith, *The Unmarried in Later Life*, New York: Praeger, 1989, p 187. At beginning of the decade, 11 per cent of women and 22 per cent of men (in their 60s) helped their children financially; at the end, it was 4 per cent of women and 5 per cent of men. At both beginning and end, 20 per cent of the women and 6 per cent of men received help from their children. The decline in income with retirement was not offset by children's contributions, however.
43)   Pat Keith, ibid, p 176.

McLanahan, in fact, found 'little evidence that important psychological rewards are derived from the later stages of parenthood.'[44] A study by AT Day found white American women, even at 77 to 87 years, had a strong desire to be independent.[45] Living with children or moving into an institution were considered equally undesirable. It was affective and social relationships more than instrumental or economic support that was wanted, and this agrees with other findings that the aged would rather engage professionals to provide instrumental care than to depend on family members. In sum, there is much evidence that, whatever the financial, medical or social conditions of the elderly, their management, in the future as well as in the past, is more a political than a demographic issue, and really part of the more general issue of disablement.[46] In low-fertility societies, an increasing proportion of the population will tend to have few relatives, but there is no reason to think that the shortage of blood ties would not be compensated by other forms of social, medical and financial arrangements, if the larger society has the will to admit them.

In developing countries, however, the outlook is still of a different sort. The growth in the numbers and length of old-age dependency must weigh upon traditional systems of family care, where it is still assumed that children, often sons, must bear the primary responsibility for both aspects. In addition to extra burdens on families with children, where fertility levels are decreasing along with the growth in life expectancy, the question is, will the demographic changes not result in many more of the dependent aged with no families to shoulder the burden?

Such worries have recently become a focus of debate in China, where the economy remains in many ways largely a poor and agricultural one, although it has seen the most precipitate decline in fertility of any developing country. At present, both rural and urban elderly usually live with a married child, and financial support is

---

44) N Glenn and S McLanahan, 'The Effects of Offspring on the Psychological well-being of older adults', *Journal of Marriage and Family*, 1981, pp 409–21, p 409.

45) AT Day, *Remarkable survivors: insights about successful aging among women*, Washington, DC: Urban Institute Press, 1991. Fewer than 9 per cent lived in institutions, while 55 per cent lived alone, 21 per cent with husbands, 16 per cent with children, and 3 per cent with siblings.

46) See Kingsley Davis, 'Low fertility in perspective', in *Below Replacement Fertility in Industrialized Societies*, K Davis, MS Bernstam and R Ricardo-Campbell, eds, Cambridge University Press, 1987, p 60. Davis points out that, in any case, a change in the TFR from 2.0 to 1.6 changes the proportion of the elderly from 20 per cent to 26 per cent. Geoffrey McNicoll, in 'Economic growth with low fertility', in the same volume points out that a population declining by 1 per cent per year (as in the asymptotic case of TFR = 1.6) has no greater total dependency burden by the conventional definition in comparison to [one with] replacement fertility, although it has a 50 per cent higher proportion of the over 65s.

provided by children for over half the men and 80 per cent of women over 60. But even here personal care is self-administered to 80 per cent of both sexes, which implies that in most cases they do not drain, but may even contribute to household labour.

According to calculations by Lin Jiang, the number of the over 65s will increase from 49 million in 1982 to 198 million in 2030, that is, from 4.9 per cent to 13.5 per cent, in an economy still too poor to contemplate universal pensions.[47] Can the traditional system of family support accommodate the increasing proportion? How should help be targeted at the most stressed families? Under the assumptions of the current fertility and infant and child mortality rates and various assumptions about marriage ages, Lin concludes that, thanks to improved survival rates among children, even though women have many fewer births larger numbers of them will have between one and three surviving children than the present elderly cohort, and fewer women will have no surviving children. At present, 8 per cent of elderly women have none, although this cohort averaged 6 births apiece and 3 surviving children. In 2030, 2.5 per cent of the old will be childless (about 4 million).

By these calculations, each household would have to foresee supporting some elderly parents for a longer period, but children for less of the time, and only 1.7 per cent of households will have to support two or more of the elderly. Thus the overall dependency ratio will remain almost unchanged between 1990 and 2030, but the proportion of support given to the elderly will shift from 9 per cent to 23 per cent. In addition, the burden of care for the elderly will peak at 45 to 54 rather than 35 to 45 as now. These predictions mean that it would be perfectly feasible for the state to institute a pensions policy which would target aid on the most stressed families, acting as a 'second insurer'. Moreover, he suggests that assistance could be given in such a way as to reinforce current demographic policy: promising more help to the childless and one-child elderly, especially to the elderly with one daughter. Aid to the childless at 100 per cent of current per capita consumption, for example, would take only 0.19 per cent of societal disposable income. Under these assumptions, the total tax rate needed would come to only 3.5 per cent of income, even including extra income for those with daughters but no sons. Lin feels such a policy would substantially reduce son preference; freed from the need for the financial support sons could provide, most of the elderly really prefer the companionship and care of daughters.

Vaclav Smil claimed that fewer than one in a thousand Chinese

---

47)   Lin Jiang, 'Parity and Security: A Simulation Study of Old-Age Support in Rural China', *Population and Development Review*, June, 1994, pp 423–48.

women wish to remain childless.[48] But Smil's assertion referred to a 1985 survey of married women in the relatively poor agricultural provinces of Hebei and Shaanxi. Fertility rates all over China have fallen since then to less than two children per woman, and, as China rapidly urbanizes, voluntary childlessness will surely increase. In the large cities, a few 'dink-er' [double income, no kids] couples have already been noted. Articles on this phenomenon have begun to appear in the Chinese press, generally favourable but often with a flavour of sexual sauciness that makes them susceptible to sale along with the burgeoning tide of sensationalist literature on Chinese newsstands.

POLICY IMPLICATIONS OF CHILDLESSNESS

Perhaps the greatest drawback that the voluntarily childless themselves experience is the lack of social support and approval in the wider society. Even those groups who might have been expected to approve have been notably lacking in enthusiastic endorsement. As Veevers points out, the feminist movement, representing a general view of the interests of the majority of women as it perceives them, has not in general been anti-motherhood, but quite the contrary. And even such organizations as Planned Parenthood and ZPG (Zero Population Growth) also seemed to assume universal parenthood.[49]

Some attempts have been made by the childless themselves to organize support groups. In the United States, NON (National Organization of Non-Parents) was founded in 1972 by Shirley Radl, and her associates, John Rogers and Sherwood Wallace. Later, strains developed within the organization between those who wished simply to stress freedom of choice in the option of parenthood, and those who felt they should be campaigning for childlessness as a superior lifestyle. The first group won out, and the name was changed to NAOP (Nation Association for Optional Parenthood), but, according to Veevers, the activist fire died down (and the organization has since expired). In Britain, a corresponding group, BON, was founded in 1978, emerging from ISSUE, a support group of the infertile, as it became clear that the positive aspects of being without children were not sufficiently attended to. The membership of BON, like the American counterpart, tends to stagnate and to have a high turnover, since many people join when they need support, only to drift away when their own crisis or difficulty has been resolved.

---

48) Vaclav Smil, *China's Environmental Crisis*, New York: ME Sharpe, 1993, p 31.
49) Jean E Veevers, *Childless by Choice*, Toronto: Butterworth, 1980, pp 180–1.

In addition to offering support to those who decide to remain childless and help for those trying to decide, BON has attempted to raise public consciousness and acceptance of non-parents by media exposure. Media approval has not been forthcoming, however. Even exposure has been difficult to obtain and almost invariably circumscribed. When 'representative' members of BON are interviewed for radio or television, it is often in a context in which their statements are neutralized or negated by the presenter, and promptly forgotten as the programme moves on under conventional assumptions about family life.

Of all the reports and investigations, only that of Veevers has spelled out a set of possible implications for social policy on the basis of her findings. These are essentially the BON programme:

- more general public acceptance that the voluntarily childless are no more maladjusted than the rest of society;
- raising public consciousness that parenthood is optional rather than compulsory;
- increase of rational debate regarding the pros and cons of childbearing;
- maintenance of a full range of both contraceptive and fertility services; and
- support, respect and solidarity with those who do not choose to have children.

Chapter 5

The myths of the only child

It may no longer be expected that a woman should want a large number of children, but a great deal of normative pressure is still exerted by governments, churches and the popular culture (let alone friends and family) on women to 'fulfil themselves' by having a child. Or, rather, two. A past president of the Planned Parenthood Federation of America once complained that she experienced more pressure to have a second child than to have her first, and in the recent American electoral campaign, Hillary Clinton was occasionally accused of not being sufficiently 'into motherhood', since she had mothered only one. The general acceptance of this sentiment is shown by polls citing the most frequent reason in favour of having a second child is the provision of companionship for the first. In this respect, and despite the steep drop in family size since then, conventional opinion does not seem to have changed since 1956.[1] A recent letter to a newspaper psychologist ran as follows:

> I have a son aged four. I would love to provide him with a brother or sister but my husband says it is out of the question for financial reasons and that we cannot have more children. I am

---

1) ES Solomon, JE Clare and CF Westoff, 'Fear of childlessness, desire to avoid having an only child, and children's desires for siblings', *Milbank Memorial Fund Quarterly*, April, 1956, pp 160–77. However, in a small sample survey of parents of two children Sharryl Hawke and David Knox (*One Child by Choice*, New Jersey: Prentice-Hall, 1977) found this was the second reason given, the first being insurance against childlessness.

terribly worried about my son growing up as an only child and find myself in constant conflict with my husband. I have even considered divorce because I feel so strongly about this.[2]

It is a curious footnote to the pronatalism of a low-birthrate society that, if remaining childless is pitied or condemned as 'selfish', having only one child inspires even more disapproval. Yet both conditions are fairly common and have been so for some time. In the United States, the proportion of women who had a single child at the completion of childbearing rose from 20 per cent to 30 per cent between 1920 and 1940. It then decreased to 15 per cent during the post-war baby boom. By the mid-1970s it was back to 20 per cent, and has increased still further in the past decade.[3] A poll taken in 1979 showed that, of women in the 18 to 24 range, 12 per cent expected to have no children, 10 per cent one child, 51 per cent two children and 18 per cent three children.[4]

Whereas the earlier increase in the proportion of one-child families (reflecting the general decrease in family size) was attributed to the economic pressures of the great depression, the current increase is attributed more complexly to more reliable birth control, more working mothers and greater marital instability, as well as financial considerations. The interesting thing about this set of factors is that they relate in different ways to the question of whether the resulting single-childedness is a matter of preference or reluctance. While a felt lack of money seems to point to the latter, dependable contraception indicates both control and preference; but marital instability and maternal jobholding are ambiguous. Do women have fewer children

2) 'Family Matters', *Observer Magazine*, 4 April, 1993, p 49. It is not really clear to what extent such a motivation is claimed because it is viewed as an acceptable pretext, in line with maternal self-abnegation. A more recent instance of the acceptability of such a sentiment occurred in the case of a British couple on trial in Romania for trying to smuggle a five-month-old baby over the border, in defiance of the country's adoption laws. Their lawyer said in extenuation, 'They broke the law in their desire to do good. They wanted to offer Grace [their previously adopted child] a little sister.' (Chris Stephen, 'Verdict in baby case soon', *Guardian*, 13 October, 1994, p 4).

3) 'Introduction', in Toni Falbo, ed., *The Single Child Family*, New York and London: Guildford Press, 1984, pp 1–2. These proportions seem high, and Ann Laybourn ('Only children in Britain: popular stereotype and research evidence', *Children & Society*, vol 4, no 4, 1990, p 386) reports lower proportions of only children in Britain. While 22 per cent of women born in 1925 ended up with only one child, only 17 per cent of those born in 1945 did so. More recent data (involving women not yet finished with childbearing) found that while 11 per cent definitely opted for one child in 1970, only 7 per cent did so in 1984. Laybourn states that at any time a larger proportion of children are only children than will end up being so. That is, there are more sibling additions than deaths.

4) H Theodore Groat, Jerry W Wicks and Arthur G Neal, 'Without siblings: the consequences in adult life of having been an only child', in Toni Falbo, ed., *The Single Child Family*, New York and London: Guildford Press, 1984, p 255.

because they are not certain their marriages will endure, or does the break-up of a marriage spell an early end to childbearing? Do women have fewer children because they wish to spend more time on their careers, or does jobholding force a realization that there are limits to a woman's time and energy?

The low birth rates in other industrialized countries and in the troubled economies of eastern Europe have resulted in an increase in the proportions of one-child families in these places, too, whether by choice or economic necessity. The highest European rate is found in Hungary, where one in four completed families have only one child. But while other European countries worry about national depletion, only the Anglophone countries seem to worry obsessively about the effect on the children themselves. Most of the research on this aspect has been done in the USA.

But what is considered wrong with being, and therefore with having, an only child? The prejudice is so pervasive, it hardly needs to be repeated: only children have been called: narcissistic, intolerant, inflexible, unrealistic about personal relationships, spoilt brats, lonely, conceited, self-centred, domineering, anxious, quarrelsome, over-protected and more liable to divorce – all depending on who you read or ask. In sum, only childhood was called a disadvantage by two-thirds of public opinion, when queried on a number of occasions. Why has the stereotype been so negative, and why haven't popular opinions changed even as the proportions of such persons in the population have?

EXPERT OPINION AND PSYCHOLOGICAL THEORIES

It must be said that authoritative opinion has not helped. An early expert statement was that of EW Bohannon, who in 1898 pronounced only children unhealthy, nervous, below average scholastically, socially immature, selfish and over-indulged. In 1907 G Stanley Hall, another pioneer of child psychology, gave it as his opinion that, 'Being an only child is a disease in itself.' In 1922 AA Brill wrote, 'It would be best for the individual and the race that there be no only children.'[5] And even now many child psychologists, and even more psychiatrists, tend to agree. 'There's a danger that the child is made a companion to the parent and catapulted into adult status', according to one clinical

---

5)   G Stanley Hall in TL Smith, ed., *Aspects of Childhood life and Education*, Boston: Ginn, 1907; AA Brill, in *Psychoanalysis, its Theories and Practical Applications*, Philadelphia: Saunders, 1922.

psychologist.[6] 'The child may compare itself with the parents, rather than with a sibling, and see itself as insufficient and incapable', says another child psychologist.

The 'counselling' approach   Many people are not clearly aware that there are two general types of expert who call themselves psychologists. The first is the sort who most often writes newspaper columns and gives advice or does counselling or 'therapy' in a clinical setting. These psychologists work by analysing the patient's or enquirer's particular circumstances and relating these to their complaints or problems, often using one or some combination of theories also developed by practitioners in a clinical setting. Confidence in the correctness of his or her explanations is built up in the practitioner's mind by experience over time. Freud is the best known exemplar of clinical practice, and his theories the most influential of this type of psychologist. The nature of the way his followers and imitators proceed makes their explanations peculiarly apt to focus on any unusual element of the situation, especially one that concerns the relationship between parents and children, which, thanks again to Freud's influence, the overwhelming majority of the western population believe is the key to all later developments. It follows easily that any divergence from the 'normal' or usual family configuration must lead to problems in child development. So such experts and their only-child clients are easily convinced that many of their woes stem from this source, and, once having decided the source or the trouble, it is easy enough to work out a story that leads to the difficulty.

The ready acceptance of this approach in the popular culture has the added advantage that although many of its adherents do have training and degrees, academic qualifications are by no means necessary for authoring books along these lines, such as a recent one that begins:

> Childhood without siblings leaves a legacy of burdens which present themselves as 'problems' with far greater force [in adulthood] than even they do in childhood .... Most certainly all is far from rosy behind the assured and confident exterior that only children usually present to the world. But if it is so difficult, why hasn't the only child experience been identified before?[7]

---

6)   This and the following quotation appear in Markie Robson-Scott, 'Only baloney', *Guardian*, 28 February, 1994, G2, p 10.

7)   Jill Pitkeathley and David Emerson, *Only child: how to survive being one*, London: Souvenir Press, 1994, p 2. The book is organized around 60 or so 'in depth' interviews, with never a

The 'scientific' approach   The other type of psychological approach involves the investigation of behaviour in a fashion that is modelled as closely as possible on procedures accepted in various natural and social sciences. Because much of human behaviour is not experimentally controllable for both ethical and practical reasons, and because the nature of mental processes is still little known, large groups of individuals must be compared with each other to determine sometimes small differences in particular tendencies or attributes, and very little can be said about any given individual. Nor can the results obtained by this method be used to advise individual decisions – such as whether to limit one's family to a single child in specific cases. But the results *can* be used to refute (or support) folk wisdom and stereotypes, since these are also general statements about groups of people sharing particular attributes. Moreover, results that contravene the stereotypes held by the researcher, or are at least controlled for the researcher's bias, are more credible than those that confirm the researcher's beliefs, both because of the human tendency to pick up and emphasize results that agree with preconceptions, and because stereotypes may act as self-fulfilling prophecies.

RESEARCH ON THE ONLY CHILD

The concerns over only children in the western world have to do with what might be called psychological development: in the areas of intellect, personality, marital adjustment, professional success, and general happiness or contentment. If one wishes to investigate these psychological qualities by more or less scientific methods, the more clearly the behaviours that indicate these qualities can be defined and measured, the more likely it is that a generally agreed result will be found. Because of the vagueness of 'personality', where children are concerned, tests of school achievement and the IQ test (which was actually developed to predict school achievement) yield the most reliable, that is, repeatable, results when groups of children who differ in various ways are compared to each other. In the case of the only child, not only must such things as class, which have been shown to affect the result, be the same, but a decision must be made about the

———————————————◇———————————————

cont.

      hint that any of the answers might have been influenced by conventional stereotypes and beliefs rather than by the assumed cause and effect relationship between only-childhood experiences and 'problems'. There are tips for parents and partners as well as for sufferers from this terrible handicap. Not only are the authors completely unaware of the large literature on the subject, but so is a journalist who interviewed them and announced that 'very little data is available'.

comparable kind of non-only child. The oldest? The youngest? And what effects do various amounts of intersibling spacing or family size have?

In many research studies, the only child is simply treated as one category of a range of family sizes. A number of studies over the past 40 years have found a negative relationship between the physical and intellectual development of children and family size. In 1956, for example, one study reported a tenfold increase in the incidence of mental deficiency as one went from the single child to the sixth in birth order.[8] The Scottish Mental Survey of 1953 found that children in larger families tended to be shorter in stature, even when the father's occupation (that is, social class) was taken into account.[9] Yet another survey found that height, weight, vital capacity and strength all decline with increasing family size and that, in general, prematurity and its attendant problems become more frequent with increasing birth order.[10] And another corroborated these findings in detail and also reported greater incidence of illness and death, both in early childhood and later, in larger families.[11] In general, the outcome is worse for all members of large families, but in particular for those of higher birth order.

It is easy enough to rationalize (especially in retrospect) the advantages in health and general development of being a member of a small as against a large clutch of siblings in terms of the ease of transmission of infections and the health, time and energy of mothers, even when such factors as income and social class are taken into account. What is of real interest where the two-child family is preferred, however, is how the only child compares with the child who has one sibling. Some early American studies found that, although the rise in IQ as family size decreases is one of the most reliable results obtained, only children seemed to do less well on such tests than the first-born of two children.[12] Ingenious theories were devised to explain this strange reversal, until it was found that the effect disappears when children with single parents, who suffer the

8)   B Passamanick and AM Lilienfeld, 'The association of maternal and fetal factors with the development of mental deficiency', *American Journal of Mental Deficiency*, vol 60, 1956, p 557.
9)   See JWB Douglas and JM Blomfield, *Children Under Five*, London: Allen and Unwin, 1958.
10)   A Benech, B Mathieu, and E Schreider, 'Family size and biological characteristics of the children', *Biotypoligie*, vol 21, 1960, pp 4–36
11)   Joel Wray, 'Population Pressures on Families', in R Revelle, ed., *Rapid Population Growth: Consequences and Policy Implications*, Baltimore: Johns Hopkins Press, 1971.
12)   For example, EW Reed and SC Reed, *Mental Retardation: A Family Study*, Philadelphia: WB Saunders, 1965; and RB Zajonc and GB Marcus, 'Birth order and intellectual development', *Psychological Review*, vol 82, pp 74–88.

effects of family conflict, were dropped from consideration.[13] In any case, this effect was not found in British studies, where only children scored better than those with one sibling.[14] When it comes to educational achievement (what the IQ test was supposed to predict), the results from both American and British studies are even more clear-cut. Only children have been found to have higher achievement in both length of education and quality of academic work.[15]

The current stereotype of only children has more to do with emotional adjustment and personality than with intellect, and Americans have been as interested in the final outcome as manifested in adults as in the problems of the young. Here the results are somewhat less clear-cut; however, when they do not favour the only child, they generally find no difference between onlies and those with siblings. Again, while earlier studies tended to be more negative, those carried out more recently come up with the more favourable findings. For example, while a 1928 study found that only children

---

13) At least one more recent American study comparing only and two-child children in intact families found that the only children did better in 25 out of 32 intellectual tasks, performed equally in a further four, and were worse in only three (John Claudy, 'The only child as a young adult', Chapter 7 in Toni Falbo, ed., *The Single Child Family*, New York and London: Guildford Press, 1984). Despite the deleterious effect of family break-up on children's academic achievement, Denise Polit found that only children and their mothers are less negatively affected than members of larger families ('The only child in single-parent families', pp 178–210, in *The Single Child Family*, ibid). The relatively poor academic showing of children in father-absent families was put in perspective by Louie Boughes (*Lone Parenthood and Family Disruption*, London: Family Policy Studies Centre, 1994), who reported the relative retardation in reading for children born outside marriage was 10 months, while that of children in large families (more than three children) was 11 months compared to children from smaller families; the reading retardation of boys relative to girls was 8 months.

14) JWB Douglas, JM Ross and HR Simpson, *All our Future*, London: Peter Davies, 1968; PE Vernon, 'Recent investigations of intelligence and its measurement', *Eugenics Review*, vol 43, 1951, pp 125–37. In the United States, only children with single parents tend to come from disadvantaged homes, while those only children with two parents tend to come from highly educated families, with a high proportion of working mothers. In a recent Scottish study, however, Ann Laybourn ('Only children in Britain: popular stereotype and research evidence', *Children & Society*, vol 4, no 4, 1990, p 395) found 16- and 17-year-old Scottish only children came from more average family backgrounds, with the two-child families tending to be the more advantaged. Nevertheless, the single children in this study were less likely to have truanted (in the 4th year), and were more likely to have found the previous six months 'very worthwhile'. They were just about as likely to continue in full time education as the more advantaged children from two-child families.

15) SL Chopra ('Family size and sib position as related to IQ and academic achievement', *Journal of Social Psychology*, vol 70, 1966, pp 133–7) found this true even when IQ was partialled out. In this study, differences were slight, but where they existed, they favoured the onlies. See also Judith Blake, 'The Only Child in America: Prejudice versus Performance', *Population and Development Review*, March, 1981, pp 43–54; Ann Laybourn, 'Only children in Britain: popular stereotype and research evidence', *Children and Society*, vol 4, 1990, pp 386–400. The higher academic achievement of only and first-born children is usually explained as resulting from the continuous relationship with parents, who expect more mature behavior from them.

were conceited and too self-confident, later research has found this was true only for upper-class white males.[16] Yet other studies found onlies were middling in self-esteem and self-confidence. Blake found onlies were not more lonely, unhappy or unpopular than others, although they were less sociable, while Hawke and Knox found them neither lonelier nor less popular than others. A number of other studies have found no differences in willingness to share or various measures of mental health (or illness).[17] And, in a kind of grand summing up, Toni Falbo and Denise Polit did a meta-analysis of the only-child literature, using 115 (out of 200) studies that had enough data to arrive at statistically significant results. Comparing onlies to the average of non-onlies, they too found onlies not only superior in achievement and IQ but also in various measures of character. There was no difference in emotional adjustment and sociability.[18]

In studies of adults, only children were found to have married at the same ages as the others, but ended up having fewer children, while members of large families tended to have fewer children than their parents did (but this may reflect the general trend towards smaller broods, concentrated around two children).[19] These results might indicate that, 'in depth' interviews to the contrary, single children are actually relatively satisfied with their condition.

The findings concerning only children are so predominantly favourable, or at least undifferentiating, that the conclusion that only children are 'more maligned than maladjusted'[20] is often explicitly expressed at the end of technical reports of research complete with graphs and tables. As Laybourn put it:

---◇---

16) N Fenton, *Journal of Genetic Psychology*, 35, 1928, pp 546–56; Toni Falbo, 'Introduction', in Toni Falbo, ed., *The Single Child Family*, New York and London: Guildford Press, 1984, p 13. The slight excess (beyond the usual ratio) of male only children over female found by researchers was, like the longer spacing between births that occurs after a boy is born, explained as a sign of male preference in firstborns even in western countries. In Britain, the only children in the National Child Development Study (born in March, 1958) were mostly girls.

17) See the reviews in Toni Falbo, ed., *The Single Child Family*, New York and London: Guildford Press, 1984; and Sharryl Hawke and David Knox, *One Child by Choice*, New Jersey: Prentice-Hall, 1977.

18) See Toni Falbo, 'Only children in the United States and China', in S Oskamp, ed., *Family Processes and Problems*, New York and London: Sage Publications, 1987, pp 159–83.

19) Sharryl Hawke and David Knox (*One Child by Choice*, New Jersey: Prentice-Hall, 1977, pp 139–40) reported that single children tend to have smaller than average families, while children from large families tend to have smaller ones than those they grew up in; H Theodore Groat, Jerry W Wicks and Arthur G Neal ('Without siblings: the consequences in adult life of having been an only child', Chapter 8 in Tony Falbo, ed., *The Single Child Family*, New York and London: Guildford Press, 1984) found only-child adults spaced their children more, and wanted fewer children than others.

20) Kenneth Terhune, *A Review of the Actual and Expected Consequences of Family Size*, Washington, DC: Govt Printing Office, 1974, p 80.

> Only children and their families are not a problem to society; quite the reverse …. Although there is some reason to believe that prejudice largely passes [them] by, there is considerable evidence that their parents, many of whom have no choice in the matter, do suffer from it; they feel stigmatised, are criticised for being selfish, and feel under considerable pressure to have another child. They may … worry that perfectly normal behaviour problems are due to their child being 'the only one'. Prejudice may thus cause problems indirectly for their children, too; for example, anxiety to avoid their child growing up spoiled may actually lead parents to be over strict.[21]

Unusually for an American researcher, Blake noted the more public and ethical aspects of the outcome of only-childhood, remarking 'They have no obvious character or personality defects: they have attitudes appropriate to good citizens of the body politic, their family behavior is not disruptive, and they are unlikely to be public charges.'[22] Also unusually, Hawke and Knox related the decision to have only one child to social reasons, that is, to rising concerns about overpopulation.[23]

Then why the folklore? And why does it persist to the point of denying so much evidence? Researchers have racked their brains over this one. Hawke and Knox proffer 'insurance against childlessness' as a reason people urge multi-child families, but this could not explain why single children have so bad an image. Judith Blake put it down to the pronatalism of American popular culture.[24] But 'pronatalism' as a reason for rejecting the single child could not explain why two children should be the ideal family size for the majority. Ann Laybourn, taking a cue from the 'emotional investment' some individuals have in maintaining the stereotype, and the accusations of 'selfishness' and 'having it easier' hurled at singlechild parents, suggests that the psychological mechanism of 'cognitive dissonance' might be at work: parents of more than one child would like to think their extra investment of time, effort and money were not

<hr/>

21) Ann Laybourn, 'Only children in Britain: popular stereotype and research evidence', *Children and Society*, vol 4, no 4, 1990, p 399.

22) Judith Blake, 'The Only Child in America', *Population and Development Review*, March, 1981, p 53. Kenneth Terhune (*A Review of the Actual and Expected Consequences of Family Size*, Washington, DC: Govt Printing Office, 1974, p 72) concluded that dependency was more characteristic of children from large families, while Bernice Moore and Wayne Holtzman found the latter to be more socially inadequate and alienated.

23) Sharryl Hawke and David Knox, *One Child by Choice*, New Jersey: Prentice-Hall, 1977, p 96. They also noted that while 15 per cent of births in the United States were 'unwanted', this was true of only 1 per cent of first births.

24) Judith Blake, 'Coercive pronatalism and American population policy', in R Parke and CF Westoff, *US Commission on Population Growth and the American Future*, 1972.

in vain, and dislike thinking that others could have produced comparable or better results with less strain.

There may be something in a 'misery loves company' theory that is also involved in criticisms of those who choose not to have any children at all; however it seems equally likely to me that once more the pervasive and almost unconscious acceptance, in both popular experts and popular culture, of psychoanalytic notions of the overwhelming importance of the family drama is once more at work. Just as it is believed that the crucial role in forming adult identity and behaviour is to be found in the child's relationship with its parents, so the really important peer relations are thought to be those with siblings: unrelated friends, rivals and playmates simply cannot be as definitive in learning such matters as 'sharing'.

CHINESE ONLY-CHILD RESEARCH

When we attempt to go beyond the concerns of personal happiness and psychological 'adjustment' to include considerations of social and environmental welfare, another light can be thrown on the question of attitudes toward only children by a consideration of Chinese society, in which the only child has also become an object of discussion and study. In China the proportions of only children have increased dramatically over the past decade and a half, and worries about the problematic character of such children have been gleefully repeated in the western press and on television without any pause to consider the differences in childrearing aims between western parents and Chinese parents.[25] The former are supposedly willing to settle for pride and occasional companionship from their children, while over 40 years of communist rule have not been able to eradicate the traditional Chinese belief that 'filiality' – honouring, obeying and serving parents (or, in the case of girls, in-laws) – is the overriding virtue of life.

A mass of research has predictably been conducted by teachers, professors of education and psychologists, the counterparts of the western researchers whose work I have reported above, as well as by

---

25) Recent newspaper and television reports still echo faithfully those of the mid-1980s, where reports of Chinese concerns appear under such headlines as: 'Fat brats worry the Chinese' and 'China's brat-pack: generation of only children'. Obesity is a particular worry: in a poor and often hungry country, Chinese parents are said to cherish their only permitted child by overfeeding it. Interestingly, Ann Laybourn (*The Only Child: Myths and Reality*, Edinburgh: HMSO, 1994, p 72) reported that only children in the National Child Development Study tended to be overweight – but only those from a 'skilled working class' background.

some western researchers. It is interesting to compare not only results, but assumptions, goals, interpretations, and methods of exposition as well as the findings of this research.[26]

In general, Chinese research compares only children with 'non-only children', without specifying the family size of the non-onlies. However, the cohort size of only children (at least among the younger ones studied) so overbalances the numbers of non-onlies in most of these studies (especially in the cities) that it may safely be assumed that the non-onlies belong to small families, probably mostly comprising two children. None of the studies is of adult onlies.

Most of the studies of behaviour used teacher and/or parent ratings. One, however, asked children to rate each other as well, and in addition matched each only child with a non-only for sex, age and family background.[27] Although the authors start out by observing 'it has been discovered that only children really do have some personality defects' and are under the impression that 'abroad, there are many studies which indicate that only children have little that is favourable, and it has been discovered that they lack opportunities for social activity compared to other children', their own findings do not bear this out. On parent and teacher ratings, they observe:

> only children who had not gone to nursery school were much weaker than those who had gone to nursery schools (both only and non-only) in sociability, adaptability, and independence. However, non-only children who had not gone to nursery school were not significantly weaker. From this it can be seen that a collective environment plays an important role in developing collective thinking, and is an important reason why our country has not developed unsociability in its only children. In addition, our nation emphasizes family traditions and treasures children, and only children free the parents to spend relatively more time looking after the growing up of their children.

They pointed out that 77 per cent of Beijing pre-school children attend nursery school. While the 'main study' was a sermon on the

---

26) Since little Chinese research has appeared in English language journals, I rely here mainly on a set of 26 studies, theses and articles, published and unpublished, which were very kindly compiled for me by Liu Ruping, a psychologist, and Jia Gailian, an educationalist, and translated by David Kellogg. All are on the faculty of the Shaanxi Provincial Institute of Education in Xi'an.

27) Chen Kewen, *Guanyu dusheng zinu heyangxing de tantuo* ('On exploring the sociability of only children'), a report on a study of 1000 children in the Beijing area, Beijing University Sociology Department, first published in *Xinli Kexue Tongxun* (*Psychological Science Bulletin*), 1985, no 4.

People who count

virtues of nursery school (with Chinese characteristics), the children
rated each other on peer prestige and popularity. 'The result was that
in one class, only children were not preferred to non-only children,
but in the other two classes, on the contrary, only children were
significantly preferred. This also demonstrates that only children are
not significantly more lonely, hard to make friends with, and, at the
elementary school level, this is even more true [that is, as compared
with kindergartners].'

The above study contrasts oddly with one of the few Chinese
studies to be published in the West, carried out in Beijing at about the
same time and place, and using peer ratings and similarly matched
pairs of children.[28] This study found only children were more
egocentric and had lower ratings on a variety of positive behaviours,
including competence, co-operation, and peer prestige. The authors
concluded sadly that only children were selfish and did not like to
share things.

The question of sharing is a very fraught one in China, as illustrated
by a study of what is termed 'modestly declining' behaviour in only
children, who were assumed to be in particular need of training.[29] The
experiment involved having the teacher announce, 'Today's baozi
[stuffed steamed buns] are really good; but unfortunately three of you
won't get any, so you'll have to eat noodles.' The authors found the
overwhelming majority of children correctly understood 'modestly
declining' behaviour, but were disappointed (and the western reader
is shamefully relieved) to note that the understanding was seldom put
into practice:

---

28)   Shulan Jiao, Guiping Ji and Qicheng Jing, 'Comparative study of behavioral qualities of
      only children and sibling children', *Child Development*, vol 57, 1986, pp 357–61.

29)   Lan Guanhong and Yan Biduan, *Xiaoban dusheng youer 'qianrang' xingwei de diaocha* ('A
      study of "modestly declining" behaviour in only children in the bottom class of
      kindergarten'), Fuzhou Municipal Institute for Child Studies, first published in *Shanghai
      Jiaoyu Keyan* (*Shanghai Education Research*), 1985, no 4. ['There is a slight confusion in
      terminology here. When guests are offered something in China, it is polite to modestly
      decline the gift an indeterminate number of times before accepting. Children are often
      taught to decline gifts from neighbours, particularly since accepting such gifts reflects
      poorly on the ability of parents to provide and causes them to lose face. Why this behavior,
      which makes social (let alone communal) life extremely inconvenient and is basically
      feudal in origin, is considered "socialist" has never been explained to me, but it is a Maoist
      commonplace. For example, in the seventies a film was popularized in which a foreign
      child psychologist did a test on children in which he told them to try to remove balls on a
      string from a bottle. If all the children tried to remove them at the same time, of course, no
      one could do so. The foreign child psychologist is amazed by Chinese children, who never
      have this problem (presumably because they know the pecking order so well).
      Fortunately, it is apparent that what is meant in the study is not this kind of modesty,
      but simply an ability to share and play – as equals – with other children. This particular
      article considers that "modestly declining" is a key to socializing children.' Translator]

The bottom class put their personal needs first, and their feelings of friendship, love, and modesty are relatively weak, so their behavior is relatively poor. For example, if asked: 'If another child likes the toy you have in your hand, what would you do?', 90 per cent of the children replied 'I'd give it to him.' But in reality they do not. If asked 'Why didn't you give it to him?', some replied, 'I wanted it', while some replied, 'I like it.' If asked: 'If you have baozi to eat, and your little friend at the table doesn't, what do you do?', 89.6 per cent answer, 'Give him half', but in reality only 24 per cent of the children did this. If asked 'XX didn't have any baozi to eat, why didn't you give him any?', the children replied, 'I wanted it' or 'I forgot to do it.'

In only one paper is birth order considered – in a study of juvenile delinquents and of the mentally ill – and in both cases the only child is likened to the youngest child, in contrast to western studies which find the only child most resembles the eldest.[30] While conceding that for the general child population, only children seem no different from the others, the authors go on, on the basis of a very small number of deviants, to say:

A large proportion of only children appear to be lazy or have poor attitudes towards work. In our study of only children, 18.8 per cent were 'three goods' (good health, good study, good relationships) students, while 3.3 per cent were students of poor moral character. This is about the same as the proportion of 'three goods' children and of children of poor moral character in their schools generally. But of 70 juvenile delinquents, 37, or 53 per cent, were youngest or only children, with 7 only children, or 10 per cent of the total. In this age group, only children are only around 3 per cent of the population in general, so the crime rate of only children is relatively high. As for the youngest-in-the-family delinquents, they were a mirror of the only children. These juvenile delinquents have one thing in common: an avid pursuit of individual 'eat, drink, and be merry' pursuits. From their childhood, they had received doting, preference, protection from their parents …. Of 80 mentally ill inpatients, 17 per cent were only children and 33 per cent youngest children. Compared to 3 per cent only children in the same age group of the general population, this is very high. The causation of mental illness is

30) Wu Jing and Lin Chongde, *Dusheng zinu xinli tedian fenxi* ('An analysis of the psychological characteristics of only children'), *Fumu Bidu* (*Required Reading for Parents*), 1981, no 3. A survey of only children in 120 kindergartens, elementary and middle schools in Beijing. The 'three goods' award is in practise often given for political conformity, participation in the youth league, etc.

extremely complex, but what links these youngest-in-the-family criminals and the mentally ill is the common psychological traits: irritability, excitability, moodiness, stubbornness and oversensitivity. These are the result of pampering, spoiling, doting by their parents; having never had any big setbacks or disappointments, they are not able to withstand emotional blows. Although youthful mental illness and only-child status are not necessarily linked, the spoiling of children by their parents is dangerous.

Another article presents no evidence at all regarding the prevalence of delinquency among only children, but concludes, 'The criminal behavior of only children may be examined from various objective or subjective points of view, but if we look deeply into the problem from the angle of social psychology, it is not difficult to discover that the main cause of criminal only-child behavior is doting and spoiling.'[31] Thus, although western research is referred to, the western belief that deviant behaviour in children stems from too little love is firmly reversed in China. Whole articles, as well as the obligatory sermons at the end of research papers, are given over to lecturing parents sternly against the evils of overindulging their young.

Surprisingly enough, given this negative predisposition, the most general finding among the research (as contrasted with the advice-giving) articles was that there seemed to be no differences between only and non-only children (five studies), at least after both had been subjected to at least a year of nursery schooling.[32] The other most usual conclusion is that boys tend to be more problematic than girls. Chinese researchers invariably put this down to the surviving feudal attitude of 'cherish the sons and despise the daughters', seldom recognizing the universal nature of this finding. The only finding favouring the only child seems to be that of independence (four studies). But this conclusion runs so much against the stereotype that another article was devoted to the importance of independence training for only children, rather quaintly designated 'labour

---

31) Xue Dunfang, *Luelun dusheng zinu jiatingzhong de qingshaonian fanzui wenti* ('Briefly on the question of juvenile delinquency in single-child families'), first published in *Qingnian yanjiu (Youth Research)*, 1986, no 4. The author first summarizes foreign literature, concluding that there seem to be many personality problems associated with only children, 'such as stubbornness, egotism, arrogance, unsociability, etc.'

32) The virtues of schooling for socializing children are again and again cried up. Xiao Fulan (*Dusheng zinu xue lingqian jiaoyu wenti tansu*, [Exploring preschool care for only children], in *Xibei Renkou* [*Northwestern Population*] 1981, issue 2, reprinted in *Ertong Jiaoyu, (Child Education)*, 1981, issue 9) explicitly compared several methods of preschool childcare (for only children) and found that intelligence and verbal ability were better among those who had been to nursery school than among those who had been left with a childminder (*tuoerhu*). Surprisingly, they found that being left with grandmother was even better (though it could cause 'stubbornness and being headstrong')!

education' but covering such matters as dressing and personal care.[33] Nevertheless, the authors feel such training has definite bearing on future work attitudes:

> It is possible to carry out labour education at a very early stage. This sort of capability suits the physical and mental character-istics of the children, and can quench their thirst to take part in adult pursuits. At three years old work and play have not yet become differentiated, and they are interested in the processes of work. With correct teaching from students, they can gradually come to emphasize the fruits of labour, and understand the meaning of labour.

There was surprisingly little interest in the question of intelligence and school achievement, but two studies found the only child superior in this respect, and one found no difference.

The Chinese researchers are in general very well aware of the findings and opinions of their western counterparts, with their emphasis on this aspect. Four articles begin with discussions of the changes in western attitudes to the only child from Bohannon on. Another is entirely devoted to a review of western research, which is pronounced inconclusive.[34] Yet another, of the same date (1984) is actually written by an American whose research is currently devoted to the subject, and is quite positive.[35] And, finally, two are devoted to the work of a Japanese researcher. One of the latter starts with reference to a 50-year-old American finding that only children are superior in IQ, and goes on to arrive at a similar conclusion.[36] The

---

33) Li Kuihua and Zhao Meisun, *Dusheng zinu zaoqi laodong jiaoyu de diaocha yu chubu shiyan* ('A survey and preliminary experiment on the early labour education of only children'), Beijing Municipal Child Education Research Office, first published in *Beijing shi youer jiaoyu yanjiu hui diyi ju nianhui cailiao huibian,* (*Beijing First Annual Child Education Research Symposium Edited Proceedings*), February, 1982. (The children in this study were born before the one-child policy.)

34) Chen Jialin, *Dusheng zinu jiaoyu de xinlixue yanjiu* ('Research into the psychology of the education of only children'), first published in *Xibei Renkou* (*Northwestern Population*), Gansu, no 11, 1984.

35) Toni Falbo, *Xifang de dusheng zinu: dui zhongguo de qifa* ('Western Only Children: Enlightenment for China'), first published in *Guangming Ribao* (*Enlightenment Daily*) 10 May, 1985.

36) *Guowai guanyu dusheng zinu de diaocha yanjiu* ('Studies on only children abroad'), by the Beijing People's Broadcasting 'World Knowledge' staff, first published in *Waiguo jiaoyu ziliao* (*Foreign Education Material*), 1981, no 4. The only children, particularly the 'net only children' (those living with both natural parents), have a clear advantage in intelligence: 'On a comparative scale of 100, the non-only children, on the average, scored 50, while the only children scored 69.5.'

other examines the satisfaction of Japanese onlies with their status, with inconclusive results.[37]

Somewhat unexpectedly, only one paper deals with another aspect of the social anxieties and aspirations aroused by the prospect of a large proportion of only children.[38] This article found that 60 per cent of the parents of only children hoped that their children would, after growing up, have 'relatively high social status', and 40.7 per cent of one-child families had special savings accounts for their children. As in other countries, the restriction in numbers of offspring leads inevitably to the prospect of higher per capita consumption.

If nothing else, the above discussion shows that there is a great deal of concern in China about learning and educating parents in the techniques of proper child rearing, as well as a great deal of worry about the effects of being an only child and a lack of sophistication about research in which stereotyping is pervasive.[39] Moreover, studies done in China in association with western researchers tended to replicate the western only-child results, rather than Chinese beliefs, despite the presumed cultural differences. In an attempt to remedy some of what they saw as shortcomings in the Chinese research, Dudley Poston and Toni Falbo (helped by sociologists and demographers from a Chinese university) conducted a study which included a better designed questionnaire and more sophisticated statistical analysis. Like some of the Chinese studies, they also included only children born before the one-child policy. They found that only children performed better than those with siblings in mathematics and Chinese. Teachers rated them more 'virtuous' and competent as well, but there were no differences in mothers' ratings,

37) Zhong Qiquan, *Dusheng xinu de xinli ji qi jiaoyu* ('The psychology and education of the only child'), first published in *Waiguo jiaoyu ziliao* (*Foreign Education Material*), 1981, no 5: 'According to one study, 17.5% of only children who would like to be the oldest child, 38.0% would like to be a middle child, while 31.8% would like to be the youngest. Those who prefer being only children, who are satisfied with their own status, are only 12.%, a very small minority. But according to another study, 2.3% want to be the oldest; 1.2% want to be the second, and 4% want to be the youngest. Here the vast majority of only children are satisfied with their status ....'

38) Chen Kewen, *Dusheng zinu de jiating guanxi ji qi shehui houguo* ('The family relationships of only children and the social consequences'), first published in *Hunyin yu jiating*, (*Marriage and the Family*), 1986, no 6.

39) It should also be remembered that Chinese social scientists to not have the money and other resources available that their western counterparts do. In some cases, the researchers admitted with disarming frankness that they chose their test group because it was conveniently close at hand.

and even the teachers' differences were significant only for urban children.[40]

The overall outcome from these Chinese studies, as from the Japanese, American and British ones, seems to be that it is not the nature of only children that is problematic, but what is expected from them by the families and societies in which they live; if they are at all different from other children, it is in the concern, expectations and anxieties that others have of them. If Chinese studies are mostly concerned with how well children fit into the collective environment, it must be admitted that westerners, for all their vaunted individualism, approve of deviance in only very restricted directions, such as high achievement. And if the western experience and Chinese investigation mean anything, Chinese only children will grow up to be at least as worthy as any other group of people.

---

40) Dudley Poston and Toni Falbo, 'Effects of the one-child policy on the children of China', in Dudley Poston and David Yaukey, eds, *The Population of Modern China*, New York and London: Plenum, 1992. There is also concern in China over the universal finding that city children seem to do better than their country counterparts. Professor Gong Yaoxian has been lauded for producing both an urban and rural revision of the standard Wechsler IQ test in which both sets of children achieved the same average result.

PART III
Population Policy

Chapter 6
India: forty trying years

Until very recently governments invariably took pride in the size of the populations over which they ruled, and historians measured economic success by the rate of population growth. When governments engaged in population policy, it was only to encourage the increase of the native-born and ethnically dominant portion. In 1952, India became the first sovereign nation to pursue a policy of limiting its numbers.[1] As a pioneer, India's progress has been monitored, criticized and interfered with, from both within and without, to such an extent that paradoxically it has become almost a by-word for overpopulation. China, on the other hand, with an even larger population but sharing many of India's social and economic characteristics, and with a population policy that has seen many of the same vicissitudes, has become a by-word for a deplorable solution.

China and India, with per capita yearly incomes of $370 and $300 respectively are among the poorest countries in the world.[2] China has

---

1) The number of governments with such policies is now well over 100, but stayed under 10 until 1965, at which point the number shot up to 15 (Dolores Foley, *NGOs as Catalysts of Policy Reform and Social Change*, unpublished thesis, University of Southern California, 1989).

2) This and most of the statistics that follow were taken from a variety of sources; the exact numbers cited tend to vary somewhat with the source, but agree in both relative and approximate magnitudes. See, for example: *The State of World Population, 1992*, United Nations Population Fund; *China's Family Planning Program in India's Family Planning Challenge*, both Washington, DC: Population Action International, 1992; V Narain, 'Population Policy: Some Critical Issues', in SK Lal and A Chandini, *India's Population Policy*, Meerut: 21st Century Publications, 1987; G Narayana and John F Kantner, *Doing the*

22 per cent of the world's population but 7 per cent of its arable land; India has 16 per cent of the world's population but 2.4 per cent of its land area. Both are now barely self-sufficient in grain production, and both face declining yields. Both are afflicted by increasing water shortages. Both were notable in the past for bizarre forms of extreme denigration and cruelty to women. Both are characterized by near-universal female marriage and strong preferences for sons, in both cases against stated government policy. The next four chapters examine the course of population policy in these two vast countries, and in a special area within each.

EVOLUTION OF A POLICY

India is a theatre in which all the themes, conflicts and dilemmas relating to both population control policy and the means through which it is achieved, whether directly through contraception or indirectly through social and economic development, have been played out. Like the remainder of the Third World, it has a poverty-stricken and rapidly growing underclass and an increasingly affluent élite.[3] Like western countries, it has a free and sometimes radically critical press, a vocal and active women's movement, and a government even more willing to accommodate minority and special interest pressure groups of many kinds by legislation.

India's population problem was conceived as a creature of the 20th century. Between the censuses of 1911 and 1921, there was actually a decline of 0.3 per cent due to the 1918–20 influenza pandemic, but the next census, in 1931, showed an increase of 11 per cent, which rose thereafter to over 20 per cent in censuses after 1961.[4] By the mid-1930s, both the then British rulers and the future Indian premier, Pandit Nehru, foresaw difficulties in maintaining the food supply. Growth was also mentioned as a problem in the Bengal Famine Commission Report of 1945. Nevertheless, after Independence in 1947, the Health Ministry was placed in the hands of Rajkumari Amrit Kaur,

———————————————◇———————————————

cont.

    Needful, Boulder Co.: Westview Press, 1992. Estimates of China's real per capita income are subject to particularly wide variation. China claimed a per capita GDP of $240 in 1980 in order to qualify for soft loans; estimates using 'purchasing power parity' rather than formal exchange rates put it at more like $1000. See Vaclav Smil, *China's Environmental Crisis*, London: ME Sharpe, 1993, pp 70–3, for an extended discussion of this point.

3)   India is also supposed to contain the world's most rapidly growing middle class. The size and distribution of this middle class is somewhat unclear, but it is roughly considered to comprise those who financially are able to respond to the increased consumption aspirations inspired by films and television advertising.

4)   *Statistics for Planning*, Trivandrum: Bureau of Economics an Statistics, Table 1.1, 1988.

who, as both a Christian and Gandhian, was inflexibly opposed to contraceptive devices.

With the advice of a World Health Organization consultant, Dr Abraham Stone, a programme was launched in 1952 to popularize the 'rhythm method' with a budget of $31,000.[5] Although the family planning budget was sharply increased in every successive five-year plan, both absolutely and relative to the health budget as a whole, the programme remained narrow and rather diffident. In 1957, the Health Minister rejected sterilization as a contraception measure because of its irreversibility, and in November 1959, Prime Minister Nehru opined in a television interview: 'Food must be a top priority. Some people imagine that we will solve India's problems by family planning. I do not agree.'[6]

Yet 1959 saw a shift to an emphasis on sterilization, with a corresponding change in objective from child spacing to family size limitation. At the same time, paradoxically, the term 'population control' gave way to 'family planning' (which in due course made the latter term anathema to population control rejecters). A concerted effort was put into education supposedly designed to strengthen the voluntary nature of the programme, and, shortly thereafter, cash incentives were introduced, at first under the rubric of 'compensation'.

The 1961 census brought home the shocking realization that the annual rate of population increase had risen from 1.5 per cent in the 1940s to 2 per cent in the 1950s, and an intensification of effort seemed urgent. An ambitious goal was set to reduce the annual birth rate of 41 per thousand to 25 by 1973. (This goal has yet to be reached; in 1993, the all-India birth rate still stood at about 30, but 'goals' and 'targets' have been officially abandoned.) In 1971, abortion was legalized, and the minimum age of marriage was raised from 15 to 18 for women, and from 18 to 21 for men. The actual average age for women to marry is still 16, but slowly rising. Nevertheless, India's peak fertility was reached in 1974, and has since begun to drift downward.

Input from foreign agencies   Over the years there have been numerous inputs to India's family planning programme from a variety of foreign agencies including USAID, UNDP, the Ford Foundation, the Population Council, WHO, Unicef, and bilaterally from countries like Japan and Sweden. It is not surprising that relations between some of these agencies and the Indian government sometimes became rather sticky when the advisers wanted to stress birth control above other

———————————————————⟨⟩———————————————————

5)   K R Rao, *Society, Culture and Population Policy in India*, Delhi: Ajanta Publications, 1989.
6)   K R Rao, ibid., p 150.

health measures. In 1966, a visiting AID group from Washington ordered, over the objections of the Indian Health Minister, that ongoing AID projects be halted and the funds shifted to population control.[7] On another occasion, resentment was caused when the Ford Foundation reneged on promised funding. On yet another, AID officials ordered that population funds be pressed on the Indian government 'whether it wanted them or not'.[8] In 1971, USAID was involved in a no-birth bonus scheme in the Nilgiri tea-gardens, which was abruptly called off a year ahead of schedule, with no reason given.

In 1973 the Indian government closed the USAID office in Delhi because of America's tilt toward Pakistan during the Indo–Pakistan war of 1971. Multi-lateral funding was to be preferred. Yet such instances of sensitivity to arm-twisting and interference from foreign powers did not prevent a number of countries, including such strange allies as Switzerland, Belgium, the Philippines, Peru, Senegal, the USSR and Ethiopia, voting against giving India UN support for its family planning programme on the hotly denied grounds of coercion.

Many Indian critics, and not just those on the left, were highly suspicious of the involvement of western experts, accusing them of commercial interests in marketing contraceptive devices, racist interests in wishing to reduce the number of non-white people, and political interests in wishing to distract attention from their own culpability in dominating and consuming the world's resources. Indira Gandhi herself occasionally took such a line. When, at the 1974 World Conference, Huang Shuzhi, the leader of the Chinese delegation, declared there that Third World overpopulation was a fallacy of the superpowers,[9] Mrs Gandhi joined the attack. It was poverty, not population, that was the real enemy, they said. But China, like India,

---

7) See M Minklar, 'Consultants or Colleagues: the role of US population advisers in India', *Population and Development Review*, December, 1977, p 412. Also *Radical Health Journal* (Bombay), June, 1988, p 22, stated that in the same year, a visiting UN advisory mission reported:

    The directorate [of Health and Family Welfare] should be relieved from other responsibilities such as maternal and child health and nutrition .... [U]ntil the family planning campaign has picked up momentum and made real progress in the states, the Director General concerned should be responsible for family planning only. This recommendation is reinforced by the fear that the programme may otherwise be used in some states to expand the much needed and neglected Maternal and Child Welfare Services (*Report of the Family Planning Programme in India*, 1966).

8) John Lewis, Director of USAID, quoted in: M Minklar, 'Consultants or Colleagues: the role of US population advisers in India', *Population and Development Review*, December, 1977, p 414.
9) *Beijing Review*, 30 August, 1974.

was by then actively pursuing a policy of trying to limit its own numbers.

Internal considerations   The Indian policy itself was not without internal contradictions. It was accompanied by no real attempt to redistribute wealth; in fact, the ceiling placed on individual land-holding backfired by actually encouraging large families for those who had property. Moreover, both regional and communal demographic competition swiftly made themselves felt. Even at the village level, caste competition militated against family size limitation.

From very early on, Hindus worried out loud that contraceptive success in their community might erode their numerical advantage over the Muslims. But although the 1961 census noted differential growth among different groups, the interpretation of these differences was another matter: many changes probably reflected conversions rather than natural increase. For example, the decline among the Hindus probably reflected the sharp increase noted among Buddhists. On the other hand, refugees from East Pakistan at first swelled Hindu numbers rather than Muslim. Yet as Hindu communalism has become more organized, violent and vocal, fears of increased demographic competition have been more stridently repeated.[10]

In addition to communal considerations, some states feared that relative family planning success would be punished by a reallocation of some of their central funds and parliamentary seats to the less successful states. It was not until 1976 that such considerations were integrated into a policy that included education and health care for women and children as well as clinics and the provision of contraceptive devices. The distribution of seats was then frozen at the 1971 level until the year 2000, and central assistance to states was partially delinked from numbers and tied instead to family planning success. For the first time, India had a comprehensive family planning policy, but under circumstances that could only generate hysteria over the entire subject.

---◇---

10) The controversy over the site of a mosque in north India has widely publicized this aspect of Hindu fundamentalist politics. Referring to claims that excessive Muslim fertility will soon reverse Hindu numerical dominance (now about 85 per cent of the Indian population), in the riots following the destruction of the Ayodhya mosque in December, 1992, a number of Muslim women were raped and mutilated 'so they would no longer bear Muslim babies'. Vibhuti Patel reports that communal Hindu organizations now parody the 'We Two, Our Two' Family planning slogan of the government of India by putting up posters saying, 'We Five, Our 25', and depicting a supposedly polygamous Muslim man with his permissible four wives: 'By the logic of this demographic argument that ... Muslims multiply in geometrical progression, the Muslims are perceived as a threat to India's population problem and thereby to the country's economic progress' ('Gender Implications of Communalisation of Socio-political Life of India', unpublished paper, March, 1993).

TWO STEPS BACK

In June, 1975, Mrs Gandhi, having been found guilty of electoral irregularities by the Allahabad High Court, declared an 'Emergency' and ruled by diktat for the next year and a half. Civil rights were abrogated, the press censored, many organizations banned, and many thousands were jailed. It was while in prison that a number of educated women political activists found time to read and reflect on the report of the Committee of the Status of Women in India, *Toward Equality*, which had been issued shortly before, and to realize the dire condition of most of their countrywomen. After release, some of these women went on to found a number of organizations intended to redress the injustices revealed.[11]

The Emergency was a watershed in the Indian family planning movement, to such an extent that many westerners are under the impression that Mrs Gandhi's role – or that of Sanjay, her son and presumed heir – was the only or chief cause of her electoral defeat when it ended. But several writers have pointed out that the change in the population policy during the Emergency was mainly that of bureaucratic implementation of a policy that had been evolving for some time and had earlier received little political opposition.[12] In fact, much of the criticism had been against the timidity with which the policy had been pursued, and Mrs Gandhi at first did little to change this. Family planning was not even included in her 20-point economic programme released shortly after the Emergency was imposed.

The National Population Policy, promulgated in April, 1976, seemed to take for granted that family limitation was broadly acceptable to the masses. It asserted that family planning was to be included in an integrated package of health care and nutrition, education about population issues, and more emphasis on the education of girls. In order eventually to stabilize the population, an average family size of two children was the goal, with incentives that were graded accordingly. Thus 150 rupees was offered for vasectomies when two or fewer children were living, 100 rupees for three, and 70 rupees thereafter. Clearly these flat rates would have looked more desirable

---

11) The report stressed that birth control *per se* could raise not the status of women; rather, it argued that 'a rise in marriage age, education, employment, better living conditions and greater general awareness' would lead to the adoption of birth control (pp 321–2).

12) See M Vicziany, 'Coercion in a Soft State', *Pacific Affairs*, 55, no 3, pp 373–402, no 4, pp 557–92, 1982; and KR Rao, *Society, Culture and Population Policy in India*, 1989, p 135ff. Rao points out, for example, that the first All-India Anti-Family Planning Conference was held as late as 1972. Objections centred on (a) harmful side-effects of existing methods; (b) danger of tilting the religious balance; (c) 'the attack on masculinity and fertility, which degraded the humanity of those sterilized' (p 155).

the poorer the recipient. No central government compulsory sterilization legislation was planned, but the states were specifically permitted to pass their own laws, commencing with three children. (Nevertheless, when Maharashtra passed such a law, it was blocked by Mrs Gandhi.)

Targets for 'acceptance' (either sterilization or IUD insertion) were set for each state, but the policy was implemented by the various states with varying levels of enthusiasm and widely varying measures. Delhi itself, under Sanjay Gandhi's personal control, had the highest reported sterilization 'performance'. Territories and states 'performed' in relationship to their distance from Delhi. Kerala, which of all the Indian states and territories has had the only real success in negotiating the demographic transition, as well as Tamil Nadu and Kashmir, all of which were distant from and had governments hostile to that of the 'centre', virtually ignored the directives.[13]

Closer to Delhi, many abuses, never denied and later apologized for, took place. People were bribed or even coerced into vasectomy booths, regardless of age, medical or marital status, or the number of children they already had, just to fulfil the allotted quotas. As a result, some hundreds of people actually died, either from infection or in riots provoked by the campaign. Potential 'acceptors' were recruited from many walks of life, using whatever means seemed efficacious: civil servants, for example, could be threatened with everything from loss of vacation pay or perks to loss of promotion and career prospects. But of course the poorer the citizen, the more vulnerable he or she was to petty forms of bribes or threats from such disparate quarters as the police, labour contractors, school teachers and ration shops. In any case, millions of people were harassed or frightened enough to alter the normal course of their lives or travel plans in order to evade the pressure. The distortions of the policy were such that not only were many aspects of the health and welfare systems sacrificed to the one area of birth control targets, but even that failed to be humanely and effectively delivered. As Gwatkin commented:

> No serious effort was made to activate the government's minimum needs program, to which the policy referred, or to implement such other fertility-related development programs proposed in the policy as improved female education, nutrition, and health ... little was done to foster adult literacy, dowry abolition, reforestation, or equality among castes. Other development work was sharply curtailed ... school teachers were

---

13) Davidson R Gwatkin, 'Political will and family planning: The implications of India's emergency experience', *Population and Development Review*, March, 1979, pp 55–6.

driven to attach greater importance to the recruitment of contraceptive acceptors than to the instruction of children; labor contractors were pressed harder to produce sterilization cases than to build roads; agricultural extension agents were goaded to increase family planning performance as a matter of higher priority than the distribution of fertilizer ...[14]

Such methods, and the evasions they provoked, make it particularly hard to decide exactly what was accomplished, even in population limitation terms: documents and statistics were said to have been falsified, those with money were said to have bribed others to 'stand in' for them in receiving vasectomies.

But that was nothing compared to the backlash that followed. In the latter half of 1976, about 8 million sterilizations, or half as many as in the previous 25 years were said to have been performed. But in the following year, the number fell to one-tenth as many, and never recovered to anything like the peak level. Similarly, the number of IUDs inserted was halved, and the number of conventional contraceptive users also declined.

What had happened? In January, 1977, apparently satisfied with the economic progress the country had made, and the increased availability of external loans (thanks to tough labour policies), Mrs Gandhi called off the Emergency and announced that elections would be held. At the same time, the birth control drive was eased. In the ensuing political campaign, none of the major political parties opposed family planning, and all but the more leftist of the communist parties explicitly supported it. Yet Mrs Gandhi's party was defeated most decisively in those states where the programme had been pursued most aggressively, and, although the victorious Janata Party kept the previous government's family planning policy intact and even increased the family planning budget by over 50 per cent, it was renamed 'family welfare' and little was done to implement it. In 1979, a report of the Working Group on Population Policy recommended that mortality decline should become a population objective equal to fertility decline in importance, and, in particular, that the infant mortality rate of 120 per thousand should be halved by 1996. In 1994 it still averages over 90.

In 1980, Mrs Gandhi swept back into office; Sanjay too was elected to parliament. Yet family planning did not regain its high profile and even Sanjay dropped it from his plans because 'people don't like it'.[15]

14) Davidson R Gwatkin, ibid, p 52.
15) J Kocher, 'Population policy in India: recent developments and current prospects', *Population and Development Review*, June, 1980, p 310.

Since then, vasectomy has remained in low esteem, and the emphasis has shifted to female sterilization and hormonal treatments, perhaps felt to be politically and socially more acceptable.[16]

CONTRACEPTIVE CONTROVERSY

Despite the number and variety of participants, the course of India's family planning activities has been marked by emphasis on a single method of contraception at a time. In the 1960s, under the urging of foreign experts, IUDs were enthusiastically promoted without adequate screening; many insertions had to be subsequently removed because of the prevalence of reproductive tract infections. Not surprisingly, the later emphasis on female sterilization has been opposed by many women's groups on a number of counts. They argue:

- it strengthens the tendency to look at women in a stereotyped fashion, as primarily mothers or prospective mothers, and women's health as primarily reproductive functioning (to the neglect of nutritional and occupational aspects, for example);
- the contraceptive methods which have been promoted so far, tubectomies, IUDs, injections and hormonal implants, are those under the control of medical practitioners, rather than of the woman herself, and therefore tend to reinforce the general powerlessness of women, especially poor women;
- for cultural reasons, most of India has had a shortage of well-trained nurses and other health workers (as is so frequently the case, 'cultural' here refers to sexual taboos: the opportunities that nurses have for coming into intimate contact with strange men, whether as colleagues or patients, has meant that women from any community with social aspirations may not nurse any but family members); and

---

16) A study by Carole Vlassoff ('Progress and stagnation: changes in fertility and women's position in an Indian village', *Population Studies*, 46, 1991, pp 195–212), although confined to the changes between 1975 and 1987 in a single village in the state of Maharashtra, is suggestive in this respect. Vlassoff found that, while female sterilization had been the most common birth control method in 1975, it was used almost exclusively in 1987. The average age of marriage was up to 17.6, but the average age of the sterilized cohort was 23. Thus many women began to bear children in adolescence, and continued to bear them as rapidly as possible up to the desired number, despite the grave health risks of such early and close-spaced pregnancies. The need for more popularization of non-terminal contraceptives was underlined by a study from the neighbouring state of Karnataka, where women tended to refuse contraception until their preferred sex distribution – usually including at least one or two sons – was achieved. Contraceptive users had more living sons than daughters, indicating that the 'desired number' is influenced by sex preferences (T Rajararetnam and RV Deshpande, *International Family Planning Perspectives*, September, 1944).

- the stress on targets has often meant inadequate sympathy and attention to the complaints, side-effects or complications attending the various forms of contraception.

Practical difficulties   On the other side, the kinds of difficulties facing the implementation of family planning programmes, even in communities already interested in controlling family sizes, is well illustrated in a thesis carried out by Rosamund Ebdon in a rural area of Bangladesh.[17] The villagers she studied were devout Muslims, but many of their beliefs and circumstances are widely shared elsewhere. Many families had accepted the need for contraception, but were severely limited in their choice by a range of cultural, practical and medical concerns. Although the husbands, and even the husbands' parents, reserved the right to make contraceptive decisions, few husbands were willing to use condoms or undergo vasectomy themselves. But even among female methods, the choice is fraught with drawbacks. Many of the villagers believe that sterilization is sinful and a woman who has been sterilized is sometimes shunned. Many women also fear that if they suddenly die with an IUD lodged in the body, they will not be acceptable to God. Excessive bleeding is both a physical and a social and religious problem, since to be menstruating is to be 'impure' and disqualifies a woman both from practical duties, such as food preparation (to the annoyance of her mother-in-law, with whom she lives) and from religious rituals, which are socially important and psychologically comforting. Yet the absence of menstruation, which can also occur, causes anxieties too and is a reason for discontinuance.

In general, methods which subject women to internal examination threaten their modesty; in addition, women who are in purdah (the custom whereby women remain in seclusion and wear clothing that completely conceals them when they go out) prefer methods that do not require them to leave their homes. Consequently, in this study the oral pill was by far the most popular method, followed at some distance by the contraceptive injection. Both of these methods are chemical or hormonal in their action, and both are conceptualized within a traditional medical system whose elements are not only widespread throughout South Asia, but reach back millennia to

---

17) Rosamund Ebdon, 'Community-Based Health Care the NGO Way: An Anthropological Study of a Maternal–Child Health and Family Planning Programme in Rural Bangladesh', Department of Social Anthropology, Edinburgh University, 1994. I am grateful to the author for permitting me to make use of a draft of her dissertation. Bangladesh, although a separate country, is in many ways still culturally similar to the Indian state of Bengal.

ancient Greece and Egypt.[18] According to this system, health and well-being require a balance between substances affecting the body that are classified 'hot', 'cold', 'wet' and 'dry'. Various medicines, as well as foods and activities, affect this balance in ways that are 'powerful' or 'weak'. Pills, and even more so injections, are considered very strong medicine, and supposedly have their effect by heating and drying the uterus, preventing the growth of the male seed.

The symptoms and side effects, such as menstrual irregularities, headaches, nausea and constipation, are also interpreted within this system; moreover, the 'allopathic' (modern) contraceptives are often taken in conjunction or alternation with traditional remedies of herbs, charms and amulets (as is also the case in some African communities). Another problem is the belief that free or low cost pills are of poor quality, while expensive ones are good. Eradicating this belief is not made easier by the fact that the free pills provided by the government are of the high-dose variety, which have been superseded in many western countries by low-dose pills found to cause fewer side-effects.[19] Finally, problems are caused by health workers who are insufficiently skilled or trained at working within the women's belief system to convince them that the pills must be taken as prescribed.[20]

The ideal contraceptive for women – one that is effective, safe, cheap, comfortable, easily accessible and completely under the user's control – does not yet exist. For women whose nutritional status is poor, who may lack adequate sanitary facilities, who engage in backbreaking physical labour, who are frequently anaemic, who are under affinal pressure to produce sons, and for whom menstruation spells impurity and additional inconvenience, this is all the more true. Tubectomies have been followed by infections, and postoperative complaints of backache and excessive bleeding; the same is true of IUDs, which, when ineptly inserted, have sometimes perforated the uterus. Pessaries and caps may present difficulties where water is in short supply and handling one's own genitals is frowned on. Condoms

---

18) See BF Musallam, *Sex and Society in Islam: Birth Control Before the Nineteenth Century*, Cambridge: Cambridge University Press, 1983; also, John M Riddle, *Contraception and Abortion from the Ancient World to the Renaissance*, Cambridge, Mass: Harvard University Press, 1992.

19) Although the recent review of prescriptions available through the National Health Service may bring back their use in Britain as a money-saving measure. See Karen Zagor, 'Your money or a life', *Guardian*, 6 June, 1944.

20) For example, some women took large doses of the pills in the hope of inducing abortion, or gave them to men or even chickens to treat for various indispositions. Although extra doses of birth control pills are in fact used as a 'morning-after' remedy, they must be consumed within 72 hours of unprotected sex to be effective and safe. Belated use by the village women was often ineffective and made the users very ill.

pose disposal problems, and, like coitus interruptus, require good communication between husband and wife – never an easy matter in any culture. Birth control pills, which must be carefully matched to the user to minimize side-effects, and have been associated in developed countries with causing cardiovascular diseases, have not been promoted in India and other underdeveloped countries until recently because of a belief that many women would be unable to store and use them properly (or, perhaps, that it would be too easy to decide for themselves to discontinue their use).

There is also, despite the possibilities of educating and bringing men into active partnership in birth control practice, still need for discreet female contraception, which may be used by women without the knowledge of their sexual partners, if women are to be able to exercise independent control over their own bodies. This is strikingly illustrated by Taslima Nasrin, upon being asked to name her heroine:

> Her name is Amina. She is 30 years old, mother of four. She carries drinking water from a community well far from home. She cooks, she washes, she feeds the children and waits on her husband. The poor girl does not know what is love, or even what is the pleasure of sex ... I am waiting to see my poor heroine rebel some day in the future. She would not do something heroic in a general sense, but simply say no when the possibility of a fifth child arises. I taught her the tricks, and Amina nodded. I knew it as a sign of rebellion.[21]

Amina and others like her could use some tricks. Until the political solutions arrive, the technical ones may be of some help. Despite the large-scale withdrawal of funding by pharmaceutical companies (which have retreated from the financial risks and controversies during the past two decades, while still using them to justify high profits), there are now a number of new types of contraceptives and refinements of older ones in prospect. These include the female condom, spermicides that give protection against diseases such as

---

21) Taslima Nasrin, *Guardian*, 27 December, 1994, S2, p 11. Other evidence comes from Latin America, where Mexican family planning clinics report 'between five and ten per cent of women attend without their husband's knowledge .... Women's greatest fear, aside from physical violence, was that husbands would leave them if they discovered they had been using family planning services' (*IPPF Open File*, August, 1993, p 11). The need for concealment has also been implicated in the excessive number of deliveries by Caesarean section in Brazil. Although it is illegal, a woman can obtain a surreptitious sterilization during the procedure by bribing the doctor. In addition to the obvious drawbacks in terms of expense and risk in performing unnecessary Caesareans, it appears that many women do not fully appreciate at the time the significance of the permanence of the method.

gonorrhoea, chlamydia and HIV infection, a hormonal IUD that reduces instead of increasing cramps and menstrual bleeding, a vaginal ring that can be inserted or removed by the user, and a variety of antifertility vaccines.

Research and testing   Although many of the prospective methods improve on those already in use, none is totally without drawbacks, and so should be considered as potential supplements to rather than replacements for the current armamentarium. It might have seemed that women's and grassroots health groups of all political stripes would welcome research and development leading to new and improved methods and the prospects of a greater range of individual choice. The reality has been quite different. For years, radical women's and health groups in India, Europe and the United States have mounted an especially strenuous campaign against hormonal contraceptives, particularly injectables and subdermal implants, charging that the trials had been carried out in an unethical and sloppy fashion, and that adequate consideration had not been given to the long-term effects of interference with the endocrinological systems, or of the possibility of fibrosis.[22]

Equally strong objections have been mounted in opposition to the development and even research towards the development of antifertility vaccines. Although the immunological approach offers many sites for highly specific and localized action on the reproductive process in both men and women, fears have been expressed over the particular dangers which lurk in interfering with the ' "sensitive, delicately balanced" immune system .... The risks include the induction of auto-immune diseases and allergies and exacerbation of infectious diseases and immune disturbances.'[23]

In the age of AIDS, no one can simply brush aside such cautions. However, while these and strictures concerning full information and consent, proper checking and monitoring before, during and after trials, and proper medical and hygienic precautions are well taken, many believe it is counterproductive to the empowerment of women

---

22) Lekha Rattanani, 'Statement on Contraception', *Research Centre for Women's Studies*, (Bombay), Summer, 1992, p 6; also, UBINIG (Policy Research for Alternative Development, a feminist collective, ranged along with FINRRAGE against hormonal contraception) 'Norplant: "The Five-Year Needle", an Investigation of the Bangladesh Trial', *Radical Journal of Health*, March, 1988, p 101. Norplant is a slow release hormone implanted in pellets under the skin. It requires medical training to implant and remove it. Their objections have been paralleled by American women's groups who see the enthusiasm of state governments for Norplant as a way of controlling welfare budgets as particularly aimed at poor and unmarried black women. See 'Women in US sue makers of Norplant', *British Medical Journal*, vol 309, 16 July, 1994.

23) R Padmanabhan, 'Women at risk', *Frontline*, 25 February, 1994, p 79.

to insist, as some Indian health activists are doing, on the discontinuation of all such research.

Much of the general objection derives from the view that all products of highly developed international medical technology are tainted with an imperialist and sexist desire for control. Yet most of the hormonal and immunological contraceptives have been tested in such developed places as Sweden, Finland and Australia, as well as in Chile, India and Brazil. Norplant, for example, was first tested in Finland in 1983. Moreover, one example of 'South–South' co-operation, the interuterine injection of quinacrine pellets which produced irreversible sterility, was developed in Chile; but trials in Vietnam were halted after criticism by an American panel.[24]

It is impossible to establish the long-term safety, efficacy and acceptability of a new contraceptive without widespread field trials. In addition, to forbid new contraceptive research and testing – and to forbid it in any site where it is intended for use – is to ignore or underestimate the drawbacks of the alternatives, which include unwanted pregnancy and recourse to traditional methods which have records of far less controlled use and testing and even more drawbacks and side-effects. In addition, objections to hormonal and chemical contraceptive research and implementation often overlook the widespread use of herbs in folk medicine, both in the past and present, which are also hormonal in their effect, as well as the mingling of 'modern' and 'folk' remedies and practices in current contraceptive usage and development.[25]

---

24) *The Lancet*, vol 343, 12 March, 1994, p 662.
25) See John M Riddle, *Contraception and Abortion from the Ancient World to the Renaissance*, Cambridge, Mass: Harvard University Press, 1992; and, for example, Caroline Bledsoe, Allan Hill, Umberto D'Alessandro and Patricia Langerock ('Constructing Natural Fertility: The Use of Western Contraceptive Technologies in Rural Gambia', *Population and Development Review*, March, 1994, pp 84–5) who found younger women relied more on traditional herbs, charms and abstinence, while 'older women with no education were the most common users of the "high-tech" method, Depo-provera' (an injection whose use is controversial in western countries).

That women continue to use untested and perhaps dangerous chemicals in the absence (or in addition to) medically approved ones is illustrated by reports from Brazil that the use of a drug originally intended for the treatment of gastric ulcers to procure abortions in Brazil – without medical supervision, as abortion is illegal – is now suspected of causing birth defects (*British Medical Journal*, 24 September, 1994, p 758).

On the other hand, the mass production of the contraceptive pill was made possible by the discovery of appropriate chemicals in the Mexican yam, and some of the most promising compounds now being studied for their antifertility properties come from seeds of the Neem tree, which is common and even revered in the Indian subcontinent. Extracts from the seeds are able to prevent implantation in one uterine horn without affecting either ovulation or the other horn.

THE CONUNDRUM OF THE SEX-RATIO IN INDIA

Women's groups have also fought to ban the increasingly common practice of foetal sex determination by amniocentesis and chorion villi sampling (and, more recently, ultrasound scanning) followed by abortion, citing a well-known finding that, of 8000 such abortions in Bombay in 1986 (reported by the Harkishan Das hospital), only one was of a male foetus. The resulting increase in the preponderance of males, they argue, would only worsen the social status of women, whatever the desires of the individual woman seeking the abortion. For this purpose, it is assumed that the woman is not a free agent, but pressured into her decision by strong family and religious pressures. (Among Hindus, for example, a son is required to light the funeral pyre of the deceased.) Yet there is much evidence that for the majority of women as well as men, the preference for sons is strong, and higher levels of education in women are followed by higher ratios of boys to girls among their children. The pretext often given is the devastation that the payment of dowry can mean, but, even before the practice of dowry penetrated through the entire social structure, the bearing of a daughter was associated with guilt and shame for both parents, even among communities which practised brideprice and where women customarily worked. The basis of this preference may be economic, since sons but not daughters are expected to contribute to their natal family's finances for life. Yet whatever investment (often considerable) a family may have to make in a son's education or establishment in life seems to be anticipated with equanimity, and the dowry phenomenon itself is a symptom of the low status of women.[26]

Nevertheless, there is something slightly mysterious from both an economic and demographic point of view in the ability of males to command excessive and growing prices in a marriage market in communities where there is a lifetime surplus of males, and the marriage of widows but not widowers is frowned on in the respectable castes. Some writers have attributed this to a 'marriage squeeze'. Where the population is increasing, younger cohorts are always larger than older ones, and since in India marriages are almost universally arranged, and arranged according to rules that require brides to be some years younger than their husbands, in the marriageable ages females may actually outnumber males; but a more important reason

26) See D Stein, 'Burning Widows, Burning Brides: the Perils of Daughterhood in India', *Pacific Affairs*, 61, no 3, 1988, pp 465–85.

may be the urgency of marrying off a daughter before some rather arbitrarily set age.[27]

THE PERPLEXITIES OF POPULATION POLICY IN INDIA

Indian feminists do not necessarily disapprove of contraception *per se*, though compared to western feminists they have been markedly slow to demand it as a right; nor do they deny that frequent pregnancies, lactation and childcare can be debilitating in themselves, all the more so when piled on top of other burdens. However, they tend to view the issue of childbearing (in contrast with that of foetal sex selection, for example) more as a need to protect women against unsafe or untried contraception than as a need to increase choice and access.[28] These considerations, they feel, should override national policy or environmental concerns, both of which are viewed with grave suspicion.

Suspicion may be merited on both counts: the Indian population policy was based on the premise that it was necessary for 'development', yet it has failed noticeably to redistribute the benefits of development or any other wealth to the most needy. Talk of the need for population control in poor countries is frequently found on the lips of those who refuse to recognize their own. Nevertheless, the arguments used when (rarely) the idea of overpopulation is not dismissed out of hand are misleading in the extreme.[29]

---

27) See V Rao, 'Dowry "Inflation" in Rural India: a Statistical Investigation', *Population Studies*, 47, no 2, July, 1993, pp 283–9. Rao, however, considers only women in the age range 15 to 20 and men in the range 20 to 25. In fact, males may marry in a much wider range than that; indeed, there is almost no age at which a man is considered too old to marry, whereas women have a much more limited 'sell-by' date before the family suffers a severe loss of status in the neighbours' eyes.

28) See, for example, 'Politics of Population and Development', *Economic and Political Weekly*, 17 September, 1994, pp 2470–2. After admitting that, 'Early, late, numerous and closely spaced pregnancies are major contributors to high infant and child mortality and morbidity rates, especially where health care facilities are scarce', the article goes on to aver that, 'A policy that attempts to give individuals the right to choose contraceptives and plan their family without providing an enabling environment that would render the choice to be automatically "safe" and "risk free" cannot, for obvious reasons, go very far.' The risks acceptable for contraception are far more stringent than those for pregnancy.

29) For example, Nagmani Rao (*FRCH [Forum for Research in Community Health] Newsletter*, Bombay, Jan–Feb, 1992, p 8) points out that between 1951 and 1981, the Indian population increased by 83 per cent, while foodgrain production rose by 135 per cent. This period conveniently covers the 'green revolution', now running out of steam, which uniquely was able to raise production by startling amounts over a very short period, but involved heavy inputs of fertilizer and irrigation. It is doubtful that this can be repeated, let alone several times. Rao also points out that the average population density of India (233/sq km in an overwhelmingly agricultural country) in 1981 was still below Japan (311) and West Germany (246) and similar to England (228) – all highly industrialized states. Comparisons

Recently the Indian government admitted that, despite the estimated averting of 143 million births, the past 40 years of family planning have failed to reduce the average annual population growth below 2 per cent, and less than 45 per cent of the country's fertile couples practice contraception. In an effort to learn from past experience, it has decided to abandon targets (for numbers of 'acceptors'), while decentralizing and improving the quality of services, offering a wider choice of contraceptives and linking birth control programmes to female literacy, employment, social security and maternal and child health.[30] Such intentions have been announced many times in the past, and were embodied in the 1976 policy declaration. Unfortunately, there is reason to believe that policy realization is if anything even less likely to occur in the future than in the past. In 1990, in response to a balance of payments crisis, India adopted a structural adjustment programme intended to make the economy more free-market-oriented. Accordingly, food and fertilizer subsidies and public sector investment have been slashed, as has the health budget – except for family planning! In a country where the age-specific death rates, nutrition and health care have generally favoured the male, such stringencies are bound to fall particularly hard upon women and girls – and to contradict the announced strategy of the population control policy.[31]

◇

---

cont.

not made include: Bangladesh (698), Kerala (660), Netherlands (354), and United States (26), according to 1987 World Bank figures. Her point that there is no simple correlation between either development or environmental degradation and population density is, however, well taken. But Rao then passes on to the total irrelevancy of claiming that 'Countries such as Canada, at their highest fertility, had a Total Fertility Rate of 8, whereas the Indian TFR has never exceeded 6.'

30) *British Medical Journal*, 15 May, 1993, p 1290.

31) In a review of the effects of the structural adjustment programme upon women, Vibhuti Patel (unpublished paper presented to the Development Studies Institute, London School of Economics, 27 November, 1992) says:

Amount of food-grains needed to provide the 'really poor' (according to the World Bank's standard – 235 million Indians) is 46.5 million tonnes. [The actual amount distributed through the public distribution system (i.e., 'fair price')] for 1991–92 is 19.1 million tonnes, ... a shortfall of nearly 59 per cent .... Studies on intra-household distribution of resources reveal that among the poorer households with gross malnutrition and nutritional deficiency, the deficiency among girls and women was 25 per cent more than that for men. For every three men who avail [themselves of] health care facilities in India, only one woman does so ... [According to the] 1991 census, the sex-ratio [number of women per 1000 men] is 929, the lowest [since census-taking began]. In the 0–19 age-group, the age-specific death rate among girls is higher than among boys. In this context, budgetary cuts in public health ... will have dire consequences for women and girls ... [The] allocation for the treatment of tuberculosis, malaria, filaria and goitre eradication programmes has been reduced .... Reductions in funds for rural sanitation ... clean water, toilets and sewerage gave rise to increased incidence of water-borne

---◇---

cont.

diseases and increased the [nursing] burden on women. Reduction in quota for
clean water resources by 38 per cent in urban areas and 36 per cent in rural areas
has increased the drudgery of working class women ... standing in long queues for
hours together for one bucket of water .... The only items for which budgetary
provision has increased are family planning (34 per cent), defence (7 per cent) and
police force (14 per cent). [A] lot has been documented on the coercive aspect of
population control programmes that force poor women to adopt contraceptives
without informed consent or proper follow-up by the medical staff (p 4).

The recent return to India of such scourges as plague and cerebral malaria only
underscores the woeful inadequacy of Indian public health measures.

Chapter 7

Kerala: the economical model

Though by no means perfect, the ratio of females to males in a society is some measure of the value of women in that society.[1] In Europe and North America, the ratio of females to males is about 1.05; in sub-Saharan Africa about 1.02; in China 0.94; in Pakistan 0.91; in Kerala 1.04.[2] In India as a whole, with Kerala averaged in, the ratio is 0.93, but there are wide differences among the states. In Tamil Nadu and Orissa, for example, the ratio is about 0.98; in Uttar Pradesh and Kashmir it is below 0.90.[3]

Kerala seems to be different from the rest of India in many ways, yet, even though it has less than 3 per cent of the population, many of the differences seem to be related to the striking difference in fertility behaviour, contrasting with the rest of India, and, until recently, the rest of the developing world. Life expectancy in Kerala is now 73 years for females and 68 for males at birth. In the rest of India it is 59 years for both. Female literacy is now nearly equal to that of the male, and

---

1) This ratio also depends on the life expectancy, since, although at birth males outnumber females by about 5 per cent, with equal care female mortality at any age tends to be lower than that of the male. That is why a ratio above unity is not a sign that females are more highly valued than males. Confusingly, a 'high' sex-ratio means that the ratio of males to females is greater than 1.

2) See Amartya Sen, 'The Economics of Life and Death', *Scientific American*, May, 1993, p 24. The figure for Kerala may be somewhat elevated because of the large amount of male migration.

3) Robin Jeffrey, *Politics, Women and Well-being: How Kerala Became a Model*, Macmillan, 1992, p 5. Jeffrey assembled a table of these ratios from a variety of sources. He also points out that even within Kerala, the sex ratios of the different religious communities vary: for the Nayar caste it is 1.002, while for Syrian Christians, 0.98 (p 98).

nearly universal. In India as whole, it is about 26 per cent, half that of males. The infant mortality rate is less than one-quarter, and the TFR now stands below two children, having fallen from six in the past 30 years, while for the Indian average it still stands at almost four.[4]

Yet Kerala is one of India's poorer states, with a per capita income of less than $200 per year, two-thirds of the all-India average; moreover, it has not really industrialized, and, until the mid-1970s, Kerala's rate of population growth exceeded that of India as a whole.[5] Paradoxically, the population control methods which proved so unpopular in the rest of India during the 'Emergency' were actually pioneered in Kerala in the early 1970s and pronounced a great success.[6]

A HISTORY OF DIFFERENCE

Many of Kerala's people belong to castes that were matrilineal from

---

4) KC Zachariah, 'Demographic transition in Kerala', paper presented to the International Congress on Kerala Studies at Thiruvananthapurum, 27–29 August, 1994. The marriage age has risen to 28 years for men and 23 for women.

5) The crude birth rates in South India (roughly Kerala, Tamil Nadu, Mysore and Andhra Pradesh) have always been lower than in the rest of India, but the mortality rates have also been lower. See, D Kumar, and M Desai, *Cambridge Economic History of India*, vol 2, pp 505 and 509. For annual growth rates, listed as of each census year, see, KC Zachariah, *The Anomaly of the Fertility Decline in India's Kerala State*, World Bank Staff Working Papers no 700, Population and Development Series no 25, 1984. Zachariah attributes about 30 per cent of the decline in fertility between 1965 and 1980, when most of it took place, to the increased age of women at marriage (which averaged almost 21, while the all-India average is 16).

> The more years of schooling a woman had, or the better off she was economically, the more likely she was to marry at an older age …. Employment of the prospective husband is emerging as a prerequisite to marriage; most women would rather wait than marry someone who is unemployed. Dowry problems also cause delays, as the price goes up in response to the increased cost of educating a boy and his increased difficulties in securing a job. (p xxv)

6) Zachariah, ibid, p 25:

> The third phase, covering the period from the end of 1970 to April, 1973, saw the conduct of mass sterilization camps. These camps not only proved to be pacesetters for the country as a whole, but were responsible in large measure for the popularity of sterilization in Kerala. Nine-month long camps were held during these years in seven of the then 11 districts in the State. The most ambitious and impressive in terms of achievement were the three camps in Ernakulam district, where the target was 85,000 sterilizations and the actual total was 93,254

Nevertheless, the camps were abandoned and in the following two years, the rate of male sterilizations in Ernakulam District fell to 5500, 4000 below the two-year period preceding the camps. Since then, Kerala followed the surge and drop-back in vasectomies found in the rest of India during the Emergency and after. Female sterilizations, however, showed a fairly steady increase until 1983. Non-terminal female methods, such as abortion and IUDs have risen fairly steadily.

the 10th or 11th centuries. According to one origin theory, other castes modelled their social system on the high-status warrior Nayars, who were off fighting each other so frequently, and at home so uncertainly, that it became convenient for women to remain always in their natal households. They formed liaisons of shorter or longer duration with men of appropriate rank, who, however, also remained part of their own natal households. Descent was reckoned through the maternal line. This did not result in a matriarchy, since the manager and head of each household was invariably male; however, as long as a woman did not violate the rules of her caste status by sexual involvement with a male of inferior rank, she had a guaranteed place and support within a usually communal family household. Furthermore, since she was not confined and controlled by a single man to whom it was of surpassing importance that her sexuality be devoted to him alone, she had a certain liberty and status in her own right; in particular, women were never confined to the house but could move freely about in public.

Sexual relationships with non-resident males could be easily broken off without affecting the welfare of children or subjecting women to social stigma – in stark contrast with the rest of India. The matrilineal model was so predominant that even the Muslims of Kerala followed the matrilocal residence pattern. Christian missionaries of course abhorred it, but in the 18th century a gentleman of the Enlightenment could urge Europe to adopt the Nayar system, to 'rescue your sisters and manumit your wives from an oppressive yoke' and 'increase the liberty and happiness of both sexes'.[7]

Although the proportions varied among the three traditional states that made up the modern one, in the 20th century Hindus constituted only 60 per cent of the population, Christians about 20 per cent and Muslims 20 per cent. Of the Hindus, the relatively higher caste Nayars constituted about one-third, or about 20 per cent of the total.[8] The remainder were lower caste, (themselves often matrilineal), or otherwise beneath the caste system. These lower groups were subjected to extreme social disabilities, since it was believed that even the sight of them could be polluting to their betters.

---

7)   James Lawrence, *Essay on the Nair System of Gallantry and Inheritance, Shewing Its Superiority Over Marriage* ..., 1792, quoted in Robin Jeffrey, *Politics, Women and Well-being: How Kerala Became a Model*, Macmillan, 1992, p 34.

8)   R Jayasree, *Religion, Social Change and Fertility Behaviour: A Study of Kerala*, New Delhi: Concept, 1989, p 30. The existence of both Christians and Muslims in Kerala goes back very far. The Syrian Christians claim residence from the time of Christ and are certainly attested before the 16th century. The Muslims likewise seem to have been converted peacefully by Arab traders whose ancestors were visiting the Kerala coast since well before the founding of Islam.

By the beginning of the 20th century, matrilineality had begun to be eroded, though it left certain residues in female freedom and independence which are still evident (in the near normal sex-ratio, for example). The breakdown of the matrilineal system was a function of British rule and factors going further back in history. By disarming the warrior Nayars early in the 19th century the British triggered a crisis in the social system, and, according to Robin Jeffrey, the controversies surrounding the system's legal break-up were important in the politicizing of the entire Keralan population. Politicization in turn transformed a rigidly hierarchical and deferential society into a demanding and contentious one.[9]

Peace, stability and an increased male presence produced a growing population and a shortage of land for the enlarged households to branch and expand into. British insistence on codifying a previously fluid system only made things worse:

> Population grew. Cash transactions spread. English law froze custom into brittle, contorted forms. New systems of administration sucked children into costly, formal schools which in turn exposed them to the likelihood of hearing matriliny mocked.[10]

Beginning in 1896 and periodically until its last vestiges were swept away in 1976, the matrilineal and collective system of marriage, inheritance and property rights was 'reformed' out of existence. The consequence of this overturn of the traditional family system was that the Communist Party of India was able to make many recruits among high caste rural Nayars in the 1940s.

Meanwhile, Party recruitment among the lower castes was aided not only by the brutal social disabilities they suffered, but by the unusually high level of education that had subsisted there since the latter part of the 19th century, thanks to the double efforts of Christian missionaries and enlightened Maharajas. By 1911, the princely states of Travancore and Cochin boasted three times the all-India literacy rate; even the British-administered Malabar state had twice that rate. Girls were included in some of this school-going right from the beginning, so that even a clergyman who characterized the Nayar women as 'grossly immoral as they don't know the sanctity of

9)   Robin Jeffrey, *Politics, Women and Well-being: How Kerala Became a Model*, Macmillan, 1992. His account, from a left-wing perspective, is matched by equally admiring and more 'liberal' accounts which tend to give more credit to enlightened native rulers. See, for example, Jayasree, note 8.

10)   Robin Jeffrey, ibid, p 40.

marriage' had to admit that they were 'learned in their own literature, music ... and ladylike and refined in their manners'.[11]

Among the teachers were members of the lower castes who constituted a ready-made core of diffusers of subversive ideas, since they were both articulate and possessed of grievances over the poor rates of pay and working conditions that are always the lot of educators of the masses. The early decades of the 20th century were also the decades of the Independence movement, and the Congress Party competed with the Communists to further stir up and increase political awareness among all the classes.

Under British rule, the growing of cash crops for export – cashews, rubber, and above all coconuts – was encouraged. By the 1930s, when the world-wide economic depression drove down prices, population growth had reached the point where the region was growing only half the grain it needed to consume. The prices of export crops under such conditions drop further than do food crops. Since it is easier to do without coconut mats than without rice, Kerala was particularly hard hit, and the bad times increased the appeal of the Communist Party. During World War II, the loss of Burma meant the loss of much of Kerala's rice supply. The threat of a hungry and politically organized population impelled Keralan governments to introduce rationing; the joint efforts of government 'fair price shops' and political 'food committees' ensured that distribution was relatively equitable and hoarding and profiteering kept to a minimum. While Bengal, which had grown 90 per cent of its own food, suffered a major famine, Kerala was hungry but few people starved. A concern for an adequate and equitable food distribution remained a legacy, as did a controversy over the state's nutritional status.

After independence, the politicized population continued to make demands upon its elected representatives in several areas. The education budget rose from 20 per cent of state outlay in the late 1950s to 40 per cent in the late 1970s (by which time the primary school intake cohort was shrinking), while the all-India average education budget was only 25 per cent. Successive governments tried to cut back, but found it politically unacceptable. Education was popular because it provided steady jobs for women and reserved places for the formerly deprived castes. For women, it provided some compensation for the loss of status that accompanied the downfall

---

◇

11) Jeffrey, ibid, p 33. See also R Jayasree, *Religion, Social Change and Fertility Behaviour: A Study of Kerala*, New Delhi: Concept, 1989, p 42. Jayasree points out that, even in 1901, Travancore (the site of his study and the southernmost of Kerala's three regions) was ahead of other Indian states in both general and women's education. Although missionaries ran schools and colleges, education is most nearly universal among Hindus.

of matrilineality and matrilocality; almost 50 per cent of Kerala's teachers were female, as against the all-India average of 25 per cent. But education was also valued for its own sake; this was demonstrated by the widespread and largely co-operative library system.[12]

Another demand, most enthusiastically espoused by the Communists, but also forced upon coalitions of various stripes in Kerala's intensely competitive political climate, was for land reform. Yet the upshot of a 30-year process, begun in 1957, was not really an equitable distribution of land to the tiller: 4 per cent of the population still own 35 per cent of cultivable land. Land was not collectivized and productivity was, if anything, reduced; but tenants became owners, middle-class and lower middle-class proprietors appeared, and over 90 per cent of rural workers (about 40 per cent female) own at least a tenth of an acre: not enough to live off, but enough to put up a hut from which they cannot be evicted. Thanks to yet other campaigns, tile roofs also began to replace verminous and leaky thatch over many of their heads.

Public health   Still another element of welfare that has a long history in Kerala is that of public health. The region is subject to most of the usual water- and insect-borne diseases, although the relatively abundant water supply has meant that most of the population was able to engage in the frequent washing and bathing that remains an all-India ideal. Even before the influence of western medicine began to make itself felt, people had availed themselves of practitioners of schools of native medicine which are still very popular. And again the princely rulers had thoughtfully provided enough smallpox vaccination services and hospital beds so that the death rates in the mid-1950s were half what they were in the previously British-administered portion. But even there, in Malabar, when cholera raged during World War II, the Communists had formed teams that went from house to house to advise people on cleanliness and disease prevention.[13]

As in education, the provision of high quality public health services depends on the availability of well-trained and dedicated professionals willing to work for low wages: usually women. Hence, possibly as important a factor as any that eventually made medical services in Kerala better than those in any other state was the combination of the sizable Christian community, among whom nursing was considered a

---

12)   R Jayasree, ibid, p 44. Another early princely project, the public library at Trivandrum was
        established in 1829. As of 1985, there were 5000 libraries around the state, mostly run on a
        co-operative basis.
13)   Robin Jeffrey, *Politics, Women and Well-being: How Kerala Became a Model*, Macmillan,
        1992, p 191.

worthy endeavour, and, once more, the willingness of parents to send their daughters out to be trained for steady employment once the facilities for training and the certainty of employment were available.[14] Despite the rather spread-out pattern of residence, health centres have been sited within easy walking distance of almost the entire population.[15] From 1970 onward, the western medical hospitals and dispensaries alone were treating an average of each member of the population once a year. In the 1960s the death rate began to fall, until by the 1970s it had fallen to 9 per 1000, about half the all-India rate. Consequently, until the mid-1970s, the population grew faster than the rest of India. (According to the 1981 census, the average density of the population was 660 per square kilometre, almost three times the all-India average.)[16]

When it came to birth control, if Kerala is different, even Kerala's Communists were different from their anti-Malthusian counterparts in other parts of the world. Jeffrey again:

> From the mid-1930s, troubled at the growth of population, men and women of various political persuasions publicly advocated artificial contraception. Such discussion came at a time when matrilineal people were being forced to adjust their entire system of family organisation. If one were asking, 'What is a family?', why not consider the appropriate size of a family as well? At the same time, social reformers sometimes exhorted their lower-caste

---

14) In contrast with the rest of India, where nursing is considered a very low-status occupation, since it involves women in contact with unrelated men, the traditionally greater freedom of Keralan women meant that they were not so subject to stigma. From an as yet incomplete study of the history of nursing in South India, Meera Abraham (personal communication) reports that nursing was a particularly attractive profession for young Christian women because:

    1) Christian families often had low incomes, and nursing training required lesser educational qualifications than medicine;
    2) inheritance law in the Syrian Christian community was very unfavourable to women; and
    3) a salaried daughter was often an acceptable substitute for a dowered one.

If women benefited personally from the employment opportunities, this was an almost accidental by-product of family calculation. Nevertheless, because bodily secretions are considered polluting, few upper-caste Hindu women have gone into nursing. (The caste system is based on notions of purity and pollution that have both temporary and permanent manifestations. The upper castes, inherently 'purer', also refuse to engage in polluting occupations.)

15) 'Basic Amenities in Villages', *Economic and Political Weekly*, 6 April, 1985, p 615. Almost all Keralan births are now medically attended. There has also been a recent growth in private medical facilities.

16) This is one of the highest densities in the world, almost twice that of Holland, and more than 20 times that of the United States (*World Development Report*, 1987, Washington, DC: World Bank).

listeners to reject Hinduism, embrace Lenin – and practise birth control.[17]

TROUBLE AT THE MODEL

If it seems difficult even now to write of Kerala without giving way to partiality and admiration, nevertheless criticism of many sorts (intended or not) can certainly be found. Feminist criticism has not been wanting. Keralan women, for all their educational and occupational achievements and involvement in public affairs, have never been able to break the male stranglehold on leadership in politics; those who tried, such as Akkamma Cheriyan in the 1950s and KR Gouri in the 1980s, have been subjected to 'innuendo, ridicule and disappointment' as severe as anywhere else. Jayasree's study reveals that here too the 'value of children' equates to the 'value of sons'.[18] Olga Nieuwenhuys' study of child labour among the poor Muslims and Ezhevas (low-caste Hindus) in a small coastal Keralan village argues that poverty and both economic and gender inequality still take their toll despite notional access to education and medical care.[19] And, finally, a recent article by K Saradamoni claims that Kerala too is increasingly adopting other models of development (including almost universal arranged marriage) in its increasing despair over high rates of unemployment.[20]

From the conventional economic side, Zachariah notes the severe and worsening problem of educated unemployment. Jeffrey deplores the fragility and economic distortions produced by remittances from those who had emigrated to work in the Gulf States, underlined when

---

17) Robin Jeffrey, *Politics, Women and Well-being: How Kerala Became a Model*, Macmillan, 1992, p 196.

18) R Jayasree, *Religion, Social Change and Fertility Behaviour: A Study of Kerala*, New Delhi: Concept, 1989, Chapter 4. It should be said too, especially in the light of the recent rise in communal agitation, that Jayasree's almost entirely laudatory book inspires some suspicion of bias in the alert reader who notes that, in the four photographic illustrations provided, both upper and lower caste Hindu families are pictured neatly grouped with their two children, a Muslim pair with seven, and a Christian fisherman family with a disorderly brood of at least seven strung out along a beach.

19) Olga Nieuwenhuys, *Children's World: Gender, Welfare and Labour in the Developing World*, London: Routledge, 1994, Chapter 7.

20) K Saradamoni, 'Women, Kerala and Some Development Issues', *Economic and Political Weekly*, 26 February, 1994, pp 501–5. The higher female educated unemployment rates are driving women back into the home (Rachel Kumar, 'Emerging trends in female unemployment in Kerala', paper presented to the International Congress on Kerala Studies at Thiruvananthapurum, 27–29 August, 1994).

these dried up in the crisis of 1990–91.[21] He also claims that the high proportion of state funds spent on education and health leave too little available for productive investment in such things as roads and water management. What state enterprises there are are unproductive and unprofitable.

Few private entrepreneurs, even wealthy natives returned from the Gulf, have cared to invest in industries in the state; they are said to fear a militant labour force. However, a thoughtful analysis of the puzzle of Kerala's lack of development has been made by Darryl D'Monte in the context of the Silent Valley dam controversy, which became a *cause célèbre* all over India and beyond. The dam plan was finally scrapped for environmental reasons thanks to the intervention of Mrs Gandhi. D'Monte thinks Mrs Gandhi was more sensitive to her image abroad than swayed by the arguments, yet he does question the previously accepted postulates of 'development', meaning modern industrialization, and suggests several alternative paths for Kerala. He points out, for example, that Idukki district produces 75 per cent of the state's power, yet has the lowest industrial growth, measured in terms of number of industrial units and employment. Pointing to Kerala's unique 'rural–urban' mix, and very high population density, he suggests small-scale and decentralized industries planned to produce the most jobs and benefit from the state's highly educated workforce, which exports professional labour (including nurses) to the West; he thinks there is scope for agro-based industries and processing. As to the usual reason given for Kerala's lagging development, he also thinks the workforce would be less militant if there were more employment opportunities at home![22]

The greatest and most important controversies, however, have swirled around the nutritional status and illness statistics. Can a society be said to be happy even if poor if large numbers of its members are sick and hungry despite long lives and high educational standards? The National Sample Survey of India of 1973–74, which used reports of household heads concerning current illnesses, found

---

21) Leela Gulati ('Male migration from Kerala: some effects on Women', *Manushi*, no 38, Jan–Feb 1987, pp 14–9) graphically spelled out the vulnerabilities of the Keralan remittance economy. One in twelve Kerala households has a migrant member, and remittance receipts rose from 5 to 17 per cent of the state income between 1976 and 1981. 'Gulf boys' command higher dowries than stay-at-homes. While wives of migrant workers have had to become more independent and capable of managing both decisions and dealing with the outside world, they have also become vulnerable to slurs against their chastity and conflicts with in-laws over allocation of remittance money, the expectation of which is liable to disappointment, not only by world events out of the migrant's control, but by his own changing allegiances.

22) Darryl D'Monte, *Temples or Tombs: Industry versus Environment*, New Delhi: Centre for Science and Environment, 1985.

Kerala had three times the all-India average for acute sickness, and several times that for such assorted conditions as epilepsy, hypertension, asthma, rheumatism – and haemorrhoids.[23] A 1987 study found the morbidity index almost three times that of 1974.[24] These results may indicate the increasing illness of an ageing population (although higher rates of sickness were found at all ages) and the increased awareness of illness in a society with easy access to medical treatment.[25] An all-India survey of causes of death in rural areas[26] shows that Kerala has lower rates of death from some of the diseases for which it has higher rates of sickness, such as asthma and gastroenteritis, as well as those for which it has lower rates, such as typhoid. It also has higher death rates from the diseases of age such as cancer and heart attacks.

The paradox of greater reported morbidity in a longer-lived, better medicated society may be no contradiction at all, but a longer-lasting puzzle has been the issue of nutrition. Surveys taken during the 1950s and 1960s seemed to indicate that the average diet in Kerala was only 1600 calories per person per day, far below the 2400 calories the Indian government considered a minimum for an agricultural people.[27] Later consideration adjusted the amounts for the high female to male ratio, the greater proportion of office workers and the amounts of coconut and cassava consumed, to bring the average to 6

---

23) Sarvekshana *Journal of the National Sample Survey Organization*, July–October 1980, vol 4, nos 1 and 2, Government of India, Department of Statistics, Ministry of Planning. See also C Murray and L Chen, 'Understanding Morbidity Change', *Population and Development Review*, September, 1992. Some of the explanation may lie in the particular selection of reported conditions of high incidence in Kerala. Murray and Chen compare the Indian findings with those in the United States, where the richer the family the more illness was reported for children and the elderly, but the less for those between 18 and 44 years. Unlike the United States, however, more Indian men than women were reported ill, and Kerala followed the Indian pattern. In India, apparently, the female tends to be the stoical sex.

24) KP Kannan, KR Thankapan, and VR Kutty, *Health and Development in Rural Kerala*, Trivandrum: Integrated Rural Technology Centre, 1991. See also BG Kumar, 'Low Mortality and High Morbidity in Kerala Reconsidered', *Population and Development Review*, 19, no 1, March, 1993, pp 103–21.

25) Olga Nieuwenhuys (*Children's World: Gender, Welfare and Labour in the Developing World*, London: Routledge, 1994, pp 67–8) points out, however, that even though medical care may be available, medicines still cost, and the poor often neglect children's minor ailments on this account.

26) *Survey of Causes of Deaths*, 1981, (New Delhi, Office of the Registrar General). See also BG Kumar, 'Low Mortality and High Morbidity in Kerala Reconsidered', *Population and Development Review*, 19, no 1, March, 1993, pp 103–21, for a discussion of these figures.

27) In the 1983 round, the National Sample Survey found the Keralan calorie intake still 15 per cent below the Indian average, and still below the minimum daily requirement. Yet according to the 1981 survey of rural Kerala, death rates from 'malnutrition and debility' are unknown, while they constitute 2 per cent of deaths in India in general. Kumar, ibid, pp 103 and 106.

per cent above minimum. It was also suggested that the better sanitary and medical conditions lowered the incidence of such diseases and worms and dysentery, permitting Keralans to make better use of the food they got.[28] Other studies found fewer Keralan children were severely undernourished in comparison with other relatively poor Indian states, and that, among lower-income village children, while 60 per cent were below the Indian average weight, 70 per cent were above the average height, indicating that their prenatal and neonatal nutrition had been superior.[29] Hence the evidence of nutritional deficiency is inconclusive.

Efforts at redistribution, while they have not eliminated poverty or ensured gender equality, have still paid off, and insistently suggest there is more to economics than growth and more to the quality of life than consumption. Nevertheless, as Mencher warns:

> Kerala seems like a 'cheap' model for development. This could easily be used to support the view that those in Western countries can have their cake and eat it too; that they can ease their consciences by encouraging patterns of development which will neither involve large transfers of funds from the wealthier countries to the poorer, nor rock the boat in which we all are sitting.[30]

Her caution is well-grounded especially since western countries do all they can to discourage any pattern of development based, as Kerala's has been, on socialist principles and practices. And also

---

28) The National Sample Survey, cited above, somewhat surprisingly reports greater incidence and prevalence of both dysentery and diarrhoea at all ages for Kerala than for India as a whole, but the average duration of each spell is less, suggesting the better availability of medical treatment. Joan Mencher, ('The Lessons and Non-lessons of Kerala: Agricultural Labourers and Poverty', *Economic and Political Weekly*, 5 October, 1980, pp 1781–4) describes the better operation of the primary health care system in Kerala (compared with that of the adjacent Tamil Nadu) in providing prompt and reliable treatment for the infant diarrhoeas and fever that are the major causes of infant mortality. This would also have a positive effect on child (and adult) nutritional status if these acute conditions are perceived and treated expeditiously. The end result, Mencher feels, is that, along with the availability of contraception and the lack of employment opportunities for children, even poor Keralan labourers limit their families.

29) See RW Franke, 'Feeding Programmes and Food Intake in a Kerala Village', *Economic and Political Weekly*, 20–27 February, 1993, p 355. Franke's own, more detailed, study examined other nutrients as well as seasonal and socioeconomic variation in the diets of a single Kerala village and found that many of the poorer people did indeed fall below the minimum during at least some parts of the year, but that ration shop rice and lunches, given to school and nursery children and their mothers, helped to raise the total calories consumed for the poorer households by between 5 and 13 per cent.

30) Joan Mencher, 'The Lessons and Non-lessons of Kerala: Agricultural Labourers and Poverty', *Economic and Political Weekly*, 5 October, 1980, p 1781.

since a pattern of dropping birth rates in conditions of continuing poverty has now developed in many other parts of the world, which will increasingly suggest to the suggestible that transfers of wealth from the richer to the poorer may after all not be necessary.

The puzzles posed by the 'Kerala model' and its comforting or worrying (depending on the observer's viewpoint) implications for fertility decline have only been heightened by the rather sharply falling birth rates in the neighbouring state of Tamil Nadu in the past decade. Tamil Nadu instituted a free midday school meal programme in the 1970s, which encourages families to keep their girl children in school. Some observers credit the sharp fall in birth rates from the mid-1980s to the lower fertility of this cohort of better educated girls.[31] However, an analysis of 1981 Tamil Nadu census data correlating fertility rates with a variety of other factors within the state indicates that fertility did not seem to be clearly related to female literacy, but was instead related to lower child mortality and the availability of road facilities.[32] It seemed that the march of communications, associated with the opportunity for women to earn money by travelling to urban areas, and the rise of educational aspirations were more effective in lowering the desired family size than female literacy. Moreover, poorer families had fewer, not more children, suggesting once more that women in many conditions of life, once given the opportunity, would regulate their fertility to accord with their resources.

---

31)   Jessica Mathews ('Population Control That Really Works', *Weekly Guardian*, 10 February, 1994) says, rather chillingly, 'A little girl became more valuable to the family by going to school and getting a nutritious meal (especially if she brought some home to share) than staying home taking care of younger siblings.'
32)   R Savitri, 'Fertility Rate Decline in Tamil Nadu', *Economic and Political Weekly*, 16 July, 1994, pp 1850–2.

Chapter 8

China: bearing pressure

Even in China, the issue of population size and growth has been debated only in the narrowest economic terms; frequently the only calculations made are of the amounts of food, whether in grain or in calories, necessary to support a given number of people, with little recognition either of the other resources a population must necessarily consume, or of the long-term environmental effects of intensive food production. Yet it is obvious that the arable land, instead of increasing to meet the growing Chinese population, is actually decreasing as more rural housing is constructed, and more topsoil is converted into bricks.

Very often, not even water resources are considered. China, although her overall precipitation is not much below the global average, has a water run-off (that is, the proportion of rainwater that runs into streams, rivers and so on and is not absorbed by the soil) of only one-fifth of the average.[1] Thus the prospects of water availability for an increasing population, let alone a rising standard of living, are ominous.

China's population size and change are of importance from environmental considerations alone. But, in addition, the Chinese reproductive policy has been the most controversial in the world, not excluding that of Romania. For example, no Romanian woman was given political asylum on account of Ceaucescu's coercive pronatal regulations, but several Chinese women were granted refugee status

---

1) Vaclav Smil, *The Bad Earth*, London: Zed Press, 1984, p 79–80.

in the United States on the grounds that, against government directives, they wished to have more than one child.[2] But the involvement of the Chinese government with its population goes back a very long way.

DEMOGRAPHIC HISTORY

The Chinese government has concerned itself with assessing, if not interfering with, the numbers of its subjects for some four thousand years. Nor has China been without its worry warts and theorists of relationship between national fecundity, prosperity and harmony. In the Zhou dynasty, about 500 BC, one Han Fei-zi remarked:

> In ancient times, people were few, but wealthy and without strife. People at present think that five sons are not too many, and each son has five sons also, and before the death of the grandfather there are already 25 descendants. Therefore, people are more and wealth is less; they work hard and receive little. The life of a nation depends upon having enough food, not upon the number of people.[3]

Over 2000 years later, Hong Liangzhi, a contemporary of Thomas Malthus but even more pessimistic, held that not even the natural scourges of war, famine and disease, let alone government policies, could hold the geometric growth in check:

> Someone will probably tell me that by the time we have reached great grandsons, new previously vacant land and new houses will be available. Even so ... [t]he number of families will always be excessive .... Does Heaven know a remedy? Flood and drought, plague and pestilence are what nature offers as remedies, though the percentage that die in natural calamities rarely exceeds one or two tenths of the population.
>
> Do emperors and state officials possess remedies? They can

---

2)   The State Family Planning Commission in 1987 found that the average family had 2.4 children. See K Forestier, 'The degreening of China', *New Scientist*, 1 July, 1989, p 53. Since then fertility rates have declined further to below replacement (although Vaclav Smil [*China's Environmental Crisis*, London: ME Sharpe, 1993, p 18] argues that official estimates have consistently underreported birth rates). Estimates by environmentalists of the total population of China have consistently been higher than official figures, and recently China has admitted that it now has 400 million more people than it can support.

3)   Quoted in G Hardin, *Population, Evolution and Birth Control*, San Francisco: WH Freeman, 1969.

see to it that there is no uncultivated land and no unused labour in the realm. When land is reclaimed they can move people on to it to cultivate there .... They can forbid luxurious living and suppress speculation in land. In the case of flood, drought and plague, they can open granaries and allow the treasury to relieve the masses. But that is all .... In short, in a long reign of peace, the emperor and his officials can neither stop human reproduction, nor are the measures they do dispose of adequate to provide the people with sustenance ...[4]

Nevertheless, according to the very dubious figures that were produced from counts ranging from the year 2 CE (Christian Era) until the latter half of the 18th century (Hong Liangzhi's time), the Chinese population hovered at or below some 60 million persons (except for some counts during the Song dynasty that ranged as high as 120 million, only to fall back during the 13th century Mongol period). Since then, although the exact totals were often unknown, especially in times of political turmoil, it is clear that growth has been relentless, doubling from some 200 million in 1750 to 400 million a century later. Another 200 million were added by 1954, but it required only 15 years to add another 200 million after that, despite the fact that the intervening years included the famine years of 1959–61, during which the increased mortality is estimated to have been between 16 and 30 million.[5]

Because of the great famine, the year 1960 actually witnessed a preponderance of deaths over births of 0.5 per cent (or 1.5 per cent or 2 per cent),[6] which was followed by a sharp increase in birth rates to unprecedented highs in the early 1960s. Since then, a decade and a half before the institution of the one-child policy, birth rates began a steep decline.

Traditionally, the Chinese patriarchal ideal was an extended joint patrilocal household, which included the family plus retainers. Data gathered in 1920s showed that average family and household sizes were quite moderate: 5.25 and 5.42 persons respectively. Child mortality then averaged 50 per cent and most families had between

---

4) Hong Liangzhi, 'Causerie on a Peaceful Reign', translated in L Silberman, 'Hung Liang-chi: a Chinese Malthus', *Population Studies*, 13, 1960, p 262.

5) For short accounts of Chinese demographic history, see, Penny Kane, *The Second Billion*, Penguin Books, 1987, and Peng Xizhe, *Demographic Transition in China*, Oxford: Clarendon Press, 1991. For estimates of the famine mortality, see Robert MacFarquhar, *The Origins of the Cultural Revolution, Vol II, The Great Leap Forward 1958–1960*, Oxford: Oxford University Press, 1983, p 330.

6) For an analysis of the inconsistencies in reporting the demographic consequences of the famine, see 'The Feast of Lies', in *Starving in Silence*, London: Article 19, 1990.

one and three surviving children.[7] When the oldest generation in a household died, the household often split, if it had not done so previously.

The poor had always availed themselves of folk contraception, abortion and female infanticide, and female mortality was 30 per cent higher than that of the male. In addition to neglect and infanticide, other ways of getting rid of unwanted daughters including selling them into marriage, slavery or prostitution. But although sons were (and are) preferred, daughters were not as unwelcome as in India: they were sources of labour and brideprice. The comparative mutability of sex preferences in China is also suggested by the existence in the 19th and early 20th centuries of a strong preference for girls in the silk district of the Pearl River delta. The silk industry offered more employment to women than men (although men's jobs were better paid), with the result that many women acquired the social and economic independence that enabled them to resist marriage successfully. Interestingly, although marriage resistance in the area is a thing of the past and son preference has reasserted itself, in Shunde, where the movement was particularly strong, as late as 1972 the birth rate was significantly lower and there were many more nurseries for young children than in a nearby area outside the movement.[8]

Nevertheless, the Chinese government's attempts to promote marriages in which the couple lives with the wife's family, have so far met with great difficulty, and the recent economic changes, which tend to increase sex discrimination, have meant that having a son still (and perhaps increasingly) spells greater economic security in old age than having a daughter.

It must be noted that the formidable difficulty of limiting the natural increase of the Chinese population is also in part an outcome of success of the government's health campaigns which have resulted in life expectancy more than doubling since 1949. A second major obstacle has been the influence of Marxist ideology, with its fierce anti-Malthusianism. Yet a third was the isolation and hostility that surrounded the country until the 1970s, including the defection of the Soviet Union, its major ally of the early years. So it is not surprising, if unfortunate, that China came so late to a serious programme of birth

7)   See Elizabeth Croll, Delia Davin, and Penny Kane, eds, *China's One-child Family Policy*, New York: Macmillan, 1985.

8)   See M Topley, 'Marriage Resistance in Rural Kwangtung', in M Wolf and R Witke eds, *Women in Chinese Society*, Stanford: Stanford University Press, 1975; also, AY So, *The South China Silk District*, Albany: State University of New York Press, 1986.

limitation that the policies eventually adopted out of desperation were too draconian to be successfully enforced.

In the early years of the People's Republic, the notion that China was overpopulated was bitterly resented by Chinese leaders as a hostile western plot. As Mao Zedong (who shortly after became an advocate of population limitation) put it in response to a letter by American Secretary of State Dean Acheson claiming that, along with the impact of the West and western ideas, China's inexorable population growth had played a major role in the problems shaping modern China:

> It is a very good thing that China has a large population. Even if China's population multiplies many times, she is fully capable of finding a solution: the solution is production. The absurd argument of Western bourgeois economists, like Malthus, that increase in production cannot keep pace with increase in population was not only thoroughly refuted in theory by Marxists long ago, but has also been completely exploded by the realities in the Soviet Union and the Liberated areas of China after their revolutions …. Under the leadership of the Communist Party, as long as there are people, every kind of miracle can be performed.[9]

Indeed, as late as August, 1974, Huang Shuzhi, the leader of the Chinese delegation to the UN World Population Conference, declared there that Third World overpopulation was a fallacy of the superpowers. So great was the suspicion of American motives that on another occasion the American ambassador was accused of *underestimating* the Chinese population in order to encourage Japan to send its excess population to China rather than the United States.[10]

Early family planning measures   When first addressed in the 1950s, family planning was presented only as a measure promoting maternal and child health. At that point, moreover, there were still shortages of contraceptives suited to poor and crowded conditions and the trained staff necessary to administer them. Until 1957, sterilization was restricted to couples who had six or more children. Nevertheless, research on contraception was pursued, and the vacuum aspiration method of abortion, later adopted all over the world, was pioneered at that time, while the 'no-scalpel' method of

---

9)   *People's Daily*, August, 1949.
10) See Penny Kane, *The Second Billion: Population and Family Planning in China*, Penguin, 1987.

vasectomy was developed in 1974. In the 1960s, China became self-sufficient in the production of contraceptive devices, and they have since been supplied free to individual couples.

POLITICS AND THE ONE-CHILD POLICY

In a pattern that was to be repeated in succeeding decades, the birth control movement became entangled in political struggles. In the late 1950s, it was the 'anti-rightist' campaign. Enthusiastic population controllers, such as Professor Ma Yinchu of Beijing University, fell victim to the repression that followed the Hundred Flowers movement, and, after the euphoria of the Great Leap, in which, once more, anything seemed possible, the 'three terrible years' of 1959–61 were years in which natural disasters and famine temporarily decreased birth rates and raised death rates. Except for the famine years, the 1950s and 1960s produced yearly rates of natural increase averaging 2.5 per cent, while death rates fell from 2 per cent to 0.7 per cent.

So, in the early years, the family planning campaign was impeded by both hubris and disaster, and the disruptions of the Cultural Revolution between 1966 and 1969 meant that population planning was not really addressed in a sustained fashion until the 1970s. At that point, despite Huang Shuzhi's fulminations, alluded to above, long-term goals announced were of achieving a 1 per cent overall growth by 1980, 0.5 per cent by 1985, and a stable population by the end of the century. These were to be achieved through the 'longer, later, fewer' policy: delayed marriage, spaced births, and a reduction of overall fertility. By 1980, the plan seemed to be having considerable success.[11] The rate of natural increase was down to 1.2 per cent, although death rates had fallen still further to about 0.6 per cent.

Thus, the Chinese rates at the beginning of the 1980s already compared very favourably with the then overall world birth rate of 2.8 per cent, and death rate of 1.1 per cent. One writer estimated that the

---

11) These are the current recommendations of the Cairo conference plan of action as conducing to the optimum health and survival of both mothers and children. But exactly what the long-term effects of such a policy were is one of the uncertainties of interpreting the data. For example, when overall fertility is low, the babies postponed in one year tend to show up later on, making it then look like a new trend toward higher fertility. This puzzle now bedevils the interpretation of data from Europe which seem to indicate an upward trend in fertility in some western European countries and the United States. See, for example, J Craig, 'Recent fertility trends in Europe', *Population Trends*, Summer, 1992, pp 20–3. In China, however, whatever the effect of delayed marriage, almost all couples proceeded to the first birth within a year, and the recommended four year spacing was generally ignored.

increasing marriage age (which had been optimistically set at 22 for women and 30 for men) accounted for more than 40 per cent of the rapid fertility decline during the preceding decade.[12] Despite this success, in 1979 a one-child policy for a large proportion of the population was instituted. In the words of Peng Xizhe:

> According to the government's long-term plan, the per capita GNP should be increased from about $US250 in 1979 to $800–$1000 by the end of the century. To achieve this goal, the population target by the year 2000 was set at 1.2 billion. In August 1978 vice-premier Chen Muhua, then head of the State Family Planning Commission, provided the statistical rationale for the new campaign. She concluded that even if every couple only had two children the population target could still not be attained. Hence, some couples would have to have only one child.[13]

Chinese officials were well aware that such a limit would be resisted by most of the population, and deliberately made the goal more restrictive than what they really believed they could achieve. Since then, they have been engaged in what might be called a kind of game with large sections of the people, who have used every loophole or relaxation to evade or avoid the government plan, including reclassification where possible to take advantage of the larger families permitted to the national minorities.

The Chinese population policy has been accompanied by energetic campaigns to explain the economic reasons behind what are admitted to be extraordinary (and temporary, to cover 30 years and compensate for the high fertility of the post-famine baby boom) demands for individual sacrifice for the collective good. It was also supposed to be implemented within a context of welfare and benefits which included rather generous pensions for the old in the cities and wealthier communes, housing, cheap food, free medical care and education, and lifetime employment, almost unheard of in an underdeveloped country. Even in the countryside, the destitute were

---

12)   Peng Xizhe, *Demographic Transition in China*, Oxford: Clarendon Press, 1991, p 151. Peng's book contains a detailed analysis of the effect of marriage age on fertility. Higher marriage age among women has the important concomitant effects of increased female education, income, choice and independence. Thus the current trend toward lower marriage ages is ominous. Increasing the marriage age for men, incidentally, is often accompanied by increasing fertility attributed to increased male income. See R Wright, 'The Easterlin Hypothesis and European Fertility Rates', *Population and Development Review*, March, 1989, p 107–19.

13)   Peng Xizhe, *Demographic Transition in China*, Oxford: Clarendon Press, 1991, p 24.

entitled to 'five guarantees', which included fuel, a grain ration, clothing, a small monthly cash income, and burial.[14]

Adoption of the single-child policy   The single-child policy was adopted with some recognition of the many problems, real (such as the prospect of a small young cohort being obliged to support a far larger ageing one), all too likely (such as the resurgence of female infanticide), and imaginary (the prospect of only children becoming 'spoiled' through excessive pampering) that success would bring. In the event, the policy was never applied very stringently in much of the countryside; in particular, couples whose first child was female were usually permitted to try again.

Many of the fluctuations in the crude birth rate during the 1980s have arguably been a result of other factors; for example, the entry of the small birth cohort of the famine years 1959–61 into childbearing produced a dip in the birth rates in the mid-1980s. At other points, birth rates have risen for a variety of reasons, including a lowering of the legal marriage age in 1982, which permitted more marriages and births to be registered.

Contrary to western misconceptions, there was never any overall law requiring couples to have no more than one child, but only various sets of schemes designed to increase the numbers of single children. Minorities were exempted from the outset. Indeed, in the early years after Liberation, government policy had been directed toward increasing minority populations, the smallest of which seemed in danger of extinction. It was not until the 1970s that they were routinely offered family planning services, and then with the purpose of improving maternal and child health and survival. Application of the one-child policy even to the Han (ethnic majority) population was adapted to local circumstances, using a combination of rewards for those taking the one-child pledge and increasingly severe fines and punishment for births subsequent to the first.

'One-child certificated' families, those that pledge to have no more, are entitled to further benefits including a medical care fund, and priority consideration for schooling and employment: that is, there was an attempt to substitute quality for quantity. The better educated the couple, the greater was the take-up of certificates. Unfortunately, the benefits as well as the penalties have been unevenly administered, and insufficient funds often resulted in cutbacks. Surveys found that

---

14)   The extent to which these (and other) entitlements were actually implemented has been
      questioned. One informant reports that, in the course of extensive travels through many
      parts of rural China in the mid-1980s he never came across a rural commune where all of
      the 'five guarantees' were honoured.

only 60 per cent of certificate holders seemed satisfied; others complained they had been promised benefits they hadn't received, the benefits varied widely geographically, and were not always fairly awarded by cadres. For those who exceeded the allowed number of children, an increasingly severe set of fines lay in store. For those who did not or could not pay, sanctions could include sealing up the family home until the fines are received.[15]

Goals   At first the goal was set for 80 per cent of urban couples and 50 per cent of rural couples to have only one child. Later the goal was shifted to 95 per cent and 90 per cent respectively. However, at almost the same time as the policy was announced, a drastic change in economic direction was also instituted. Whether from this cause, or more general ones, by 1990 it seemed that, while it was easy to reduce average fertility rates from 6 to 2.5 children in circumstances of low infant mortality, it was more difficult to reduce them much further.[16] Nevertheless, in 1993, it was announced that between 1987 and 1992 fertility rates had fallen another 25 per cent, to 1.90 births per woman. Some of this fall may be due to the increasing urbanization of the Chinese people – the rural population has fallen from 80 to 70 per cent – but there is some evidence that even in the countryside, the preferred family size is approaching two children.[17]

Urban uptake   Although the policy was applied more strictly in the cities than in the countryside, rural and urban birth rates had already begun to diverge by the mid-1960s. In the cities, incentives for taking the single-child pledge included a small monthly allowance for health care and housing allotted as for two-child families. Shanghai offered one year's paid maternity leave as well as 70 per cent pensions

------

15) John Aird (*Slaughter of the Innocents: Coercive Birth Control in China*, Washington, DC: American Enterprise Institute, 1990) and others go a good deal further and level accusations that not only forced contraception and sterilization, but even infanticide, are part of the official birth control policy and conveyed as such to local officials. The government denies this, and claims that any instances of such coercion are excesses on the part of individual family planning workers. Another controversy involves the term 'quality births', the official meaning of which relates to the health care given to mothers and babies born within plan; however, it must be said that the Chinese do openly disdain the disabled. Ascertaining, let alone interpreting, the actual policy is complicated by the political motivation of many of the accusers, most notably right-wing members of the American government.

16) Peng Xizhe, *Demographic Transition in China*, Oxford: Clarendon Press, 1991, p 295. A survey conducted in Shandong province shows that only 4 per cent of rural couples declared that they desired only one child, while 70 per cent opted for two, and 26 per cent three or more. And this in response to an official government survey after almost a decade of propaganda, education and incentives recommending the one-child family!

17) See Susan Greenhalgh, Zhu Chuzhu and Li Nan, 'Restraining Population Growth in Three Chinese Villages', *Population and Development Review*, June, 1994.

to one-child families, while in Beijing pensions amounted to as much as 100 per cent to those who reached retirement age without children. By mid 1983, most suburban communes also pensioned the childless.

The 1980s was a decade of consumerism, and city girls demanded ever-larger amounts of furniture upon marriage as part of their traditional brideprice, which put additional pressure on urban housing. While in the countryside housing was usually occupier-owned and prosperity often took the form of housebuilding, housing in cities was usually rented and has always been extremely inadequate. Average urban living space per person actually declined from 4.5 square metres to 3.6 square metres between 1952 and 1977. Employment in the cities was often in state-owned industries or services, one perquisite of which was the 'ding-ti' system, by which one child was permitted to replace a retiring parent. Consequently, it was relatively easy to reduce fertility rates to two children in the cities, and some couples had already opted for a single child before the institution of the policy. In Beijing, as early as 1979, 19 per cent of one-child families considered the family complete. As a result of the lowered birth rate, the teacher/pupil ratio improved, though there were still creche places for only one-fifth of the under sevens.[18]

ASSESSING THE POLICY

The history and motivation behind China's population policy raises insistently two questions which can be asked about the implementation of any policy: how effective has it been, and how necessary are elements of compulsion to achieve its effects? Despite the dramatic reductions in fertility rates, the questions are not easy to answer.

Many critics point to such examples as Kerala and Thailand, where birth rates have dropped to near replacement without the harsh measures employed by the Chinese. These comparisons neglect important differences. In the former case, the rest of India, with its huge illiterate population and disappointing 40-year population policy is more comparable to China than is Kerala, with its small highly educated population and relatively liberated women. As for Thailand, its sharp fertility decline may owe much to international assistance and the modelling effect alluded to in Chapter 1, which in China were precluded by her long isolation and the hostility of the superpowers, and in any case began to be influential long after China's government perceived a need for urgent action.

18) Penny Kane, 'Single-child family policy in the cities', in E Croll, D Davin and P Kane, eds, *China's One-child Family Policy*, New York: Macmillan, 1985.

Among scholars, the issue of compulsion has been argued vehemently between John Aird, who denies even the reality of China's population problem, and Susan Greenhalgh. Somewhat uncertainly in the middle stands Vaclav Smil, who, despite his personal objection to abortion, feels the impending environmental crisis warrants a birth control policy that includes: 'insisting on a general use of contraceptives, delaying marriages, and widely spacing two births per family.'[19] This, he feels, is an improvement on a 'simplistic and rigidly enforced one-child policy.' But all of the elements he mentions are already included in the current policy, which has never been either simplistic or rigidly enforced on a country-wide basis.

For his part, Aird simplistically pictures 'population controllers', including Smil, as one-cause believers who divert attention from bad policies and leadership (presumably in the developing countries, there's no mention of western policies). They and family planning workers, he says, overlook Chinese coerciveness out of self interest: the Chinese 1982 census and fertility survey produced so much information it made China a good place to do research in.[20]

One researcher he castigates especially is Susan Greenhalgh, who believes that a measure of compulsion was necessary for the success of the policy (whose economic need she accepts).[21] Greenhalgh's most recent work indicates that Chinese women she studies have become reconciled to the policy and even appreciate its health benefits.[22] Few commentators, even those who are concerned about the human rights aspect of China's policy, have thought to consider all the benefits of low fertility to women and children, economic as well as medical.

The single-child policy and its workings have received an enormous amount of attention from scholars, scientists, writers and commentators of all political casts of mind. What is strange, therefore, is not the variety of interpretations put on it, but the uncertainty of the primary data on which the interpretations are based. For example, one pair reported that in the populous province of Jilin, between 1967 and 1987, 99.8 per cent of women of legal age were married – in some years 100 per cent! Even for a culture where universal marriage is the

---

19)   Vaclav Smil, *China's Environmental Crisis*, New York: ME Sharpe, 1993, p 35.
20)   John S Aird, *Slaughter of the Innocents*, Washington DC: The American Enterprise Institute, 1990, p 9 (and p 89).
21)   Susan Greenhalgh, 'The Evolution of the One-child Policy in Shaanxi, 1979–1988', *China Quarterly*, June, 1990, pp 191–229.
22)   Susan Greenhalgh, Zhu Chuzhu and Li Nan, 'Restraining Population Growth in Three Chinese Villages', *Population and Development Review*, June, 1994, pp 365–96.

norm, this seems incredible.[23] The degree of acceptance of the one-child policy has been fiercely debated, some writers claiming that most of the observed rise in the fertility rate during the 1980s was due to the exceptionally large cohort entering the childbearing years, others that it demonstrated that acceptance of the policy had been under duress, which was now crumbling inevitably in the climate of free-for-all economic encouragement.

From 1984, the number of exceptions to the one-child policy, which had always included a large number of seemingly disparate rationales, was gradually increased.[24] At present, in 18 of the 30 regions, rural couples can have a second child if the first is a girl. In many cases, no penalties are exacted for a second child whatever the sex of the first. Two minority regions have no formal regulations on family size, except for those of Han ethnicity. In Henan, Tibet, Xinjiang and Guizhou, couples *average* more than three children each; in Tibet alone, the average is 4.5.[25] But China is once again making efforts to tighten up its population policy, particularly in the cities, and, as will be examined in more detail in the next chapter in the case of Tibet, resistance among minorities is imbued with the politics of demographic competition found elsewhere in the world.

For the country as a whole, by 1987 a comprehensive review of the general response to the single-child policy concluded that 'although family size preferences have decreased, very few people, even in urban areas, would prefer to have only one child. Two children would be acceptable to most people in both rural and urban areas, but

---

23) For example, it assumes that no women are considered too disabled to marry, let alone too determined not to. See G Feeney and Wang Feng, 'Parity Progression and Birth Intervals in China: The influence of policy in hastening fertility decline', *Population and Development Review*, 19, no 1, March, 1993, pp 61–101, Table 12. They also report that between 97 and 99 per cent have at least one child. This is too much for the authors, who, taking the 3 per cent infertility rate of the Hutterites as a benchmark of physiological possibility, concluded that some children reported as natural may in fact be adopted.

24) There are something like fifteen of these, which also vary from province to province, but include:

- one spouse is a fisherman;
- couple resides in a remote, sparsely settled area;
- one or both spouses is an only child;
- one spouse is the child of a revolutionary martyr;
- one spouse is handicapped;
- first child is handicapped ...

25) See S Conly and S Camp, *China's Family Planning Program: Challenging the Myths*, Washington: Population Action International, 1992. One result of the more generous family targets for the minorities, according to geographer Terry Cannon, is that many Chinese of mixed descent, who were formerly classified as Han, have had themselves reclassified, and the minority population now approximates 100 million. It should also be noted that Henan is not even a minority region, but notorious as a source of migration to other regions.

preferably these should be a boy and a girl.'[26] This is very similar to preferences in industrialized countries, and the authors also note with disquiet that the lowering of fertility has been accompanied by a raising of aspirations among parents for their children, in both urban and rural areas, to heights which can scarcely be realized in any country, let alone a poor one. Yet such aspirations are common in surveys in other poor countries as well as rich ones.

The effectiveness of the one-child policy (as contrasted with large-scale changes in birth rates which arose from other causes) has been complicated not only by the variability of incentives and sanctions over space and time, but by the effects of the economic reforms themselves. While the overall and relative effectiveness of the various elements of the policy are hard to determine, perhaps increasingly hard in view of the large and growing 'floating population' who evade not only restrictive measures but all attempts to record their demographic activities as well, the overall decline of Chinese fertility rates under the policy is generally believed.

BENDING THE GENDER RATIO

Most sensitive is the question of just how many girl babies are missing in the Chinese population; but the current worsening of the sex-ratio in China should be discussed in a context wider than that of the one-child policy.

Even though men are dominant in all known societies, it is by no means true that people everywhere prefer to have sons rather than daughters. A lot of research has gone into parental preferences in various parts of the world. For example, a recent Tokyo government survey found that three-quarters of Japanese women would prefer a girl if they could choose the sex of an only child. This finding was echoed in a survey by the Cambridge Centre for Family Research, which also found a preference for girls, and in Britain, only children born in 1958 are predominantly female.[27] Attempts to set up – and counterattempts to block – a clinic devoted to the predetermination of sex in Britain have disclosed that most interested queries came from Britons of Asian descent and from orthodox Jews, both with a view to

---

26) MK Whyte and SZ Gu, 'Popular Response to China's Fertility Transition', *Population and Development Review*, 13, no 3, September, 1987, pp 471–93.

27) Ann Laybourn, *The Only Child: Myths and Realities*, Edinburgh: HMSO, 1994, p 24. Laybourn used the National Child Development Study, which has been following all the children born in England, Scotland and Wales in one week in March, 1958. The surmise that parents of girls are more likely to stop at one than parents of boys was supported by the finding that the first born of two-child families were predominantly male.

boys. Other surveys have found son preference absent in South America, in the Caribbean and in Kenya, but strong in Jordan and Syria. In the Philippines, sons are preferred for the first child, daughters thereafter. Son preference is very strong in Bangladesh, Nepal, Pakistan, Taiwan and South Korea.

In China, it has been found that the Han ethnic majority has a stronger son preference than any minority except the Manchu, and the Yi actually prefers daughters. However, in many places, including China, most parents would like at least one child of each sex.[28]

This is not the case in India, where the sex-ratio may be worsening as well. The blame for making daughters increasingly unwelcome there is usually placed on the practice of dowry, which, since it was made illegal in 1963, has continued to spread and proliferate through the population even where it was not traditional. To avoid ruinous marriage costs, Indians say they must avoid having daughters. Ultrasound screening or amniocentesis followed by abortion of unwanted female foetuses is now illegal following a sharp dispute between some (but not all) feminists, and doctors who claim it is more humane (as well as more profitable) to spare unwanted girls from a life of neglect and mistreatment, including inadequate food and medical care; rates of malnutrition among girl children are much higher than among boys, as they are among females, as compared to males, at all ages, and even girls who survive and are adequately fed and cared for have the psychic pain of knowing they are a cause of regret and distress to their families.

Yet the sudden deluge of publicity in the West about skewed gender ratios centres around the situation in China, where the reader is always told it is a result of the one-child policy. Ironically, one reason that China has figured so prominently in discussions of unnatural gender ratios is that the Chinese government has been so concerned about it. Recent reports, enthusiastically echoed in the western press under such titles as 'They are killing baby girls in Beijing', have revealed the growing official disquiet over the high and increasing proportion of boy babies.

In government birth control campaigning, efforts were made to overcome the entrenched preference for sons (which, on the other hand, was also catered to by exceptions made to the one-child policy). Slogans asserted that girls, too, could be made responsible for parental support, and posters depicted the single child as a daughter. These efforts have fallen short of success. Some researchers, however, report that at least some of the 'missing girls' show up at

28) See Fred Arnold and Liu Zhaoxiang, 'Sex Preference, Fertility and Family Planning in China', *Population and Development Review*, 12, no 2, June, 1986, pp 221–46.

age five, when schooling begins. In yet other instances, there is evidence that many of them are given away for private adoption by childless couples; one study claimed to have found about half the absent daughters from estimates taken from newly published adoption data.[29]

The sex-ratio of adoptions has always been biased against boys, and is increasingly so, varying from 55 (per 100 girls) in 1980 to 27 in 1987. In other words, the most plausible conclusion to be drawn is that many parents do not register the births of girls, either giving them away with the intention of trying again for a boy, or keeping them quietly at home, hoping for a chance to evade the one-child restriction, until they are of school age. There is reason to believe both that underreporting of girls continues and that the practice of selectively aborting females is increasing.[30] The practice is illegal, but apparently it is often possible to get around the law by means of bribery. There have also been cases of female infanticide, which the government has vehemently denounced.

Against these findings, the current strength of the persisting sex-preference itself has become a matter of some debate. Of a survey of 1000 couples who had a second child 'out of plan' in 1981, 50 per cent had wanted a boy and 11 per cent had wanted a girl. The reasons given for preferring a son in a typical survey include: 51 per cent, for old age support; 25 per cent, for the ancestral line; and 21 per cent to increase the household labour force.[31] (Among the reasons given for

29) S Johansson, and O Nygren, 'The Missing Girls of China', *Population and Development Review*, March, 1991, 17, no 1, pp 35–52. Perhaps surprisingly, the adoption of girls is a traditional practice in some parts of China, for a variety of reasons. According to Arthur Wolf, who studied this practice from records of northern Taiwan (and the adjacent mainland areas of Fujian and Guangdong) early in this century, most commonly a girl of a poor family could be adopted by another family in infancy or early childhood to be raised as a wife for the adopting family's son. Thus, brideprice, wedding and dowry expenses were avoided, and the family benefited from her labour from an early age. Alternatively, girls could be adopted for slave labour alone. The mortality rate among such adopted daughters was very high. Another reason for adoption was the belief that the adoption of a daughter would 'lead in' a son. Wolf claims the market for adoptable daughters was so great it may have exceeded the supply ('The Women of Hai-shan: a Demographic Portrait', in M Wolf and R Witke, eds, *Women in Chinese Society*, Stanford, Cal.: Stanford University Press, 1975).

30) Zeng Yi, Tu Ping, Gu Baochang, Xu Yi, Li Bohua and Li Yongping, 'Causes and Implications of the Recent Increase in the Reported Sex Ratio at Birth in China', *Population and Development Review*, June, 1993.

31) Delia Davin, 'Single-child family policy in the countryside', in E Croll, D Davin and P Kane, eds, *China's One-child Family Policy*, New York: Macmillan, 1985.
The figures are for Hebei.

wanting a girl was that they look after old people and can do embroidery!)[32]

Arnold and Zhaoxiang, after applying various tests, such as the sex-ratio of the single child among couples who later renounce their one-child pledge, concluded that while the Chinese do indeed prefer sons, the preference is not as strong as in other countries with a Confucian tradition, such as South Korea, and that it is weaker among educated women and in urban areas (and indeed, not noticeable in Beijing and Shanghai).[33] There is even evidence of a weakening of son-preference in the countryside as well. Greenhalgh, an American who, in association with scientists at the Population Studies Institute of Jiaotong University, has been following the progress of China's family planning programme since 1988 by looking in detail at three villages in central China, reports that the two-child family is the size wanted by the overwhelming majority of the villagers, but increasingly they want no more than one son (as compared to previous desires for at least one son). This change is attributed to the rising expenses involved in marriage costs and providing a second house required by the second son on marriage. There is also 'a growing sense that sons are unreliable and may not be willing to support their parents when they grow old.' And there is increasing acceptance of the practice of marrying a son into the family as well: 'married-in sons-in-law are no longer looked down upon by other villagers. Such arrangements also provide unexpected benefits for the families involved ... married-in sons-in-law, who usually come from distant places, often bring new skills with them, and they treat their parents-in-law better than real sons treat their parents.'[34]

Denigration of the females?   In countries like China and India, where population numbers and growth are serious concerns, and male preference has traditionally led to serious abuse of girls and

---

32) Zeng Yi, Tu Ping, Gu Baochang, Xu Yi, Li Bohua and Li Yongping, 'Causes and Implications of the Recent Increase in the Reported Sex Ratio at Birth in China' (*Population and Development Review*, June, 1993, p 293), reproduce a table based on the 1990 One Percent Census that indicates the reported sex-ratio (number of males per 100 females) at birth for children with no older siblings is 105.6, while that for children with one brother has dropped to 101.4. This finding implies both widespread prenatal sex determination and a rising preference for a daughter once there is a surviving son. Results of surveys are unfortunately usually quoted without distinguishing the sex of the respondents, although there is evidence from many places that women often have different wishes regarding the gender and number of the children desired.

33) Fred Arnold and Liu Zhaoxiang, 'Sex Preference, Fertility and Family Planning in China', *Population and Development Review*, 12, no 2, June, 1986, pp 221–46. This along with the adoption evidence, casts doubt on allegations of widespread female infanticide.

34) Susan Greenhalgh, Zhu Chuzhu and Li Nan, 'Restraining Population Growth in Three Chinese Villages', *Population and Development Review*, June, 1994, 365–96.

women, some observers are frightened of the prospect of mass use of sex selection. Others approve it as a population limiting measure, reasoning that some parents will go on trying until a son is born in any case. In countries which have yet to be convinced that they have a population problem, and where the prejudice against women is less overt, where the right to the know the sex of one's foetus is considered part of freedom of information and the right to abortion has been fought for as a reproductive right, and where, indeed, most childbearing decisions are largely in women's hands, the issue has taken on more of a philosophical aspect. In western countries there has been much speculation over the subtle social effects that could be produced by a trend to 'balance the family' deliberately, including inequalities in birth order, yet exactly what the actual demographic outcome is likely to be is hard to foretell, especially given the preferences for girls expressed in some surveys referred to above.

But why are governments (and the media) so concerned about the sex ratios? Why is there not equal concern about the more usual imbalance between men and women at older ages, when women outnumber men? In China, the social problems feared from an increasingly masculine population range from a mounting traffic in the kidnapping and sale of women, to increasing the choice and power devolving on them. The former is already happening, but mainly as a function of the breakdown in law and order, and the unequal distribution of the ability to pay marriage costs; and in any society where men continue to be dominant, the latter is very unlikely, as the Indian situation demonstrates.

In fact, the most frequently expressed official and media concern over the worsening gender ratio is not the denigration it implies for the female sex, but the feared shortage of wives for the excess sons. The current worry about the plight of millions of Chinese men seeking marriage partners is an echo of an earlier journalist's account of the abortion of female foetuses in India that bore the title: 'India's unborn brides'.[35] Once more, women are viewed not as full human beings in their own right, but in their potential as mates for men.

Just as I was writing this, an article appeared in the paper describing the sad case of a Chinese woman whose husband took to beating her and eventually deserted her after she gave birth to a daughter.[36] One third of Chinese divorces, the article claimed, spring from the same cause. 'The reason', says the author, 'lies in China's infamous one-child policy.' The 1991 Marriage Law prevents a child's

---

35) Eric Silver, 'India's unborn brides', *Guardian*, 14 November, 1985.
36) Debbie Taylor, 'To the divorcee, a daughter', *Guardian*, 16 November, 1994, p 13 (S2).

sex being used as grounds for divorce, so fathers now maltreat their wives until the women do the divorcing and the men are then free to try again for a boy with a new partner. Divorced women with daughters have little chance of a second marriage. Yet a not too careful perusal of the article itself revealed that the man's mother (with whom they lived) had always hated the wife, and that the beatings had begun well before the baby arrived. No matter: the author blames, not the husband, nor his mother, nor the sexism of Chinese society, nor the authorities for not ruling against a man having a second child when the first is a girl, but once more the 'infamous one-child policy'.

EFFECTS OF THE ECONOMIC REFORMS

Paradoxically, shortly after the Chinese government began significantly to relax its demographic goals by permitting an increase in second births, the American government chose to signal its displeasure with the whole policy. The United States, while continuing to pursue a policy of co-operation with China (especially against the Soviet Union) in such areas as defence, technology and trade, adopted a stance of virulent hostility to the population policy of China, but to no other country. This was particularly ironic because another Chinese policy, the 'economic reforms', which had then been underway for half a decade, featured a strong opening to trade and foreign investment with the outside world, including the United States, with whose general views they were most congenial.

Exactly what the long-term effects of the economic changes on fertility behaviour in the rural areas will be is uncertain. The return of the family as the economic unit has possibly made larger families seem an economic advantage to the winners in the agrarian reforms, and has certainly swelled the ranks of the losers: the 'floating unemployed'. Some of these had fled their homes to avoid the birth control restrictions. Others simply lost out on the rural reforms and were forced to migrate in search of employment. They are now estimated at over 50 million, who are not subject to registration or regulation, whether of residence, marriage or birth. On the other hand, the return of responsibility from the collective to the family has meant that the collective will no longer share in the costs of children, whose care may eat into the ability of women to earn money.

The reforms   The reforms began in the countryside as an attempt to hasten the modernization of the economy, and, above all, increase productivity. The change started with the 'responsibility system' in

1978, where separate households within the communes got contracts to particular pieces of land in return for selling a proportion of the crop to the state (at less than market prices). At first land could be contracted for only a year, but this was lengthened to three years to encourage peasants to put more into the land, and it rapidly became ownership, with full rights of selling, renting, inheriting, and so on. In addition, peasants, at first still unsure if they could keep land, put their profits rather into house building than land improvement, as a claim on the land and a more secure investment. Finally it became possible to lease land for 15 years, and now, with the disappearance of the communes who were the owners, the term is essentially permanent.

Some households were called 'specialized households' and contracted to take on certain services or production from the collective, using collective resources. Often they either rented or sold their contracted land, rather than return it to the collective. These have prospered, and hence have been favoured by the government, although they inspired resentment both in neighbours and in local officials. But the latter themselves soon became the overwhelming proportion of the new entrepreneurs, and it is really the loss of the egalitarian ethic and the sense of betrayal among those who have failed to 'get rich first' (or at all), that may have ultimately the most socially destructive effects. It has already resulted in a collapse of law and order such that some parts of the country are almost completely out of control.

Ensuing problems   Not surprisingly, although the initial results of the reforms in the countryside are said to have raised the incomes of most peasants, the programme ran into increasing difficulties after 1985, once the initial effects of profit taking from previous collective investment were over (and without the previous fortuitous coincidence of particularly good harvests). According to one writer, the basic problems included the failure of the privatized economy to modernize technologically and maintain and improve transportation, communication and the productivity of the land. The planned reforms in the urban industrial sector also proved harder to implement than those in the countryside, and inflation, which had been kept in check for a long time, became difficult to control.[37]

These basic problems, White argues, as well as the failure to appear of the political changes which were expected to accompany economic liberalization, led – although, interestingly, only in the cities,

------

37) Gordon White, 'Introduction', in Gordon White, ed., *The Chinese State in the Era of Economic Reform: The Road to Crisis*, London: Macmillan, 1991, p 5.

where the 'breakdown' alluded to is less apparent – to the demonstrations that climaxed in the Tiananmen Square repression.

Since then, the political climate of China has been one of tense waiting, of expectations held in check by force. Yet, paradoxically, an unintended result of the economic reforms is that the government has lost authority, as has the Party, and these were the main channels of birth control enforcement. The fixed and stable contract for land means the preferential allocation of land to one-child families is no longer enforceable. From 1979–87, the average farmer's net income went up by 150 per cent, so more of them were able to pay whatever penalties there were for excess fecundity, and clan organizations have been revived, indicating a return to traditional family ideals.

The co-operative health care system has also been affected. In many areas, no one is in charge of family planning, and sometimes the office has even been abolished. Even among the rural families who have stayed put, since policies have changed so often in past, any relaxation of controls leads couples to rush into childbearing for fear the opportunity may be lost in the future, when they might otherwise have postponed the birth(s). Hence, relaxation of the one-child policy meant at least a temporary surge in second and higher order births.

The net result of the loss of control at the centre, has been a devolution of power, both to local officials who are often corrupt, charging for what should be public services, such as education, health or roads, and to the family. In the countryside, this has meant the definitive breakdown of the 'five guarantees', formerly the responsibility of the now-disbanded communes, and with it the commune's promise of old-age security for the childless.[38]

In any case, government policy itself has been to favour the most successful, not only smiling on individual entrepreneurs, who by fortune or connections or cleverness were able to 'get rich first', but also giving special privileges to the southern coastal region whose inhabitants often had more children because of links with overseas relatives who had more traditional views.

The effects of the economic reforms in the cities, instituted some years later, are even more complex and uncertain. The decline of state industries and the rise of private employment has spelled the end of the guaranteed employment of the 'ding-ti' system, pensions and other forms of social security, all of which enhances the need for family security. Another effect of privatization and consumerism has been the return of sex discrimination as well as more traditionally

---

38)   See Elizabeth Croll, 'The State and the Single-child Policy', Chapter 12 in Gordon White, ibid.

stereotypic images of women and their role, which can encourage higher fertility rates. On the other hand, under the old dispensation, the government had seen to it that basic prices did not rise for two decades – until the late 1970s – so when they did rise, as part of the reform policy, it seemed as if the world was ending, a feeling reinforced by each new inflationary surge. In general, as demonstrated by the dropping of the birth rate in Russia and other eastern European countries in response to soaring inflation since 1989, a perceived worsening in the economic situation has an anti- rather than pronatal effect. Nor is the housing squeeze easing as a result of the transfer of state and municipal functions to the private sector. Thus, the pronatal effects of the reforms on urban dwellers are liable, if anything, to be weaker than in the countryside.

What are termed the Chinese economic reforms, without irony or quotation marks, denote the transfer of public assets into private hands with all that entails both economically and politically. Many writers are still very dubious regarding the eventual outcome, even in economic terms.[39] The social costs, not least in the effects on the status of women if not fertility rates, are likely to be high, and the continued neglect of the environment in the climate of 'business fever' may have the highest cost of all.

---

39) See, for example, Gordon White ibid; also John Gittings, Jr, 'The patient has China syndrome', *Guardian*, 10 July, 1993, p 40, and L Sun, 'Capitalism puts China's workers on their knees', *Guardian*, 17 November, 1993, p 9. Marion Jones claims that income inequality in rural areas (ratio between the richest and poorest fifths) has more than trebled between 1980 and 1990. On a microlevel, it is both cadres and those with landlord backgrounds who seem to be profiting most; however, in contrast with White, she feels that class inequality is resented less than spatial disparities (differences in prosperity between adjacent regions) (*Journal of Peasant Studies*, forthcoming). Another disturbing development reported by both residents and travellers is the hardening and intensifying of China's traditional xenophobia, primarily against the Japanese, but including all foreigners.

Chapter 9
Tibet: dragon tales

Population and politics are nowhere more heatedly connected than in Tibet. Almost everything about Tibet is disputed, including what is meant by 'Tibet', and how many Tibetans there are. The most important source of confusion arises from a distinction drawn between 'political Tibet' and 'ethnographic Tibet'. The former, which is what Chinese sources mean by 'Tibet', is the state which had been reigned over by the present Dalai Lama and his predecessor, and is now designated the Tibetan Autonomous Region (TAR); the latter refers to the TAR plus a number of regions in which substantial communities of Tibetans live. These include areas in the neighbouring Chinese provinces of Qinghai, Sichuan, Gansu, and Yunnan. The neighbouring countries of Sikkim, Bhutan, Nepal and India also contain Tibetan communities, as well as others that are ethnically and linguistically related. When the Dalai Lama, Tibetan nationalists and their western sympathizers speak of Tibet, it is to the TAR and the areas in adjacent Chinese provinces (though not to those outside China, such as Ladakh) that they refer.

Because the territorial regions designated 'Tibet' differ, so do the population figures. According to Chinese sources, the 1991 population of the TAR was 2,217,800, and the total Tibetan population in China 4,593,072. Tibetan nationalist sources usually place the latter total at 6 million, and have done so for about a decade, sometimes modified by a claim of 1.2 million deaths laid at the Chinese door.[1] Chinese

---

1)   Just how the deaths for which the Chinese are held responsible were arrived at by Tibetan

sources claim that the Han (ethnic Chinese) population of the TAR in 1991 was 81,000; Tibetan nationalist sources cite 7.5 million Han Chinese on the territory they claim. (It should be remembered that members of some of China's other 54 minority ethnic groups, including Monbas, Lopas, Naxis and Hui (Muslims), as well as other religious groups, also live in Tibet.)[2]

The status of Tibet is even more controversial. According to the Chinese government, Tibet is an inalienable and integral part of China; according to Tibetan nationalists and their sympathizers, it is an

――――――――――――――――――――◇――――――――――――――――――――

cont.

nationalists has never been made clear. They are attributed to 'figures published by the Information Office of the Central Tibetan Secretariat' in India, and include: Torture, 92,731; Battles/Uprisings, 432,705; Execution, 156,758; Starvation, 342,970; Suicide, 9002; Prisons and labour camps, 173,221. A letter to the *Tibetan Review* (April, 1989, p 22) by Jampel Senge says 'The census which resulted in the figure of 1.2 million was conducted by the Government in Exile through exiled Tibetans who travelled to meet their relatives, and through new arrivals in Tibet.' On the other hand, Graham Clarke ('Tibet today: propaganda, record and policy', *Himalayan Research Bulletin*, vol 8, no 1, 1988, p 28) says, 'The original baseline figures are estimates from a time when there were no modern census records, and the current figures for Tibet come from Chinese statistics the absolute basis of which is unclear: the million is obtained by subtracting the one from the other.' Elsewhere ('The Movement of Population to the west of China: Tibet and Qinghai' in R Foot and J Brown, eds, *Population Movement in Asia*; London: Macmillan, 1994, fn 60), Clarke (who does not consider pre-1982 census data reliable) points out that a proper assessment would require an analysis of the age distributions of post-1982 data, looking for an unexpectedly small ageing cohort, and possibly a skewed gender distribution with small numbers of males within that cohort. This is not possible on the basis of present data available.

2)   Chinese sources rely on the successive censuses of 1953, 1964, 1982 and 1990. The table below is taken from *China Statistical Yearbook, 1992*, issued by the State Statistical Bureau of the People's Republic of China.

	1953	1964	1982	1990
Total TAR	na	1,251,225	1,863,623	2,196,029
Males	na	597,296	921,238	1,098,912
Females	na	633,929	942,385	1,097,117
Tibetan nationality	2,775,622	2,501,174	3,847,875	4,593,072
Tibetan males	na	na	1,882,334	2,269,082
Tibetan females	na	na	1,965,541	2,323,990

The figure of 81,000 Han presumably does not include the Chinese forces personnel stationed there. Almost all Han are in Lhasa or the other 'cities' of Xigaze and Gyanse, or in the border areas. This figure is down considerably from 1980, when the Chinese said there were 300,000 PLA (People's Liberation Army) members and 125,000 civilian Han in Tibet, but it must be remembered that many (most?) of the resident Han have only temporary licences to reside there, and may not be included in these numbers; furthermore, the phenomenon of the 'floating population' has hit Lhasa as well as other cities; many people, both Han and non-Han have no permits to reside at all. Jack Ives and Bruno Messerli (*The Himalayan Dilemma*, Routledge, 1989, p 233) point out that the Han themselves do not like to settle in Tibet; their children are subject to pulmonary oedema, and adults to altitude sickness.

occupied country. To reinforce legal and historical claims, both sides have claimed human rights violations on the part of their opponents. The major issues in dispute have been addressed by several western and Tibetan scholars, but the works of journalists and members of western support groups and Tibetan nationalists are far better known to the international community at large. In the discussion that follows, therefore, it will be necessary to cite both types of writing. Although the focus here is on population policy, and not on the issues of nationalism, separatism, dissidence and repression, it will be necessary to provide at least some historical, economic and political background.

BACKGROUND AND HISTORY

Almost all the productive output of Tibet is agricultural. About half consists of grain and other crops, grown in the south and east; the other half is meat and milk (and hides) produced by herders distributed over by far the larger area. Traditionally, the population of the Tibetan plateau was kept in rough balance with its agricultural and pastoral productive capacity by its extreme isolation, by a very high death rate, and by the very poor standard of living of the majority, 95 per cent of whom had a low position in Tibet's traditional social hierarchy. (There are arguments over the extent to which the term 'serf' describes their status.) Despite claims on the part of Tibetan nationalists and their western supporters that Tibet never knew famine before the post-1959 Chinese interference with the agricultural system, the poor majority often ate badly. Tom Grunfeld cites 'a survey made in 1940 in eastern Tibet' which 'found that 51 per cent could not afford to use butter, and that 75 per cent of the households were forced at times to resort to eating grass cooked with cow bones and mixed with oat or pea flour.'[3] Another traditional means of limiting population growth at the family level was the familiar one of differential childcare.[4]

Unlike other Buddhist sects, the Tibetan form involved a proportion

---

3)   A Tom Grunfeld, *The Making of Modern Tibet*, London: Zed Press, 1987, p 15.
4)   Nancy E Levine ('Differential child care in three Tibetan communities: beyond son preference', *Population and Development Review*, January, 1987, pp 281–304), in a study of Tibetan communities in Nepal, concluded that more or less aggressive selective neglect and deprivation was still instrumental in raising the death rates of any children considered less desirable by their parents. Later-born children of either sex were especially affected by this treatment. Differential childcare, with effects on child death rates, is common in other parts of Asia, but it should be noted that, in contrast to the Han, Indian, Korean and Pakistani populations, Tibetan females outnumber males.

variously estimated at between one-fifth and one-third of the male population becoming monks while still children, some contributed by their families as part of their feudal obligations. Monks did no productive work but were supported by the monastic estates and pious donations. Some of the more gifted monks became scholars after years of abstruse studies, but most were barely literate, if that. Clearly, their support placed a heavy economic burden upon such a poor agricultural society.

In contrast to the hundreds of thousands of monks, before the Chinese invasion there were only about 27,000 nuns in Tibet.[5] It has been claimed that the large proportion of celibate monks was one factor in keeping the traditional population growth low; however, few women were celibate, since polygyny (as well as polyandry) was practised, and there was little or no stigma attached to sexual activity and birth outside marriage, so it is hard to see how this could have been so. In addition, lamas (priests) of the 'Red Hat' sects are permitted to marry.

Various celibate monasteries solved the problem of succession to important offices by the device of finding the re-incarnation of the previous office-holder (who was himself the incarnation of an important Buddhist saint or 'bodhisattva') in a suitable young boy who could be moulded and raised by the clergy. Until the boy's majority, the powers of the office were exercised by regents.[6] Of the large number of incarnated office holders, only one is a woman. She is the abbess of Samding Temple, and is called the 'Thunderbolt Sow'. Her saintly predecessor saved her nunnery from invaders by turning the inhabitants into a herd of pigs who escaped, and her incarnation is said to retain this power. After going into exile in 1959, the abbess Dorge Phagmo returned to China and became vice-chair of the Tibetan PPCC (legislature) and a member of the Chinese National People's Congress.

---

5)   Hannah Havnevik ('The Role of Nuns in Contemporary Tibet', in Robert Barnett and Shirin Akiner, eds, *Resistance and Reform in Tibet*, London: Hurst and Co, 1994, p 259), citing a survey carried out for the Dalai Lama's Council For Religious and Cultural Affairs. Havnevik feels that nuns are triply subordinated: as Tibetans, as women, and as nuns within the monastic structure. According to one of the less uplifting anecdotes of the Buddha's life, he was reluctant to agree to his aunt's pleas regarding the setting up of women's religious orders. Declaring that women mendicants would damage and shorten the rule of law, he shared the view of the less enlightened that a woman's place was in the home. Buddhists also believed that a woman would first have to be reborn as a male before she could make her way to final salvation. See Frances Wilson, in Diana Paul, *Women in Buddhism*, Berkeley: University of California Press, 1985, Chapter 3.

6)   The device of incarnation of the Dalai Lama did not preclude nepotism (or, according to some views, social mobility), since the new Dalai's family was immediately promoted into the high hereditary nobility, even though he usually came from the peasantry.

The conservative ruling élite (usually associated with the clergy) tried to keep Tibet isolated both to maintain power and to avoid irreligious foreign influences; however, its location between three empires inevitably led to a competition over controlling or at least influencing it, as each manoeuvred to enlarge or secure its borders. The Chinese government, having asserted a claim to sovereignty in the 18th century by military invasion at the height of the power of the Manchu Qing dynasty, did not become deeply involved in Tibetan affairs until the mid-19th century. At that point, the British, having acquired India, decided they needed a treaty to open up trade and to create a buffer zone (along with other Himalayan principalities) against the Russian empire to the north.

The exiles of the Dalai Lama   The Tibetans wanted nothing from the British, neither trade nor treaty. Instead they tried to get protection, first from the Chinese, and then from the Russians. When unsuccessful, the Dalai Lama fled, and the British invaded and forced the Tibetan government to sign a treaty giving them the trade privileges they sought. Shortly afterwards, the Qing dynasty collapsed, a Chinese republic was declared, and, in the ensuing turmoil, the Dalai was able to return and expel all Chinese officials. According to Graham Clarke, it was in the early 20th-century struggles with the Chinese Republic that the 'a Tibetan national sentiment and identity developed out of the more traditional and fluid political and religious linkages and common cultural milieux.' In other words, a pan-Tibetan identity was not formed until after the areas now incorporated into other Chinese provinces had been settled by other nationalities, especially Han.[7] Tibet, that is, the TAR, was effectively independent until 1950; other areas in which large numbers of Tibetans live have in modern times been mostly under local or Chinese control.

Although Tibet, with its distinctive language, culture and geographical homeland, seems to possess the attributes of a separate nation-state, the reality is that its rulers have for many centuries had to establish and maintain their independence by seeking a protective ally against whichever power seems to menace it most at the moment. Since the conservative religious élite sometimes feared western influence as much as or more than Chinese, these attempts during the 20th century have included Japan and the Chinese rulers of Taiwan (who also consider Tibet an integral part of China), as well as India and the United States. The victory of the communists in mainland

7)   Graham Clarke, 'The Movement of Population to the West of China: Tibet and Qinghai', in R
      Foot and J Brown, eds, *Population Movement in Asia*, London: Macmillan, 1994, p 7.

China in 1949, and the subsequent attempts of the new government not only to reassert but also to make good the Chinese claim to sovereignty over Tibet, was the worst possible development in the eyes of Tibetan rulers: for the religious, it promised the elimination of religion; for the nobility, an end to their traditional privileges, wealth and power. As for rest of the people, they had never been involved in either national or class struggle, and communist ideology often only bewildered them.

The Tibetan government appealed in vain to all the heavenly and earthly powers from Palden Lhamo, Tibet's guardian deity, to the UN ambassador from El Salvador. The regent and his advisers then decided to enthrone the 16-year-old Dalai Lama two years ahead of time. He (or the advisers who still surrounded him) simultaneously agreed to enter into negotiations with the Chinese and fled to the Indian border. After his representatives signed a '17-point Agreement for the Peaceful Liberation of Tibet' in Beijing, however, a Chinese general and one faction of his court persuaded him to return to Lhasa. The agreement, which recognized Chinese sovereignty but also guaranteed the status, functions and powers of the high lamas, and protected religious beliefs and practices, has since been repudiated by the nationalists, who also claim violations on the Chinese side.

For their part, the Chinese enlisted the help of sympathetic Tibetans, established schools, clinics, youth and women's groups with the approval of the government and modernizers, and tried to curry favour with both the lay nobility and the great monasteries. Nevertheless, they faced resistance. In 1955–56 revolts began in Kham. Since it lay outside the TAR, the Chinese had not considered eastern Kham covered by the Agreement, and had begun to implement various changes. The Khampas have a reputation among other Tibetans for being wild and lawless, and the rebellions were quelled, but once more the Dalai began to fear the future and once more fled to India. Again he was enticed back by Mao's promise not to implement changes for at least six years – indeed, not for decades, if Tibetans found them unacceptable.

In 1959, a third flight was marked by a more general uprising, and up to 100,000 Tibetans, rich and poor, have since followed their leader into exile, mostly in India, but also in Nepal, Sikkim, Bhutan, Switzerland, Canada, and, what has become increasingly significant, the United States. (Two of the Dalai's brothers eventually became American citizens.) The CIA (Central Intelligence Agency), which had begun to liaise with the Dalai Lama's brothers in the early 1950s, assisted the Dalai's 1959 flight; they also trained (in Colorado) and airdropped-in some Khampa fighters; later they helped finance guerrilla warfare launched from the tiny Nepalese principality of Mustang.[8]

Tibet since 1959   After 1959, no part of Tibet could any longer be insulated from the social, economic and political tides that swept over the rest of China (although the Chinese leadership occasionally tried). These included the great famine and the tumult of the Cultural Revolution. Many of the features of the 'old society', including Buddhism, superstition, a rigid hierarchical social structure, and rule by a small educated élite, were common to both Tibet and the rest of China. But when communist cadres believed they were engaging in class struggle in Tibet, to the Tibetans it seemed to imply a denigration of everything that was theirs, and inflamed a sense of injustice that has since been exacerbated by the inept and harsh treatment of Tibetan complaints and demonstrations. Although there is evidence that much of the destruction of religious institutions during the Cultural Revolution was in fact actually carried out by Red Guards of Tibetan ethnicity,[9] it has since been laid entirely at the Chinese door, and the tendency of Tibetans and their pro-nationalist supporters to think only in ethnic terms has hardened. Neither the government's admission of past 'mistakes' nor attempts to address Tibetan grievances and ameliorate the conditions of the Tibetan people have made much impression.[10]

In addition to history and the right to self-determination, the

---◇---

8)   See Chris Mullin, 'The CIA–Tibetan conspiracy', *Far Eastern Economic Review*, 5 September, 1975, pp 30–4; A Tom Grunfeld, *The Making of Modern Tibet*, London: Zed Press, 1987, Chapter 8; and Israel Epstein, *Tibet Transformed*, Beijing: New World Press, 1983, pp 223–5. Jamyang Norbu takes a somewhat different view, playing down the role of the CIA in arguing that Tibetan resistance has never been as non-violent as it has been presented for western consumption. See Jamyang Norbu, 'The Tibetan Resistance Movement and the Role of the CIA', in Robert Barnett and Shirin Akiner, eds, *Resistance and Reform in Tibet*, London: Hurst and Co, 1994, pp 186–96.

9)   Chris Mullin, *The Tibetans*, Minority Rights Groups Report, no 49, pp 9–10; Melvyn Goldstein, 'The dragon and the snow lion', *Tibetan Review*, April, 1991, pp 18–20; Graham Clarke, 'Tibet today: propaganda, record and policy', *Himalayan Research Bulletin*, vol 8, no 1, 1988, p 33; also *Tibet under Chinese Communist Rule*, OIIR, 1975, pp 105–6, 160–6, from the nationalist camp. Many of the wrecked religious sites were in remote areas where the Chinese seldom ventured.

10) See Ronald D Schwartz, *Circle of Protest: Political Ritual in the Tibetan Uprising*, London: Hurst and Co, 1994. Schwartz argues that repression has served to unify the people, bridging over such traditional hostilities as those between Lhasaites and Khampas, while relaxation affords them space to devise ever-more ingenious means of protest within whatever limits of ritual religious expression exist. The arbitrary reimposition of controls then only demonstrates the impossibility of true religious and cultural freedom under Chinese domination. On the economic side, while the unrelieved poverty under Chinese rule until 1980 demonstrates the inability of Chinese communism to manage the Tibetan economy, any improvement since then can be brushed aside as irrelevant beside the rights, freedoms and spiritual progress which is the true goal of Tibetan Buddhism.

nationalist cause has been and still is argued along several other fronts:

1) environmental degradation resulting from ruthless Chinese exploitation of Tibet and its resources, or mistaken Chinese development policies;
2) inadequacy of the Chinese reforms in the areas of health, education, infrastructure and the economy;
3) 'cultural genocide' in the areas of religion and language, and by population transfer;
4) human rights violations by economic and social discrimination, censorship, imprisonment and torture; and
5) physical genocide by starvation, massacre, forced abortion and sterilization, and by the application of family planning policy to an extreme degree, approaching and even exceeding its application to the Han Chinese.

The last claim is most relevant to this book.

CHINESE RULE AND STEWARDSHIP

The environment   Almost every issue of Tibetan nationalist periodicals contains some alarming article about environmental threats in the ethnic Tibetan areas, ranging from the siting of nuclear weapons and toxic waste to soil erosion and improper fertilizer use, all caused by Chinese policy.[11] The most persistent and emotional accusation, however, is that of extensive deforestation, without adequate replanting. However, a careful review of the entire Himalayan region by Jack Ives and Bruno Messerli sees the issue in geographic, historical and socioeconomic perspectives which tend to mitigate the claim of Chinese culpability. These authors argue that, contrary to general belief, the Himalayan ecology is not going into supercrisis, even in Tibet. Deforestation has been a long-term affair, not just since 1950, but may stretch back hundreds or even over a thousand years. They point out that peat deposits, and still-surviving trees at high altitudes indicate there were formerly more forests in Tibet, and besides, the society could not have supported the building

---

11) For example: Michael Alexander, 'Nuclear Weapons on the Roof of the World', *Tibetan Bulletin*, October 1989, pp 15–6; 'Poisoning the Plateau', *Tibetan Bulletin*, Nov–Dec, 1991, p 20; Sajeev Prakash, 'Do Tibetans have environmental rights?', *Tibetan Review*, June, 1992. There is also an entire journal, *Tibetan Environmental News*, devoted to the subject. The *Tibetan Bulletin* is the official journal of the Tibetan government in exile. The *Tibetan Review* is what almost amounts to a loyal opposition, and has at various times been critical of the exile government, though not of the Dalai Lama himself.

of so many large religious institutions if all the wood had to be imported.

Ives and Messerli point out, however, that vast areas of Yunnan Plateau (claimed by Tibetan nationalists but incorporated into another Chinese province) have not only been stripped of forest cover, but subsequent erosion has removed the soil cover completely over wide areas. This, too, is a long-term process, but there has been modern damage as well. Some destruction of forest resources has occurred because the Naxis (another rapidly increasing minority population), whose income doubled between 1979 and 1985, created a building boom: one-third of all the local houses were built since 1979. In addition, the logging practices used were often wasteful. In 1985, for example, lack of co-ordination between loggers and transport authorities meant many square kilometres of felled trees were left to rot on the ground.[12]

Health care   It is in the area of health care that Chinese government sources make their proudest claims with respect to Tibet, claims that the Dalai Lama himself has admitted, qualified by the somewhat unfair observation that the lengthening of life expectancy and decreases in infectious diseases have been accompanied by the appearance of the diseases of stress, such as heart trouble and strokes.[13] In 1958, according to Chinese sources, Tibet had only 174 hospital beds (or 0.15 per thousand people); in 1991, this had increased to 5000 (or 2.3 per thousand). As of 1990, the death rate was down to 7 per cent, and life expectancy had risen from 35 in the early 1950s to 65. A survey in 1982 of Tibetan children between 7 and 17 showed that boys averaged over 10 centimetres taller and 5 kilograms heavier, while girls were 8 centimetres taller and 3 kilograms heavier than in 1965.[14]

---

12)   Jack Ives and Bruno Messerli, *The Himalayan Dilemma*, Routledge, 1989, pp 53–60 and 227. Although these authors claim to have seen extensive reforested areas, Vaclav Smil (*China's Environmental Crisis*, London: ME Sharpe, 1993, pp 59–64) is particularly scathing about both the wastefulness of Chinese use of timber and the low success rates of replanting efforts.

13)   See Miriam Kaye, 'What they are saying at the Yak Restaurant', *Far Eastern Economic Review*, 19 November, 1987, p 60. These diseases are of course expected to increase with increased life expectancy.

14)   Figures for 1991 from *China Statistical Yearbook, 1992*, p 740; for 1958 from Dai Yannian, Edna Driscoll, Yan Quin Long and Zhu Yuan, eds, *Tibet: Myth vs Reality*, Beijing: Beijing Review Publications, 1988, p 58, which also carries the child height and weight figures on p 59. The number of TAR hospital beds has not increased since 1984; hence the ratio per thousand has decreased, but still compares roughly with that of, say, London. But there have also been complaints about the quality of the medical staff once the bed is occupied. Chinese sources are frequently illustrated by pictures of infants in hospital being carefully tended by white-coated and surgically masked nurses, but the only figure on infant

Education   Another area in which the Chinese government boasts progress over the feudal era is in education. Almost all schools, and certainly all secular schools and institutions of higher education were established in Tibet since 'peaceful liberation'. In that time, literacy increased from a mere 2 per cent to 48 per cent in 1984.[15] Unlike other parts of China, schooling is free. The Tibetan nationalists still ask why standards of education in Tibet are so low, and claim besides that whatever improvements have been made in education, as in health, transportation, and industrialization, are for the benefit of and taken advantage of by the Han Chinese. All higher education is conducted in the Chinese language, which doubly disadvantages Tibetans, since it is more difficult for them to gain entry to advanced education, and those who do risk neglecting their own language and culture, especially if they are picked for study in the Chinese interior.

ROLE OF THE EXILES

In the area of education, the nationalists are on somewhat shaky ground. Not only do they ignore the educational situation in the 'old society', but the pages of their own journals, as well as the writings of foreign scholars, show that education (and health) in the exile communities in India still leaves much to be desired.[16] If higher

---

◇

---

cont.

mortality I have come across is 1.8 per cent in 1987, attributed to 'leading officials of the [Chinese] State Nationalities Affairs Commission' by Ngapoi Ngawang Jigme (*On Tibetan Issues*, Beijing: New Star Publishers, 1991, p 144. [He is also the source of the life expectancies, p 14.]) This figure is utterly unbelievable: the 1993 all-China infant mortality is 5.3 per cent (Population Reference Bureau) or 2.9 per cent (Population Action International). The traditional Tibetan child mortality has been variously estimated at 50 per cent or more, and the infant mortality in one of the Tibetan agricultural settlements in South India in 1981 was reported to be 16.2 per cent (John Billington, *The Tibet Society & Relief Fund of the UK Newsletter*, Summer, 1981, pp 13–17). I suspect a misplaced decimal point. These figures (and all other Chinese health claims) are disputed by nationalists. See, for example, Paul Ingram (*Tibet: the Facts*, Dharamsala: Tibetan Young Buddhist Association, 1990, pp 44–55). Tsetse Sandup ('Health problems in Tibet today', *Tibetan Review*, July, 1988, p 16) claims Tibetan life expectancy is about 40 years, and infant mortality about 17 per cent, but this seems to be on the basis of anecdotal evidence only.

15)   In the TAR for ages over 12 years (World Bank, 1984, cited in Graham Clarke, 'China's reforms of Tibet, and their effects on pastoralism', Discussion Paper no 237, Brighton, England: Institute of Development Studies, 1987, p 51). This is still well below any other region, except Xinjiang. Qinghai, Gansu and Yunnan were all about 65 per cent literate. Once more, it depends on your sources. Wang Xiaoqiang (*China Now*, Winter, 1992/3, p 10), claims *illiteracy* in TAR is still 68 per cent, that in Qinghai 47 per cent, and in Yunnan 38 per cent.

16)   See, for example, Nawang Phuntsog Sipur, 'Tibetan secular education: a rude awakening', *Tibetan Review*, June, 1992, p 11–3; AT Grunfeld, *The Making of Modern Tibet*, London: Zed Press, 1987, pp 193–4.

education is conducted in Chinese in Tibet, in India it is in English, for roughly the same reasons: partly the remains of cultural imperialism, and partly the sheer demographic dominance of speakers of these languages, in which work in so many modern disciplines is communicated. Moreover, the wealthier exiles send their children to Anglo–Indian schools, and not to the Tibetan school system at all. If Tibetan children are sometimes sent to the Chinese interior to be educated, the more fortunate of the children of the exiled communities' destitute are in boarding schools and children's homes far from their parents, too. If Han students in Tibet have sometimes insinuated themselves into places reserved for Tibetans by means of the famous 'back door', so apparently has it happened that some wealthy *émigré* offspring 'apply for – and receive – financial assistance for higher studies on the ground that they were, after all, "poor refugees".'[17] Furthermore, it is the well-educated who are fluent in English, who now assume the roles of leaders and spokespeople for the entire exiled community. Should Tibet ever reach a political solution with China, furthermore, it is the returnees from among the English-educated who are most likely to shape the future Tibetan economy and society.

The exiles have been subsidized by many foreign international, governmental, institutional and individual contributions, as well as by the proceeds from an investment fund that the Dalai Lama prudently sent to Sikkim during the 1950s. Some have become prosperous as farmers, professionals and entrepreneurs; yet the majority remain very poor, a reproach to how the funds have been managed.

Perhaps the most unfortunate social effects, still little noted, are experienced by the young women and girls. Although always less welcome than sons, Tibetan girls grew up in a traditional society which afforded them remarkable freedom, most notably in social and sexual activities before marriage, as well as respect for their skills in such things as handling money. In India they find themselves in a far more repressive society, particularly regarding anything that can be remotely connected with female sexuality, and, according to Margaret Novak, '[t]he traditional independence of Tibetan women appears to be giving way to a more dependent style of femininity'.[18] Moreover, certain kinds of traditional commercial activity, such as the selling of barley beer, are now frowned upon as socially degrading. These

---

17) Margaret Nowak, *Tibetan Refugees*, New Jersey: Rutgers University Press, 1984, p 108.
18) Margaret Nowak, ibid, p 121. Nevertheless, as usual, the burden of sustaining cultural identity even in such matters as clothing, falls more heavily on women.

losses have not been completely compensated by, say, increased educational or religious opportunities.[19]

RESURGENCE OF TRADITIONAL ECONOMY AND CULTURE

Back in Tibet, it is still the case that over 80 per cent of the population are engaged in herding and sedentary agriculture. In 1980, a fact-finding trip by Hu Yaobang and Wan Li, which coincided with the initiation of economic liberalization in the rest of China, produced a programme of more laissez faire policies in Tibet as well. In acknowledgement of the obvious wretched poverty that still obtained, the liberalizations were extended even further in 1984. Communes were disbanded, and Tibetan agriculturalists were not only returned to 'household responsibility', but were relieved of taxes and the obligation to sell a quota of their produce to the state at controlled prices. The forced conversion of grassland to wheat was declared a 'leftist mistake' and reversed. These reforms, which resulted in Tibetan herders and farmers reverting to traditional practices, and, to some extent, to traditional cultural and social values, have succeeded in increasing the prosperity of the nomadic pastoralists (the majority) at least.[20] However, more market-oriented types of exchanges, such as those involved in supplying the cities with meat, have tended to replace traditional exchanges in kind between regions. Furthermore, the increases in flocks, particularly around the proliferating roads, are beginning to put pressure on the grasslands.

The Chinese government subsidizes the Tibetan areas to an extent that far exceeds that to any other region, and, thanks to the difficult terrain and climate, it is likely that there can be no conventional

---

19) Margaret Nowak's study of Tibetan refugees in India noted the complaint of five girls admitted to the study of Buddhist philosophy at the Central Institute of Higher Tibetan Studies: 'If we talk to the boys, they tell us we're bad girls' (ibid, p 112). All five later left the programme.

20) See Melvyn Goldstein and Cynthia Beall, 'The impact of China's reform policy on the nomads of western Tibet', *Asian Survey*, June, 1989, pp 619–41; and Graham Clarke, 'China's reforms of Tibet, and their effects on pastoralism', Discussion Paper no 237, Brighton, England: Institute of Development Studies, 1987. The taboo on women slaughtering animals has re-emerged, and, while pastoralists are increasingly hiring help to perform the killing, they are considered social inferiors. Although there is a taboo against killing among Buddhists, meat eating is permissible (particularly in the Tantric tradition which many Tibetan Buddhists follow), as long as it does not involve certain forbidden animals, and as long as the animal was not specifically killed for the benefit of the eater.

'development' in Tibet without subsidy.[21] Melvyn Goldstein and Cynthia Beall also point out that with a population now growing at a rate of about 2 per cent, the land, which was divided in 1980–81, will not long be able to sustain the increase, despite the notionally low density.[22]

Faced with a growing population and an undeveloped or unsustainable economic base, it is all too often that the development of tourism is seized upon as the obvious way to exploit what nature has bestowed while escaping from the constraints of what she has not. This is not just part of the western belief in free markets, from which it follows that the right way to make money is to sell pleasure to the rich rather than provide the basic needs of all. It has also been embraced by Deng Xiaoping's economic planners. In their study of the comparative poverty of the western regions of China in contrast to the booming east coast since economic liberalization, Wang Xiaoqiang and Bai Nanfeng, members of the group that advised Zhao Ziyang before his fall in 1989, urged tourism as a development strategy for Tibet, not only to exploit its cultural and spiritual attractions, but to entice the inhabitants into the mainstream Chinese economy by exposing them to the more consumer-oriented visitors from both China and abroad.[23] The advice was taken, but the results have not been at all what the Chinese expected.

POPULATION POLICY

If claim and counter-claim in the areas of the environment, health, education and the economy must be carefully interpreted, the situation becomes far more difficult to evaluate when we move to the even more emotive areas of population policy. Here, since the establishment of the Tibetan government in exile, a steady and

21) Graham Clarke, London China Seminar, 25 February, 1993. For the nature and extent of government subsidy, see Israel Epstein, *Tibet Transformed*, Beijing: New World Press, 1983, pp 24, 28–9; and A Tom Grunfeld, *The Making of Modern Tibet*, London: Zed Press, 1987, pp 212–13. In Clarke's opinion, Tibet is now almost self-sufficient in grain; the remainder is imported to feed the Han soldier and civilian population.

22) Melvyn Goldstein and Cynthia Beall, 'China's birth control policy in the Tibet autonomous region', *Asian Survey*, March, 1991, p 300. Birth control policy has recently been tightened all over China, including the Tibetan nationality areas.

23) Wang Xiaoqiang and Bai Nanfeng, *The Poverty of Plenty* (translated by Angela Knox), London: Macmillan, 1991. The authors attribute the failure of Tibetans to 'get rich quick' to their 'backwardness' in having so few material wants that they spend for religious purposes whatever they accumulate.

vehement stream of accusations have been levelled against the actions and motives of the Chinese government.[24]

Even before the adoption of the one-child policy, China's ethnic minority populations were increasing faster than the majority. Between 1964 and 1982, for example, while the Han population rose by 44 per cent, that of the minorities went up by 68 per cent.[25] When it was adopted, the 'minority nationalities' were explicitly excepted. Nationalities with populations below 3,000,000 were entirely exempted. For larger nationalities, birth limitation rules were implemented, if at all, according to a variety of local conditions. Those who lived in remote areas were usually not limited at all, and, in fact, often had no access to family planning services. Peasants and herders who lived in more densely populated areas were usually limited to three children, while government workers (cadres) were limited to two. Indeed, at the end of the report on their findings on Tibetan birth rates in the 1980s, Goldstein and Beall were moved to ask why the Chinese government was not attempting a more restrictive policy.[26]

Charges of genocide of Tibetan nationals began well before the promulgation of any restrictive birth control policy. As early as July 1959, a report published by the Legal Inquiry Committee (LIC) of the International Commission of Jurists (ICJ) noted that the belief that large numbers of Tibetans had been sterilized by the Chinese was widespread. The LIC found no evidence of the truth of these allegations, but they have been since accepted routinely by a succession of other nationalist and pro-nationalist sources, including the LIC parent body, the ICJ.[27]

---

24) Chinese publications attempt an air of sober fact with such titles as '100 questions about Tibet', 'On Tibetan Issues', 'Tibet: Myth vs Reality', while there is a tendency for western-authored pro-nationalist writing to appear under such titles as 'Merciless Repression', 'Tears of Blood', 'Children of Despair'. An exception is *Tibet: The Facts* (1990), which is extremely pronationalist, while claiming to be not political; it was produced by 'The Scientific Buddhist Association' (since renamed 'Optimus' and declared non-religious), and is said by its author, Paul Ingram, whose name does not appear on cover or title page, to 'provide a thorough and balanced assessment' (p xiv). Nevertheless, pro-Chinese or sceptical writings are treated very critically while pro-nationalist arguments and claims are presented unquestioningly. The allegations and arguments presented by Ingram here and in *Children of Despair* appear again and again in pronatalist statements in many contexts (including letters to the editor, interventions in meetings and so on).
25) T Cannon and A Jenkins, *The Geography of Contemporary China: The Impact of Deng Xiaoping's Decade*, London: Routledge, 1990, p 105.
26) Melvyn Goldstein and Cynthia Beall, 'China's birth control policy in the Tibet autonomous region', *Asian Survey*, March, 1991, p 300.
27) See, for example, *Children of Despair*, Eyewitness series, Report no 3, compiled by Martin Ross for Campaign Free Tibet, 1992, p 23. The ICJ itself grew out of a group created by American intelligence agents whose purpose was disseminating anti-communist propaganda. It too has received funds from the CIA, which is not a notable human

Chinese protestations regarding its birth control policies with respect to minorities were routinely brushed aside. Also ignored or rejected have been the results of the independent study conducted by Melvyn Goldstein and Cynthia Beall between 1985–90 in three different sites: Lhasa, a nearby village and a remote traditional nomad area to the northwest.[28] They found that, in Lhasa, all Han cadres (officials) were restricted to a single child (as in the rest of China), and had to ask their work units for permission to have the child. Tibetan cadres (who constitute over 60 per cent of TAR government employees, according to Chinese sources) were restricted to two children; no permission was needed for the first, and no automatic sanctions were invoked, even if the limits in spacing or number were breached. As to the other Lhasaite Tibetans, there seemed to be uncertainty among them over whether there was a policy, and, if so, what it was, until mid-1990, when the rules for the Tibetan cadres were extended to the rest of the urban population.

In the rural area, no evidence of any policy restricting the number of children that herding and farming women could bear was found, although there had been some publicity extolling the virtues of family planning and small families, especially in locations near administrative centres. Rural officials as well as nomads had very large families.[29] In the village near Lhasa, birth control was a familiar notion; however, there too average fertility rates were well above two children. In any case, no evidence of coercion was found, and no mobile sterilization gangs or complaints of forced abortions or infanticide.[30]

Even before the Goldstein and Beall report appeared, Asia Watch, an American human rights monitoring organization which had issued two reports expressing concern over the forced abortion and sterilization claims, issued a third report that made no reference to birth control, coercive or otherwise.[31] Nevertheless, some journalistic

cont.

rights organization, nor, which is more to the point, particularly noted for its interest in truth. The 1960 LIC report, *Tibet and the Chinese People's Republic* (ICJ, Geneva: 1990) shows strong signs of bias in accepting or rejecting the testimonies cited.

28) Melvyn Goldstein and Cynthia Beall, *Asian Survey*, March, 1991, pp 285–303.
29) This is illustrated by the example of the three local Communist Party members, all of whose wives had borne them at least seven children. The birth rates and death rates noted were 35 and 30 per thousand respectively, the latter far in excess of the 7 per cent reported by Chinese sources as the all-Tibet rate, far in excess of that reported from other western Tibetan regions, and reportedly due to a 1988–90 epidemic; however, the birth rates are comparable.
30) Graham Clarke ('Tibet today: propaganda, record and policy', *Himalayan Research Bulletin*, vol 8, no 1, p 32) concurs with this point, having put the question to an anti-Chinese refugee nurse in Nepal who had worked in hospitals in Chamdo and Lhasa. The Chinese do, however, pressure single women to have abortions.
31) *Merciless Repression: Human Rights in Tibet*, New York and Washington, DC: Human Rights Watch, 1990.

and propaganda claims of genocide by birth control (including coerced abortion, sterilization and medical infanticide) have become more and more strident, along with claims that the Chinese birth control rules are now more limiting for Tibetans than for the Han: 'Tibetan women are being refused permits for even one child; Chinese women suffer no such restrictions.'[32] Others claim that although the official policy is permissive, in practice all or most Tibetan women have already been sterilized.[33] Yet others note doubts but go on to write as if the allegations were true.[34]

It is therefore somewhat surprising to find the argument capped in one such account by a suggestion that many Tibetan women might actually want contraception:

> If the programme is voluntary, as the Chinese say, why do they not give Tibetan women the option of limiting their families simply by extending to them a humane programme of contraception which is cheap and effective? Such contraceptives as are available in Tibet seem to be dangerous and inefficient. It might perhaps be that considerable numbers of Tibetan women would participate in such a programme, but instead they are subjected to insidious [sic] butchery and pain.[35]

That there could actually be an unmet need for contraception among Tibetan women was indeed indicated by Goldstein and Beall's report that one of their informants asked *them* if they could help her get some birth control 'medicine' that she had heard about. They found that the nearest available contraception (in the form of injections) was three days away by horseback; IUDs and sterilization were even more distant. It was not until 1990 that contraceptives were offered locally.

---

32) William Oddie, *Sunday Telegraph*, 10 October, 1993.
33) See, for example, *Merciless Repression*, New York and Washington, DC: Human Rights Watch, 1990, p 21; *Children of Despair*, Eyewitness series, Report no 3, compiled by Martin Ross for Campaign Free Tibet, 1992, pp 5–6.
34) For example, Carol Devine (*Determination: Tibetan Women and the Struggle for an Independent Tibet*, Toronto: Vauve Press, 1993, p 69) notes: 'Robbie Barnett of TIN [Tibetan Information Network] thinks the debate on "forced" abortion has been whipped up by foreigners, particularly Western men.' Despite such demurrals, and a final plea for more research, Devine generally assumes the one-child policy applies to Tibetans.
35) Paul Ingram, *Children of Despair*, Eyewitness series, Report no 3, 1992, p 4. Amnesty International, which has documented many cases of imprisonment and torture of Tibetan protesters, many of them nuns, has no cases on file of women who were either forcibly aborted of imprisoned for refusal to have an abortion. Complaints about the poor hygiene conditions under which abortions are carried out are the same as those made for many poor regions of the world, including India, which Ingram considers 'humane'.

MIGRANTS AND TOURISTS

In June, 1988, the Dalai Lama put forth a plan in an address to the European Parliament at Strasbourg, by which he proposed that the whole of Tibet ('ethnographic Tibet', that is) would become a peaceful self-governing entity, devoted to environmental conservation. In return for autonomy, demilitarization and the reversal of 'population transfers', he agreed that defence and foreign affairs (other than cultural matters) should rest in the hands of the Beijing government. Among the sorest points of which the nationalists complain is the influx of Han and other nationalities to territories claimed as ancestrally Tibetan. They are also horrified by government encouragement of Han–Tibetan intermarriage, seeing both as attempts to dilute or overwhelm their race; and, although this has been given less publicity, Tibetan nationalists are as hostile to the presence of Hui (Chinese Muslims) in 'their' territory as they are to the Han.

Both Melvyn Goldstein and Graham Clarke, anthropologists who have done and are continuing to do fieldwork in Tibet and are intimately familiar with its history and demography, have addressed the question of population shifts, and the latter in particular has traced it in detail.[36] Both refute the impression nationalists convey that the presence of non-Tibetans is a post-1950 phenomenon, as well as the usual conflation of the TAR and the other areas with substantial Tibetan presence. In addition, as they point out, the nationalists attribute to deliberate Beijing policy population movements that are secondary effects of economic changes elsewhere in China – ironically, the result of liberalization.

But the Himalayas have always been home to a mixed set of peoples, where, for example, 'one has Tibetans at one altitude, "tribals" at another, and Hindus below, on each and every mountain slope'.[37] The Muslim presence too is not new, even in central Tibet, but was reported by Jesuit missionaries in the 17th century. Some Han presence in Qinghai (which Tibetan nationalists claim under the name of Amdo) dates back to the 18th and 19th centuries. Clarke points out that Han agriculturists have been following and settling around military outposts in north-east Qinghai for centuries, but it is only recently that there has been appreciable Han migration to the Tibetan

---

36) See Graham E Clarke, 'Tibet Today: Propaganda, Record and Policy', *Himalayan Research Bulletin*, vol 8, no 1, 1988, pp 29–30; 'The Movement of Population to the West of China: Tibet and Qinghai', in R Foot and J Brown, eds, *Population Movement in Asia*, London: Macmillan, 1994. I am grateful to Dr Clarke for allowing me to see a draft copy of this chapter.

37) Graham E Clarke, 'Tibet Today: Propaganda, Record and Policy', *Himalayan Research Bulletin*, vol 8, no 1, 1988, p 30.

plateau. Currently, about 60 per cent of the population of Qinghai is Han, and 20 per cent Tibetan. The rest belong to other ethnic groups. Both Han and Tibetans practice settled agriculture. The Han are almost all settled in the lower north-east.

In the TAR there are still no Han farmers or herders. Han are to be found almost exclusively in the cities and towns and clustered along the roads. Han (and other non-Tibetan) workers, traders and artisans are not encouraged to migrate to Tibet, and are usually there under temporary licence or even illegally. Professionals are given some economic encouragement to work in Tibet, but try to transfer their permanent residence to more desirable urban locations eastward in China. However, the increasing market economy may mean that the traders and others may be able to evade or ignore their lack of residence permits, and there is a tendency, noted elsewhere in this book, for temporary migration to become permanent. Ironically, the explosion of tourism in the 1980s was the attraction which first drew many of them to Tibet.[38]

A form of ethnic cleansing was implied in the Dalai Lama's Strasbourg proposal for the revision of 'population transfers', and has certainly been contemplated by some of his officials. David Kellogg describes an interview with 'two Tibetan officials, a former county judge and a former radio journalist ... now working with the exiled government in Dharamsala': 'I asked what [they] thought should be done with the four and a half million Han Chinese ... living in Qinghai. The reply was very succinct: all those born after 1949 would have to leave immediately; the others would have to justify their presence. I asked if the same held true for Mongols, Salahs and other minorities, and was relieved to find that these would be dealt with on a case by case basis'.[39]

TRAVEL REPORTS

In making their conflicting cases, a surprising amount of reliance is placed on the reports of travellers and tourists by both sides, but the Chinese attempts have been relatively naive. In an effort to woo the Dalai Lama into returning to Tibet, in 1979–80, the government arranged for him to send several 'fact-finding' groups on tour, to show the exiles how propitious conditions were back home. One of these was led by the Dalai's sister, who wrote after her return that she 'did

---

38) Melvyn Goldstein, 'The Dragon and the Snow Lion: The Tibet question in the 20th century', *Tibetan Review*, April, 1991, pp 19–20.

39) David Kellogg, 'Tibet, Kuwait and the New World Order', *The Insider*, July, 1991, p 2.

not see a single pregnant Tibetan woman throughout my stay and travel in Tibet. While I have no definite proof, I feel quite certain that this is another of their evil designs to wipe out our people.'[40]

Tourists have also become enmeshed in the political struggle, and it is the pronationalists who understand best that travellers see and report what they are looking for. The Tibet Support Group UK even puts out a handy sheet of suggestions, telling the tourist how to distinguish the (good) Tibetan from the (bad) Han, and how to express contempt for those in authority (who the writer seems unaware are usually Tibetan) without actually getting arrested.[41] These efforts have borne fruit. Asia Watch, for example, attempts to refute 'persistent Chinese claims that there are only 73,000 (Han) Chinese in the TAR' by noting that 'any visitor can see there are far more than that in the Lhasa area alone.'[42] More serious (and

---

40)   Quoted in *Children of Despair*, Eyewitness series, Report no 3, compiled by Martin Ross for Campaign Free Tibet, 1992, p 23. The passage goes on to quote a 1991 statement from the exiled government's Office of Information and International Relations, to the effect that: 'such practices of birth control contravene the tenets of their Buddhist faith.' The idea, frequently cited, that birth control is against the Buddhist faith has been contradicted by the Dalai Lama himself, who at the final session of the first Parliament of the World's Religions, told delegates that they should advocate family planning as a means of sustaining life on Earth: 'If you look at each individual human life as precious, it is better to control that precious life instead of having too much precious life.' (*The Washington Times*, USA, 5 September, 1993, p A3.)

    Paul Ingram, who wrote the introduction to *Children of Despair*, is equally credulous in retailing anything that seems to point to Chinese propensities for genocide. At one point he demands to know what happened to the Lolos (yet another Tibeto–burman minority), unaware that they are alive and well and living in Yunnan, and, at their own request, they are now referred to as 'Yi'.

41)   'Advice for Tourists to Tibet' unpublished 'advice sheet', enclosed in *Tibet Society of the United Kingdom Newsletter*, Summer, 1993. The advice begins, 'The more people who visit Tibet, the more committed supporters there will be for the Tibetan cause. To visit Tibet is to be convinced of the outrage perpetrated on Tibetans and their culture.' Then follows instructions on how to say 'Democracy is good' in Tibetan, after which:

> ... you may be watched or followed even when you are unaware ... Chinese stooges may appear out of nowhere: Chinese spies may dress in monks' clothes .... Tibetans live in constant fear .... If you get in trouble with the police, act. Adopt an air of complete innocence ... (hypocrisy gets you everywhere in China) .... Never get angry or assertive (unless you are an American): they want to be loved .... Use your time in Tibet to gather information if you can .... When you return to the UK, please feed back any information you think might be useful to our office or to the office of one of our allied groups. This is very important.

42)   *Merciless Repression*, p 41. It is not clear how a casual visitor could perform such a head count. It should be said, however, that more foreign comment has centred on the proportion of Han in Lhasa than any other place, and, although Chinese sources have analysed the numbers and proportions of the Han, Tibetan and other minority populations in various Tibetan autonomous areas as well as the TAR, they have never estimated the numbers or proportions in Lhasa itself. Lhasa is in any case a segregated city. (See David Kellogg, 'Tibetan tales at the World Parliamentarians Conference', *Frontline* (India), 20 May, 1994, pp 44–5). As to the rest of the Tibetan areas, such pamphlets as Zhong Quan, *Figures and Facts on the Population of Tibet*, Beijing: New Star Publishers, 1991, present some figures (p 8) from which I have constructed the following table:

dangerous) have been the activities of western visitors in encouraging, and even joining in, anti-Chinese demonstrations, which tends to
have the effect of deepening Chinese xenophobia.[43]

Government efforts   Government efforts have been less successful. When the possibilities of tourism, both financial and ideological,
began to be developed, visitors to Tibet were shown through the
Museum of the Tibetan Revolution, which was replete with reminders
of the bad old days, in the form of jewels, gold and other luxuries from
the Potala vaults, together with such grisly items as severed limbs and
serfs' bones, wine cups made of human skulls and trumpets from the
thigh bones of 16-year-old virgins – besides, of course, glowing
pictures of happy peasants and other evidence of communist
improvements. Eventually, however, the Tourist Board had to admit
that western tourists wanted to see Shangri-la, not increased output.
The Museum was dismantled, and the monasteries began to be
restored, partly with the aid of tourist donations.[44] The skull cups and
thigh-bone trumpets are now openly for sale in the Barkhor market.

It is only gradually being generally acknowledged that tourism not
only damages the physical and cultural environment it feeds on, but
carries a very high social price tag as well. Given its unique situation
and mystique in addition, Tibet, whether it remains in Chinese hands
or not, for cultural and political as well as economic reasons, is
increasingly in danger of becoming a kind of theme park for wealthy
foreign visitors; indeed, this too was implied in the Dalai Lama's vision
of developing a 'zone of peace and conservation'. Yet is it inconsistent
that a significant and increasing body of disruptive western tourists
should be considered by Tibetans more welcome or different from a

⬦

cont.

	TAR		Other Autonomous Regions		Total	
	No	*%*	*No*	*%*	*No*	*%*
Tibetans	2.1	95	2.1	53	4.2	68
Han	0.08	4	1.26	31	1.34	22
Other	0.02	1	0.6	16	0.62	10
Total	2.2		4.0		6.2	

Note: Numbers are in millions and based on the 1990 census.

43)   As did the recent attempt of the American Secretary of State to berate the Chinese prime
      minister on the issue of human rights, and to threaten him with withdrawal of 'most
      favoured nation' status. See also June Teufel Dreyer, 'Recent unrest in Tibet', in
      Contemporary Asian Studies Series, no 4, 1989 (93), p 15.
44)   See P Christiaan Klieger, 'Tourism and nationalism in Tibet', *Tibetan Bulletin*, May–July,
      1988, pp 6–10.

temporary, if constantly replenished, 'floating population', whether
licensed or not, about which Tibetan nationalists complain so
bitterly.[45]

The motives attributed to the Chinese government for its alleged
irrational, unnecessary and internationally embarrassing policies and
actions are purely racist, according to the pro-nationalists, and
regularly likened to the Nazi persecutions of Jews. Both Goldstein and
Clarke have been at pains to refute the drawing of Holocaust
parallels.[46] There is no systematic policy of genocide directed against
the Tibetan people. Birth control programmes are part of a pan-
Chinese policy of population control, implemented far more
vigorously among the Han; migrations of non-Tibetans to Tibetan
nationality areas (as elsewhere) are an unintended result of perceived
economic opportunities there. The charges of 'genocide' continue to
be made for a purpose different from that of alerting the world to a real
situation.

'GENOCIDE' AS PUBLIC RELATIONS

It is understandable that the Tibetan nationalists should avail
themselves of whatever help came to hand in trying to achieve their
ends.[47] But the western and specifically American connection that
was forged in the 1950s and continues to manifest itself has certainly
shaped many features of the campaign for independence waged by
Tibetan nationalists over the past 35 years, and has brought with it
several pitfalls (for Tibetans), as well as opportunities for an extension
of conservative social politics (by foreigners).

---

45) June Teufel Dreyer ('Recent unrest in Tibet', in *Contemporary Asian Studies Series*, no 4,
1989 [93], p 12) does list foreign tourism among Tibetan grievances. At present, however,
the main complaint is that the Han Chinese rather than Tibetans benefit from tourist-
generated income. This is now balanced by a readiness to cultivate the sympathy and
support most foreign tourists appear to give the nationalist cause.

46) Melvyn Goldstein, 'The Dragon and the Snow Lion: The Tibet question in the 20th century',
Tibetan Review, April, 1991, p 16; Graham E Clarke, 'Tibet Today: Propaganda, Record and
Policy', *Himalayan Research Bulletin*, vol 8, no 1, 1988, pp 26–7. Tibetan nationalists have
found parallels with their own situation in many other beleaguered and threatened
minorities, from Kuwaitis invaded by Saddam Hussein to both Jews and Palestinians in the
Middle East. See 'Arafat's way is our way', *Tibetan Review*, Jan–Feb, 1976, p 15; and 'Secret
of survival: Tibetan–Jewish dialogue', Tibetan Bulletin, Oct–Nov, 1990, p 17. Interestingly,
the latter account claims that while Tibetans can learn 'survival through culture and
heritage' from the Jews, the latter can learn 'to imbue any struggle with the force of moral
integrity which His Holiness has imparted to the Tibetan struggle'.

47) In August, 1982, a flutter was caused by a statement made by a Soviet official that 'the
Soviet Union would support the Tibetan cause if asked.' ('No Russian military aid for
Tibetans', *Tibetan Review*, September, 1982, p 6.)

First of all, the Dalai Lama himself has become a public relations expert, and has succeeded in enlisting the outspoken support of many well-known westerners and most of the American legislature.[48] In addition to film stars, such as Richard Gere, his supporters included the late German Green Party leader Petra Kelly, but are concentrated in the political right, whose defence of human rights and democracy has been very selective.

A surprising number of western men have taken up cudgels in defence of Chinese (and Tibetan) multiple motherhood. Some, such as Stephen Mosher, also willingly appear on anti-abortion platforms, and some of the atrocity stories retailed by pro-Tibetan nationalist (and anti-Chinese) groups are closely modelled on American anti-abortion propaganda, for example, lurid accounts of aborted foetuses being unceremoniously tossed into rubbish bins. The attempts of American anti-abortion groups to identify with Tibetan human rights protests have been particularly embarrassing to the latter.[49]

The largely western audience has also influenced the presentation of Tibetan Buddhism, for western consumption. Indeed, religion may prove to be Tibet's most successful product, both in the form of tourism and pilgrimage, and in the form of foundations and converts abroad. There are also imports. Some Tibetans, grateful for the

---

48) The US Congress has passed several resolutions supporting the nationalist cause and allegations, despite a more cautious stance taken by the White House, whether in Republican or Democrat hands. The obsessiveness with which the nationalist view has been adopted by educated westerners is illustrated by a restaurant review in *LIFE* (the colour magazine of the *Sunday Observer*, London), 8 May, 1994, p 40. At the end of a brief write-up of the new Tibetan Restaurant in Covent Garden, the writer, John Lancaster, observes that the food is not very good, 'but some things are more important than food, and any venture which helps increase interest in the betrayed and abandoned country of Tibet is a good thing'. An account of a holiday visit to Tibet, fairly critical of Chinese management, by the *Guardian's* China specialist, John Gittings ('Chinese whispers', *Guardian Weekend*, 12 November, 1994, pp 53–55) provoked a letter beginning 'John Gittings seems to suggest that not all is wrong with the Chinese occupation of Tibet. But since 1949 [sic] when they invaded Tibet the Chinese have carried out a policy of genocide ...' (Paul Veitch, *Guardian Weekend*, 19 November, 1994, p 6).

49) See Tim Cornwell, 'Gunmen of the abortion war await America's judgment', *Observer*, 20 February, 1994, p 16, and compare *Children of Despair* (Eyewitness series, Report no 3, p 17). The 'eyewitness' quoted there, Liu Yin, adds, 'Quite a few women commit suicide after they find out their aborted babies were male.' Liu's report 'strongly corresponds with reports from Tibetan refugees.' Liu Yin (like other writers used there) is really talking about China, not Tibet, but the two are easily conflated in many polemics. Nevertheless, Campaign Free Tibet (CFT) places a disclaimer on the first page: 'The report does not consider any rights or wrongs of abortion itself and CFT takes no position upon abortion, sterilisation or birth control policies *per se* ...'. And the generally uncritical Carol Devine notes cautiously: 'The recent attempts of British pro-life lobbies to join with Tibetan groups over abortion and sterilization remain questionable. Tibetan and Western pro-life groups are dealing with very different matters and the pro-life lobby appears to manipulate the Tibetan question.' (*Determination: Tibetan Women and the Struggle for an Independent Tibet*, Toronto: Vauve Press, 1993, p 82.)

sympathy, interest and support that seem to be forthcoming from the United States, are prone to contrast western values, such as human rights and democracy, which they see as compatible with Buddhist ethics, with the materialism of the Chinese, whom, ironically, they blame for corrupting the youth with alcohol, gambling and pornography. But others do see the paradox of tourists who stay in the newly built luxury hotels seeking spiritual renewal in Tibet as other westerners go swimming with dolphins for the same purpose. The more sophisticated have warned against the dangers of looking to western support, whether politically or sentimentally motivated, which has proved so illusory for eastern Europeans and Africans, whether economically or as an escape from suffering and violence.[50]

50) See Tsering Shakya, 'Tibet and the Occident: The Myth of Shangri-la', *Tibetan Review*, January, 1992, pp 13–16.

Chapter 10

Immigration: artificial increase

Throughout this book the close connection between population issues and trends in the rich and poor countries has been stressed and illustrated. But this connection is nowhere more acute, paradoxical and emotive than where population movements are concerned. The discussion of 'population transfers' in the last chapter can serve as a good introduction to an increasingly common and general view of immigration, usually from poor countries, as culturally and economically threatening, regardless of relative numbers. (By contrast, the discussion of tourism there illustrates another increasing trend, where foreign tourists, usually from wealthy countries, are welcomed with few reservations and little consideration of their cultural, social or environmental impact – *pace* 'eco-tourism'.)

The idea that migration is a basic, inalienable right is among those found, like the right to bear children, in the Universal Declaration of Human Rights.[1] But the right to enter the country of one's choice is very carefully circumscribed, and is likely to become more so in the future.

Nation-states tend to consider themselves as either 'immigrant' or 'non-immigrant' countries, that is, having a history of accepting and assimilating substantial flows of people who wish to settle in them for

<hr>

1) It was not subscribed to by the Soviet bloc or several other Communist states – and this fact was given much play during the Cold War. On the other hand, the United States did not subscribe to the International Covenant on Civil and Political Rights, to which most western and Soviet bloc states were signatories.

whatever reason, and those whose sense of nationhood is based on shared descent, race and cultural traditions. Neither position is without paradox. Increasingly, most of the 'immigrant' countries, such as the United States, Latin America, South Africa, Australia and Canada, prefer to forget their beginnings as invader or settler colonies, pushing aside the previous occupants.[2] On the other hand, the so-called non-immigrant countries, such as Germany and Britain, have in the past been both labour-exporting and labour-importing countries.

Even among those most concerned about poverty, hunger and overpopulation in the Third World, immigration is the ultimate threat; it has been used by both environmentalists and politicians from underdeveloped countries in attempts to make the rich and contented nations face up to their responsibility to 'do something': cancel debts, pay more for the commodities they import, or invest in meliorating some of the global environmental threats. It is also used by political opportunists to panic western electorates, whether comfortable or insecure, and it generally succeeds.

GIVE ME YOUR POOR ...

The United States of America is almost invariably depicted – especially in polemics urging tighter immigration controls – as a land that has always been smiling, generous and welcoming toward newcomers of every stripe. 'Can we doubt', said President Reagan in accepting the Republican nomination, 'that only a Divine Providence places this land – this island of freedom – here as a refuge for all those in the world who yearn to be free? Jews and Christians enduring persecution behind the Iron Curtain, the boat people of Southeast Asia, Cuba and of Haiti, the victims of drought and famine in Africa, the Freedom Fighters in Afghanistan and our own countrymen held in savage captivity.'[3]

Like many of Reagan's pronouncements, this was largely a myth.

2) AR Zolberg, A Suhrke and S Aguayo, *Escape from Violence: Conflict and the Refugee Crisis in the Developing World*, Oxford: Oxford University Press, 1989, p 287, n 50. France until recently was rather exceptional in its relative willingness to accept immigrants, thanks to the early near-stabilization of its population. The low birth rate was the result of a popular conspiracy to practice birth control in the face of government policy, which has since been obsessed by fears of depopulation; a recent French publication has caused a furore by claiming that the infiltration of the French statistical service by right-wing nationalists has resulted in the skewing of reported birth rates to encourage pronatalist measures. Recently, France too has joined the anti-immigration nations. See for example, P Webster, 'Pasqua aiming for "zero immigration"', *Guardian*, 2 June, 1993, p 8.

3) Quoted in L Fuchs, 'Immigration, Pluralism and Public Policy', in Mary M Kritz, ed., *US Immigration and Refugee Policy*, Lexington, Mass: Lexington Books, 1983, p 289.

Immigration has always been a divisive issue. Even while the 'frontier' (inhabited by Native Americans, who didn't count) lasted, each wave of settlers produced resentment, especially from the last wave. In 1654, for example, Peter Stuyvesant was already protesting against the admission of Jewish refugees into New Amsterdam. More recently, business interests desiring a larger supply of cheap labour and some immigrant groups urging an easier passage for their relatives and countrymen have occupied one side of the economic/ideological split over immigration, with labour unions and conservative nativists on the other: strange bedfellows on both sides.

The most open period occurred in the latter half of the 19th century, although as early as 1882 a new restrictiveness was heralded by the Chinese Exclusion Act, which violated the 1868 Burlingame Treaty with China, and also the later 1880 treaty. Chinese workers, who had been imported to the west coast to help build the railway in 1848, were always denied citizenship, but it was feared that it could not be withheld from their native-born children.

Further restrictions were added when criminals and prostitutes were barred along with the Chinese. In 1908, a 'Gentlemen's Agreement' was concluded with Japan to keep out their nationals. From 1917 no illiterates were to be admitted. This was considered a subtle way of biasing admissions in favour of northern and western Europe and against southern and eastern Europe, where mass education was less common.

After World War I, the new nation-states formed from multi-ethnic empires spawned a rich crop of dislocated minorities who fled, were expelled or exchanged; in the Balkans this precursor to ethnic cleansing was euphemistically called the 'unmixing of populations'. The American response to the situation, less subtle than the literacy requirement, was the passage of the 1924 Immigration Act, which limited the total number of European immigrants to 150,000 per year, apportioned according to the numbers from each country that had been resident in 1910.

The climax of interwar restrictiveness came in 1938 at the Evian conference called by President Roosevelt, ostensibly to help refugees from Germany and Austria, who were mostly Jewish and amounted to some 660,000, but also to relieve the pressure on American quotas. A poll had shown 67.4 per cent of Americans in favour of keeping them out and 18.2 per cent were for admission, but within the existing quotas; only 5 per cent were for raising the quotas.[4] At the conference, only Holland and Denmark agreed to receive a limited number.

---

4)   See A Dowty, *Closed Borders: The Contemporary Assault on Freedom of Movement*, New Haven: Yale University Press, 1987, p 92.

Romania and Poland attended, but asked to be considered on the 'supply side'. Australia attended to announce that it had no racial problems and did not wish to import any. The British attended but did not want the Palestine issue raised, and the sentiments of the British foreign office were reported to be: 'The pitiful condition to which German Jews will be reduced will not make them desirable immigrants.'[5] The outcome of the Evian conference was later said to have helped to bring on the 'final solution', as Germans concluded that no one wanted their despised outcasts and no one cared what happened to them. As if to underline this message, in 1939 Congress defeated the Refugee Act, which would have admitted some 20,000 'undesirables'.

The Holocaust and the aftermath of World War II influenced the readiness to admit refugees. The 1952 Walter–McCarran Act reaffirmed the national quotas but accommodated a steady accumulation of exceptions, providing for the admission of otherwise excluded persons and enhancing the power and influence of Congress and the executive who were able to effect these exceptions. Consequently, from 1952 to 1965, the now outmoded national quotas were used to only 60 per cent of capacity, and one third of entrants came in outside of quotas.

The Civil Rights movement of the 1960s and a more general acceptance of a 'cultural pluralism' model (originally propounded in 1915) to replace the 'melting pot' (which had invited discussion of the limits of assimilation) influenced a drastic change in the immigration law.[6] In 1965, all national quotas were abolished; instead, total yearly numbers were given a fixed ceiling within which each country was permitted up to 20,000 immigrants with their families. Western hemisphere migrants were given a separate allotment, but the two were later combined.

In addition to numbers, both a preference system and set of exclusionary classes were retained, and still are. There were 33

5)　R Landau, *The Nazi Holocaust*, London: IB Tauris, 1992, p 138. The admission of refugees to industrialized countries is still subject to similar considerations, which can militate against single women and those with dependent children but no husband. See S Martin, *Refugee Women*, London: Zed Press, 1991, pp 80–83.

6)　'Cultural pluralism' now seems to be heading toward a situation in which every ethnic and religious division must organize itself into self-congratulatory and self-promoting groups in order to feel part of the mainstream of American life. Arvind Rajgopal ('An unholy nexus: Expatriate anxiety and Hindu extremism', *Frontline*, 10 September, 1993, p 13) sees the answer to the paradox that successful middle-class Hindus in the United States have been attracted in large and generous numbers to the fundamentalist Hindu VHPA (Vishwa Hindu Parashad of America, Inc) precisely in the fact that 'participating in the VHP has made it easier, not harder, to be part of American society. "It's more a matter of self-confidence than culture."' Where the Jewish lobby and the black movement has led, almost anyone can follow.

classes of exclusions, among them paupers, prostitutes, homosexuals, the insane or retarded, the bodily ill, such as those with AIDS or TB, Nazis, communists and fascists. On the other hand, immediate relatives of residents, spouses, parents, and children are admitted without limit. Other relatives, such as brothers and sisters, are admitted within slightly lower orders of preference, but the immediate families of these too are admitted. The high priority given to family reunification may seem like a vote for motherhood, but it has been accused of being subtly racist in itself, as, like the quotas, it permits co-ethnics of those already settled to jump the queue.

MYTHS ABOUT MIGRANTS

What have been the effects of immigration on the receiving countries, on the immigrants and on the senders? The fears sometimes expressed that immigrants might be a drain on the economy have been countered by, among others, Julian Simon, who calculated in 1981 that each immigrant family to the United States, '[w]hen looked at by natives as an investment, similar to such social capital as dams and roads ... is worth somewhere between $15,000 and $20,000, even calculated with relatively high rates for the social cost of capital.'[7] Simon has become notorious among environmentalists for his beliefs that nothing but good can result from unlimited population and economic growth; however, in this instance later studies have concurred. David North, for example, estimated that the utilization by regular immigrants of three types of social service programmes – income transfer (food stamps, AFDC [Aid to Families with Dependent Children] and social security), education and health – were all at the same level as the population as a whole. But immigrants also contribute, both in money and in skills: their financial contribution to income transfers was about average, while their personnel contribution to education was below average, and that to health was above average. As for refugees, who are often the recipients of special programmes of assistance and training, the ratio of taxes they pay to services they consume has been estimated at $90 billion to $5 billion.[8]

---

7)   J Simon, 'Immigrants, Taxes and Welfare in the United States', *Population and Development Review*, March, 1984.
8)   See David North, 'Impact of Legal, Illegal and Refugee Migrations on US Social Service Programs', Chapter 14 in M Kritz, ed., *US Immigration and Refugee Policy*, 1983 (see note 3). Philip Martin and Elizabeth Midgley ('Immigration to the United States: Journey to an Uncertain Destination', *Population Bulletin*, September, 1994, p 33) note that: 'The political controversy arises from the fact that the bulk of the taxes immigrants pay flow to the

Britain   The history of immigration to Britain is different, largely owing to its colonial history, but current policy is driven by similar popular beliefs that those of alien race and culture take jobs, housing and social services from those of 'native' stock – and the political capital that can be made out of such fears. Whether and to what extent these beliefs are true is not known, because so little of the relevant data has been collected, but contrary to the general impression, European countries began to close their borders to migrants from the South before the 1973 'oil shock' caused a slow-down in their previously expanding economies, and did not open them again after recovery.

The 'fortress mentality' of the rest of Europe has been matched or even exceeded by Britain. Until 1971, all British subjects had the unfettered right to enter and live in the UK. At that point, such a right was reserved for citizens of the UK alone. In 1981, citizenship was narrowed to those who had at least one parent who was a citizen: those born in the UK were no longer automatically citizens. Since then, the right to settle in the UK has been largely reserved to spouses and dependent children of UK citizens and residents; their numbers exceed emigration by a mere 28,000 per year.[9] 'Primary' (male) immigration has ended, and John Major has refused to sign the Schengen agreement which would end passport checks between EC countries, in order to 'double-bolt' the doors against immigrants.[10]

———————————◇———————————

cont.

federal government, while the costs of providing immigrants and their children with schooling, health care, and public safety tends to be borne by state and local governments.' The same, of course, is true for all residents.

9)   Even for spouses, barriers are erected by the practice of asking intimate and intrusive questions to make certain that immigration was not the 'primary purpose' of the marriage. The use of DNA testing to verify the relationship of dependent children has also raised problems. Not only is the onus and cost of the tests on the (often poor) applicant, but the impact on the family should the test not confirm the claims can be devastating, particularly when the child turns out to be related to the mother but not the sponsoring father (as happened, for example, in 7 per cent of the 1043 cases carried out in Bangladesh in 1992). Elspeth Guild ('Future Immigration Policy', in Sarah Spencer, ed., *Strangers and Citizens*, London: IPPR, 1994, p 238), in discussing this situation remarks that, 'It is not the role of immigration policy to police the fidelity of wives.' Even she, however, does not consider the possibility that rape and/or incest rather than 'infidelity' might be at issue.

10)   Allan Findlay, 'An Economic Audit of Contemporary Immigration', in Sarah Spencer, ed., *Strangers and Citizens*, London: IPPR, 1994, p 165. What strikingly emerges from this article is the absence of research and data supporting the main justifications for current policy. EC and Irish migration is unfettered and not included in 'immigration' statistics. That 'immigration' is publicly viewed in racial terms is indicated by the lack of awareness of such facts as that, while 16 per cent of the (small) foreign population in Britain is Indian, 13 per cent is American (p 161). Findlay also points out that one effect of racism is that foreign-born labour is used inefficiently, with many workers unemployed or overqualified for the jobs they hold. For the history of changes to the rights of entry and abode, see Laurie Fransman, 'Future Citizenship Policy', and Elspeth Guild, 'Future Immigration Policy', both in the same volume. The fear of male migration is still mirrored in the gender

Arguments in favour of more generous immigration policies are usually framed in terms of the economic benefits carefully selected, highly skilled and wealthy immigrants or temporary workers can bring with them. These arguments have been heeded even in Britain, where the possession of £200,000 to invest or start a business can also get you permission to enter and reside, and the issuing of work permits to employees of international corporations has been speeded up.[11]

MOTIVES FOR MIGRATION: PULL FACTORS

In addition to whatever inherent attractions travel, change and new opportunities may hold for the migrants, the channels of communication, assistance and encouragement set up by earlier passages from the same family or location make it easier as well as more desirable to follow the same course. The lure often becomes so strong that discouragement by the receiving country is not very effective in shutting off or even diminishing previously established flows. So it is often taken for granted that immigration must be of benefit, economically and socially, to the immigrant. Yet the extent to which immigrants like their new surroundings well enough to settle permanently is sometimes exaggerated. Even in the case of United States, the legendary mecca and haven for immigrants, the only two groups whose members nearly all stayed on were the Irish and the Jews; about 50 per cent of the rest were, for one reason or another 'birds of passage', in effect, migrant workers.[12]

We hear more from successful immigrants than from unsuccessful ones. Nevertheless, that there are overall economic benefits to the migrant is relatively reliable. The median incomes of foreign-born earners, age for age, are slightly higher than those of the native-born. The earnings of foreign-born males reach parity with the native-born 13 years after arrival, while women, whose incomes are overwhelmingly less than men's, take only two years to equal those of native women.[13]

Ironically, the relative economic success of immigrants is some-

---

cont.

 inequality which permitted foreign male students to have their spouses with them, while female students may not.

11) Allan Findlay, 'An Economic Audit of Contemporary Immigration', in Sarah Spencer, ibid, pp 177–81. The largest numbers of non-European staff to receive these work permits are from Japan and the USA.

12) A Zolberg, 'Contemporary Transnational Migrations in Historical Perspective', in Mary M Kritz, ed., *US Immigration and Refugee Policy*, Lexington, Mass: Lexington Books, 1983, p 27.

13) See David North, 'Impact of Legal, Illegal and Refugee Migrations on US Social Service Programs', in *US Immigration and Refugee Policy*, ibid, pp 275–6.

times considered a problem. The standard rags-to-riches immigrant story is often held up to counter the claims of native-born disadvantaged groups, and these respond in turn by citing the corners cut into hard-won legislation on wages and working conditions by both immigrant workers and employers.[14] What is sometimes underestimated in immigrant success stories are the educational and financial advantages many immigrant groups have brought with them or found waiting on arrival. It is not the poorest residents of the source countries who emigrate; emigrants must, at the very least, be able to stump up the costs of passage. In many cases, as in Britain, Canada and the United States, immigration is made officially easier for those who can bring substantial amounts of capital or income with them.[15] In other cases, such as that of recent Korean settlers in the United States, they also have access to rotating credit associations which the Korean community continues to maintain.

Nor is it the least skilled who migrate; countries as diverse as Britain, Russia, India, Jamaica and Haiti have complained of a 'brain drain' depleting the national stock of trained professionals. The relatively greater economic success of Cuban compared to Mexican immigration is based upon the class cohesion and resources of the former. Indeed, with the exception of some Latin American entrants, recent immigration has exceeded the American norm in socio-economic status upon arrival.

THE IMPACT ON THE MIGRANTS ...

The social and cultural benefits of migration can be more uncertainly realized by the migrants than the economic ones. The British Asian community, for example, originally consisted mainly of lone men who mingled with each other and with the native population to a large extent. With the passage of time and family reunification, Asians have split into separate groups whose male leaders and family heads often try to recreate the village communities they left behind.

---

14) See L Light, 'Immigrant Entrepreneurs in America: Koreans in Los Angeles', in Nathan Glazer, ed., *Clamor at the Gates*, SF: Institute for Contemporary Studies Press, 1985.

15) The United States Immigration and Naturalization Service introduced an 'investor exemption' category by which people bringing at least $250,000 to invest get preference for admission. Many Hong Kongers have migrated to Canada under similar regulations, driving up house property values and causing native resentment, while a person who possesses £150,000 or more, or an income of at least £15,000 per year can settle in Britain as a 'person of independent means', provided he (or she) can also demonstrate a 'historic connection' with the country. Bank managers may number among such connections.

They are not only harassed by the white majority,[16] but are often on hostile terms with each other. Living in increasingly crowded neighbourhoods and hemmed in by religious and social prohibitions, often blighted by unemployment, young men have little to do and are increasingly slipping out of the once-vaunted Asian family control, or turning to fundamentalist religious groups. Attempts by Pakistani and Bangladeshi immigrants to keep up ties with their places of origin have included sending children there for periods of up to two years at a time, which has had disastrous effects on their educational progress.

The worst effects are probably felt by young women who were born or brought up in Britain. For them, feminine expectations like long-suffering submissiveness and bowing to family decisions about education or work, let alone arranged or even forced marriages – sometimes to grooms in villages back in the 'old country' – are increasingly unacceptable. The rate of suicide among young women with Asian parents is said to be three times that of their non-Asian-descended peers.[17] A handful of the more rebellious young women, including those already bound in unhappy marriages, have run away to women's refuges and many have been tracked down by 'vigilantes' hired by their families or working on a volunteer basis.

... AND ON SENDING COUNTRIES

Attitudes toward emigration have varied greatly across time and space. In the *Republic*, Plato said only older citizens of proven loyalty should be permitted to leave, and then as part of official delegations. The Spartan Laws of Lycurgus (800 BC), too, prohibited travel abroad to spare the city 'the infection of foreign bad habits', and this attitude has sometimes been echoed by Chinese government attitudes to those of their nationals who returned to 'build the motherland'. The enlightenment philosophy of the French revolution included the right to leave, but this was shortly reneged on when the government began to fear a shortage of soldiers. After the Russian revolution, Lenin, too, reversed his prerevolutionary stance in favour of cancelling Tsarist Russia's prohibition on emigration – on the grounds that citizens owe

---

16) The number of racial attacks and 'incidents' in Britain is rising continually. In 1993, there were 9000 such attacks registered with the police, but estimates by the Home Office and the Labour Party place the number of 'incidents' at between 130,000 and 200,000. The Home Office's British Crime survey estimates that these numbers include over 30,000 assaults.

17) Study by North Thames Health Authority. Suicide rates of Asian men, by contrast, are lower than those of the British-descended population.

the revolutionary state who nurtured them their labour, just as children owe their parents support.[18]

Nevertheless, by the end of the 19th and beginning the 20th centuries, it was clear that over- rather than underpopulation was the problem in Europe (except in France), and departures were assisted. Europe was at this time passing through what is known as the 'demographic transition' (from high to low birth and death rates). Thanks to improvements in nutrition and public health associated with the industrial revolution, the death rates were dropping and European populations had swelled.

Eventually, birth rates too began to drop. The European demographic transition is the model which the rest of the world is expected to follow as it too modernizes, but, in holding up this model, it is often neglected to mention the waves of emigration that flowed out of Europe to populate the New World, or the role of empire in relieving poverty at home. Or that in those days it was thought quite respectable, even laudable, to leave one's native land with the purpose of making one's personal fortune abroad.[19] From 1815 to 1895, about 15 (or 25 or 40 or 50, depending on who you read) million Europeans went abroad, mostly to the New World. Ireland was the only country that was severely depopulated, and even there the effects were beneficial: wages rose, farms got larger and remittances from abroad were received. From the point of view of governments, the emigration of malcontents increased social stability; moreover, some governments, such as that of Sweden, found it possible to improve domestic conditions to stem what they felt might have been an excessive outflow.

Migrant labour: temporary immigration?   Are the effects of importing labour rather than people better or worse than immigration, and for whom? It is sometimes claimed that for countries suffering a temporary or permanent problem of surplus population, exporting the surplus in the form of migrant labour is the ideal solution. Everyone supposedly benefits: the migrants who get jobs and acquire skills; their families who receive remittances; the sending countries that reap

---

18) The Russian (largely Jewish) emigration to the United States was actually illegal, though the law was not rigorously enforced. Many young Jewish men, subject to long years of army service as well as a lifetime of persecution, sought to escape in this way. In the 19th century, draft evasion was a standard reason for emigration from other countries as well, including Switzerland, whose males were citizens by descent and subject to service in perpetuity. Even now, such draft evaders are not considered real refugees, unless they can be shown to be 'true conscientious objectors'.

19) Estimates vary, but one claim is that the present population of the British Isles, about 65 million, would have been as high as 90 million had it not been for emigration (James Le Fanu, 'Must life mean death', *Sunday Telegraph*, 15 August, 1993).

social stability, hard currency and investment; the receiving countries that get exactly the kind and amount of labour they need for exactly the period of time it is necessary – without incurring the responsibility of training or assimilating foreigners.[20]

In practice it has not worked out quite that way. Receiving countries have found that migrant workers tend to turn into immigrants. Germany, for example, found that regularly rotating its Turkish 'guestworkers', which it had recruited before the oil shock of the early 1970s, was not practical, so some of the 'temporary workers' have now been resident for over 20 years without the benefits of citizenship. Attempts to bribe them to return home have been largely unsuccessful; the recessionary pressures that made their labour unwanted in Germany have affected Turkey too. And because of the 'social problems' resulting from skewed sex-ratios (the tendency of migrant workers to form relationships with German women), family reunion was eventually permitted, and many Turkish children born in Germany know no other country.

Britain actively recruited labour in the West Indies in the 1950s, even going to the extent of setting up recruitment and training agencies for prospective London Transport workers in Barbados. In 1993, the daughter of one such migrant, who also had another daughter settled in the UK, was suffocated while being forcibly evicted from the country in accordance with what the government always terms its 'firm but fair immigration policy'.

Sending countries have sometimes made attempts to control migrant labour, but many have become so dependent upon remittances, which now often constitute a substantial part of national revenue, that the control has focused more on the worker than on his or her protection.[21] China, for example, required the remission of 20 per cent of wages. Vietnam, heavily in debt to the Soviet Union after the Vietnam War, agreed to repay by exporting labour; a proportion of each worker's wages was retained by the government.[22]

---

20) In some places, such as the Middle East, foreign workers are even segregated. On the other hand, some sending countries, such as Italy before its own birth rate dropped, thought of emigration as establishing 'colonies' of influence abroad, and encouraged its nationals to keep contact with the homeland and make refreshing visits back home. Interesting discussions of migrant labour from many points of view are to be found in M Parnwell, *Population Movements in the Third World*, London: Routledge, 1993; M Kritz, L Lim, and H Zlotnik, eds, *International Migration Systems*, Oxford: Clarendon Press, 1992; A Dowty, *Closed Borders*, New Haven: Yale University Press, 1987.

21) For example, the value of remittances to India reached 30 per cent of export goods and was over 8 per cent of household savings in the early 1980s; for Pakistan, Egypt, Jordan and Yemen, remittance sums exceeded all goods exported.

22) See F Arnold, 'The Contribution of Remittances to Economic and Social Development', in M Kritz, L Lim, and H Zlotnik, eds, *International Migration Systems*, Oxford: Clarendon Press, 1992, p 208.

Many countries limit the right of women to travel without family consent; yet, until after the Gulf War, the Philippines, which by law required Filipinos working abroad to remit as much as 80 per cent of their earnings through Philippine banks (taxing both the workers and banks in the process), made no attempt to protect migrant maidservants from widespread economic, physical and sexual abuse while abroad. Before then, only Algeria had stopped its citizens from migrating to France in 1973 because of racial abuse experienced by them there.

As in the case of emigration, too, it is often not the unemployed and locally unemployable who leave to work abroad, but the skilled and sometimes even employed. Hence, it is difficult not to concur that:

> The labour export programme harms the domestic economy by syphoning off skilled workers .... To make matters worse, many of those working abroad are not even acquiring new skills, but are becoming 'de-skilled'. However many dollars and cents are earned from the labour trade, the long term costs incurred by the country are likely to outweigh any benefits.[23]

Since this was written, the Gulf War has further demonstrated the risks of becoming too dependent on remittances, and the evidence against benefits to the sending countries has become far stronger.

Effects on families of migrant workers   The effects on the families of migrant workers in many ways reflects those on the sending countries. Although there is no question that many individual families have benefited a great deal, there is always danger inherent in a household, like a country, developing a dependency upon income that may cease for a variety of reasons, including the migrant worker's change of attitude. The longer the worker is abroad, the more likely this is to happen. While they last, however, the bulk of remittances seem to go to 'consumption', including day-to-day expenses, such as food, as well as education and housing. Remittances also finance past consumption, in the form of debt repayment. Only about 10 per cent overall is invested in 'productive industry',[24] although some writers argue that education and even housing may be seen as forms of investment. The stereotyped picture of the migrant returning home with his entire savings squandered on fancy electronics and other

23) Michael Parnwell, *Population Movements in the Third World*, London: Routledge, 1993, p 93.
24) See, for example, P Martin, *The Unfinished Story: Turkish Labour Migration to Western Europe*, Geneva: ILO, 1991.

foreign luxury goods may be an exaggeration, but the stimulation given to imports, as well as the encouragement to more migration produced by the migrant's experiences (and the resulting increase in education in his or her family) cannot be discounted.[25]

The receiving countries   For the receiving countries, the economic arguments revolve about the need for cheap labour. In contrast with the developing oil-rich countries, in industrialized countries imported labour is now at best a convenience, despite fears occasionally expressed about ageing populations. Furthermore, alternatives to permitting cheap labour to cross national borders are already in place. These include the relocation of plants (in both senses), automation, increased exploitation of indigenous reserves of labour, such as women, and, as a last resort, improving the pay and conditions of the regular workforce. In any case, the actual location of certain operations, in particular those concerned with information technology, is less and less important, as in data processing, for example. What started as a flight to the suburbs and small towns, which enabled the part- or full-time employment of women who had difficulty accessing ordinary office jobs, went on to be exported to 'enterprise zones' in Third World countries, and is now coming home in the form of more sophisticated programmes that permit a good deal of automatic processing. The same process can be seen in the area of computer programming, where women who work at home – which allows them to look after their children and perform other household duties at the same time – are finding themselves displaced by cheaper labour in more distant parts of the planet now easily accessible by satellite. The same differences in pay and opportunity that drive migration can now ensure that the services of well-trained Indian computer programmers in enterprise zones are available for $3000 a year.

REASONS FOR REFUGEES

If there is general acceptance that both legal immigration and migrant labour should be under the control of the receiving country, to regulate according to its own judgement of national benefits to be derived, attitudes toward the admission of refugees and 'undocu-

---

25) See Michael Parnwell, *Population Movements in the Third World*, London: Routledge, 1993, p 110; and F Arnold, 'The Contribution of Remittances to Economic and Social Development', in M Kritz, L Lim and H Zlotnik, eds, *International Migration Systems*, Oxford: Clarendon Press, 1992, pp 209–11.

mented' migrants are not so clear-cut. In theory at least, refugees are admitted for humanitarian reasons, for their well-being and benefit. But, in countries like Britain which have closed off immigration, and countries like Germany which have never had it, refugees have become synonymous with immigration in the popular imagination and are attracting the same sort of racial hostility, their bona fides increasingly questioned. As good a summary as any of the received current view of refugees was put by WR Smyser, who was UN Deputy High Commissioner for refugees from 1981–86:

> Some migrants appear to be abusing rights intended for refugees. The nature of the refugee problem has changed so much that we must review some of our ways of dealing with it .... The structure of refugee law and care, which has been generously assembled since the dawn of our culture and particularly in the twentieth century, cannot remain in place if it is abandoned by political and popular opinion.[26]

More recently, President Clinton reacted to the discovery of a boat load of smuggled Chinese migrants in similar terms, by saying, 'We will not surrender our borders to those who wish to exploit our history of compassion and justice.'[27] The idea that it is the asylum seekers who are threatening a carefully erected, just and humane refugee policy certainly appeals to American vanity, but a closer look at the development of refugee policy creates doubt over all of these adjectives.

What was actually being exploited by the asylum seekers in the case just cited was the history of giving asylum to the overwhelming majority of migrants from 'Communist China' who tried to claim it, and the reaction was more to a realization of their ever-increasing numbers than to a change in the nature of the migrants themselves. More generally, an examination of the history of refugee protection indicates that the 'structure of law and care' was built less on compassion and justice than on the scoring of political points and the need to limit numbers as strictly as possible. Comparing the difference between the American government's treatment of Cuban asylants and the fewer but no less (indeed more) persecuted Haitians reveals the political dimension at work. (A British parallel is the readiness with which Polish refugees were received in contrast to the brusque reception given to Sri Lankan Tamils.) Finally, the numbers claiming

---

26)   WR Smyser, *Refugees: Extended Exile*, New York: Praeger, 1987, p 2.
27)   P Belluck, 'Immigration policy tide shifts against stranded Chinese', *Philadelphia Enquirer*, 11 October, 1993, p A10.

asylum from both Cuba and Haiti became so intractable (and unpopular) that political solutions to both crises were sought: with Cuba in the form of an agreement with Fidel Castro (who had always complained that by refusing to take legal immigration but accepting all who came illegally, the United States itself was encouraging illegal immigration); and with Haiti, by invasion and restoration of the legitimately elected president.

Refugees and 'economic migrants'   This year's refugees can easily become next year's economic migrants. The demand by the United States that Cuba should restrain its refugees is only one among numerous ironies that dot the history of controlling refugee numbers. Another is that it was the 1989 breakdown of the much-deplored Eastern Bloc policy of sealing their borders to would-be refugees that precipitated the reunification of Germany – and has by another twist led to a change in Germany's post-World War II generous asylum policy.

Refugee policies are based on the premise that the causes of refugee flows are different from the causes of other types of migration. Yet this notion itself flows out of fairly recent conditions and constraints on refugees, and, in fact, almost all observers agree that even so it is increasingly difficult to differentiate even in theory between 'economic migrants' and refugees.[28] The distinction has also been questioned on ethical grounds. Is it right to give help to those who meet particular, rather arbitrary criteria, while refusing it to many who might be more in need? After all, persecution may take the form of economic discrimination, while economic deprivation is often the outcome of political conflict. The deliberate defoliation and mining of the Vietnam countryside by the Americans produced starvation and hardship, yet the fleeing populace were admitted as political refugees regardless of the reason for flight.

It is not simply the practical difficulties in application and interpretation, but the criteria themselves that should receive the most careful scrutiny when dealing with refugees. Until after World War I, asylum was given to the victims of ideological expulsion or individual persecution on an *ad hoc* basis, when refugees were noticed at all. But most refugees are no longer individual political dissidents. Most 'refugees' are not even legally refugees at all, since

---

28) The best exploration of this issue I have seen is contained in Andrew Johnson's MA Thesis, 'Motives for flight: the Vietnamese refugee exodus, April, 1975–89' (University of Hull, April, 1990). In the cases of both Vietnam and Cuba, the United States put economic pressure on a country whose regime it disliked, while offering undiscriminating welcome to all migrants who claimed political asylum.

they are dislocated within the borders of their own countries. Even when they cross borders, 90 per cent of them remain in the Third World. They are the victims of threatened starvation and violence, caused by armed conflict, often made more violent and destructive by the ongoing arms trade, by poverty caused by environmental degradation and/or natural disasters and debt. All of these causes are closely linked, and the sources of these conditions usually reside in the First World.[29]

All too often, too, refugee outflows are the consequence of policies which were (and still are) very popular with the receiving countries when proposed and first implemented. These can range from attempts at development – such as large dam projects or 'structural adjustment programmes' – that displace or impoverish the already poor through to military actions such as the Gulf War. (The Gulf War polled a 92 per cent American approval at the time, yet scarcely two years later the prospect of receiving 4000 Iraqi prisoners of war and their families caused outrage in Congress.)[30]

Development of refugee conventions   The current conventions and protocols that attempt to establish international standards in the definition and treatment of refugees stem from the tentative League of Nations convention of 1933. The original refugee office had been titled 'High Commissioner on behalf of the League in connection with the problems of Russian Refugees in Europe', although Greeks, Turks and Bulgarians were also aided under Fritjof Nansen's leadership. In 1933 the League Assembly decided to appoint a High Commissioner 'for Refugees coming out of Germany', but Germany took offence and resigned from the League. Similarly, in 1938 the Soviet Union objected to the giving of any kind of protection to its exiles. Diplomats from imperial countries objected to definitions of political persecution which could possibly cover the residents of European colonies. Besides its concerns over offending 'friendly' governments, the League did not wish to encourage states to expel their unwanted groups, or, conversely, to encourage anyone to migrate who might otherwise stay put. These worries have continued through all subsequent attempts to redefine refugees.[31]

---

29) See Geoff Gilbert, 'Tackling the Causes of Refugee Flows', Sarah Spencer, ed., *Strangers and Citizens*, London: IPPR, 1994.

30) M Walker, 'Iraqi POWs fuel flames of US immigration row', *Guardian*, 24 August, 1993, p 7.

31) According to a report issued under the auspices of the UNHCR, 'the mere fact that a man has left his country because political events there are not to his liking does not suffice to confer on him the status of refugee and any ensuing advantage.' Quoted in A Zolberg, A Suhrke, and S Aguayo, *Escape From Violence*, Oxford: Oxford University Press, 1989, p 21.

The League convention was the precedent for the UN Convention of 1951, which contained the first official recognition of the rights of refugees. The intent at first was to cover only those who had been displaced or rendered stateless before 1951, and only Europeans. Like the League's efforts, it was hoped that the need would be temporary and specific. In the event, the bulk of displaced persons in Europe after World War II were, on the one hand, Jewish survivors of the Holocaust, and, on the other, Germans expelled from eastern Europe. They were mostly absorbed, symmetrically enough, by Israel and Germany, both of whom had enshrined the principle of admitting any member by descent of its respective group (in the German case, a rule that had originated before World War I).

The tides of refugees in the world, however, did not subside, but changed their natures following geopolitical events. Since the 1950s, 95 per cent of refugees have originated in the Third World. In 1967, a protocol signed by almost 100 countries removed both the time and geographical limitations. In 1969, the Organization of African Unity (OAU) negotiated a convention that broadened the 1951 definition – 'persons who are outside their country because of a well-founded fear of persecution for reasons of race, religion, nationality, membership of a particular social group or political opinion' – by adding that the term would apply also to persons whom aggression, occupation, foreign domination or violence had forced to leave their country of origin or nationality.

In the United States, since the passage of the 1980 Refugee Act, each year the president sets numerical ceilings for the number of refugees world-wide, and for Southeast Asia. For example, in 1980, the numbers were 231,700 world-wide, of which 169,200 were allotted to Southeast Asians. During the 1980s the total numbers decreased, and the Southeast Asian percentage has also fluctuated. In 1988, a total of 94,000 were admitted, of whom 53,000 were from Southeast Asia.

Most of the Southeast Asian refugees were from Vietnam. After each of the two Indochinese wars, many tried to escape the political consequences; after the 1954 partition, about 1 million moved, of whom 900,000 went from North to South.[32] The consequences of the

---

32) See A Zolberg, A Suhrke, and S Aguayo, *Escape from Violence: Conflict and the Refugee Crisis in the Developing World*, Oxford: Oxford University Press, 1989, p 162:

> ... The most determined efforts to influence refugee movements were organized by a newly formed special American unit (SMM, Saigon Military Mission) on behalf of the Southern regime. The objective was to encourage people to leave Communist Vietnam through an elaborate 'psywar' campaign conducted in the North. Two revealing incidents are described in detail in the *Pentagon Papers*. In Sept, 1954, SMM agents tried to sabotage the printing presses of a large private publishing firm that had decided to stay and work under Communist rule. The attempt to induce

second Indochinese war produced a fluctuating but continuous and intractable current of refugees. Having turned on the tap and encouraged the flow, the western powers seemed to have no way to turn it off. From Vietnam, refugees came in three waves: landlords and Catholics, similar to the ones who had come from North to South after the first war, that is supporters of the *ancien régime*, many of whose members had worked for the Americans or their collaborators. These amounted to some 125,000 plus a trickle over the years. The second wave was of some 163,000 ethnic Chinese, who were discriminated against by the new regime, and also suffered because of hostilities between Vietnam and China. When the flow of these threatened to become continuous, China closed its ports.[33]

Until mid-1979 there was little challenge to the status of more than half a million Vietnamese and Chinese claiming asylum, but neighbouring countries began to express alarm at their numbers. At a meeting in July 1979 attended by 65 countries, Vietnam pledged to control the exodus and the industrialized states pledged to take 250,000, an arrangement known as 'third country settlement'. Strangely enough, it was then that a different outflow materialized, consisting of ethnic Vietnamese drawn from the middle and lower strata, and including teachers, clerks, soldiers, peasants and fishermen. Some veterans of 're-education' camps also continued to come out, but the bulk were people the revolution was supposed to benefit. Some left because of natural or man-made disasters, or because of the war-devastated economy, which was economically shunned by the major western powers, the World Bank and the Asian Development Bank. Another factor was the collapse of the dependency economy that had been built up during the American presence, for whom a virtual client population had been created.

But perhaps most important in sustaining the refugee flows were the 'pull' factors. At first, the Vietnamese were encouraged to leave as a propaganda scoring point. This was a popular policy domestically in the United States. Some Americans favoured admission of the

---

cont.

the firm to pack up and leave failed, but a subsequent 'black psywar strike' in Hanoi was spectacularly successful. Agents distributed false leaflets 'signed' by Vietminh officials with instructions concerning the scheduled transfer of French-controlled zones in the Tonkin area to the Communist authorities. The transfer was said to affect property (to be confiscated) and money (to be devalued), and the workers (to be given a three-day holiday). The next day, refugee registration tripled.

33) Mirroring the immigration preference categories, the American Immigration and Naturalization Service set up categories of Vietnamese refugees: Chinese ethnics; Buddhist monks; US Employees; Hmong. There was no limit on the number of immediate relatives admitted (*Refuge Denied*, Lawyers Committee on Human Rights, 1989. [USA], p 95).

refugees because they felt guilt that the war had wrecked their country, while others felt guilt that it had been lost. Initially, no one distinguished the economic and political motives, which were intertwined even conceptually, since both systems had justified their ideologies by claiming they could deliver a better standard of living as well as a more just society. So no questions were asked about motives, and the earlier refugees, as all immigrants do, set up conditions that helped others to follow.

Later, when distinctions began to be made, even those who failed the persecution test could not be returned. The United States insisted for a long time that they were not to be sent back, and underwrote a large settlement programme. Because the countries of Southeast Asia refused to settle them, resettlement in the West remained the expectation, and that was enough to keep the refugees braving all kinds of dangers and long stays in squalid and dangerous camps.[34]

The so-called orderly departure programme, set up in 1984 by the Vietnamese, assisted the migration of relatives, but did not stem the flow, and, in any case, political prisoners were generally excluded from it by the Vietnamese. More recently, the political situation in Hong Kong has become such that the British have attempted various methods to get the refugees in the camps to go back; when bribery failed, forced return was tried.

The enforced return of 51 boat people in December 1989 caused an international outcry, most influentially from the United States, and there were riots in the camps. On 29 October, 1991, Vietnam, Hong Kong and Great Britain signed an accord to enable more forced repatriation. The detainees have threatened more riots and mass suicide, but the American government now seems reconciled. The narrowing interpretation of what constitutes a 'real' refugee has coincided with the compassion fatigue which has afflicted so many western nations and led to drastically reduced resettlement quotas.[35]

---

34) A Zolberg, A Suhrke, and S Aguayo, *Escape from Violence: Conflict and the Refugee Crisis in the Developing World*, Oxford: Oxford University Press, 1989, p 161 ff.

35) M Parnwell, *Population Movements and the Third World*, London: Routledge, 1993, pp 45–47. If privation and ill-treatment in refugee camps has not proved a sufficient deterrence, even the recently noted improvement in the Vietnamese economy may not be enough to discourage continued migration once the channels are so well established. Despite impressive economic growth, immigration to the United States from Taiwan, Singapore, and South Korea remains considerable. In addition, the relaxation of the American-led boycott and Vietnam's recent and much trumpeted success in entering the global capitalist system has been accompanied by the closing down of the social services and disaster assistance that sustained the rural poor. (See Philip Shenon, 'Poorest suffer in new Vietnam', *Guardian*, 22 November, 1994, p 15.)

Refugee women   No group could be more vulnerable or given less recognition than women, who actually constitute the majority of refugees and asylum seekers.[36] Famine, war, disasters and deprivation fall more heavily upon them, and often result in a loss of social status that persists even after the crisis has passed; they are the first to be forced into demeaning work, and often sold into concubinage or prostitution.[37] In addition, there are categories of voluntary behaviour which can result in women becoming outcasts or subject to persecution in their own societies – and hence likely to become refugees – that do not apply to men: for example, violation of the social rules by refusing to wear a veil or enter an arranged marriage, or by engaging in or being suspected of sexual activity outside of marriage.[38]

Women refugees are even more subject to violence than men. In addition to those who are killed or die *en route*, many arrive at the place of sanctuary after having been raped and abused.[39] Even after arrival at refugee camps, women are often at risk of further rape and violence on the part of other inmates, police, soldiers or bandits. Because of traditional attitudes, aside from other physical injuries, the social aftermath of rape alone may be so devastating as to ruin their lives. In the Somali refugee camp at Dadaab in Kenya, women who are raped are not only rejected by husbands and prospective husbands, but are ostracized by other women.[40]

While being a refugee can be more oppressive, it is sometimes more constructive for women than for men.[41] Women may be able to pursue their customary tasks, such as foraging, cooking and childcare, while men have lost their trades and must often sit idle. Administrators of refugee programmes and camps have found that if women are

---

36) See Genevieve Camus-Jacques, 'Refugee women: the forgotten majority', in G Loescher and L Monahan, eds, *Refugees and International Relations*, Oxford: Oxford University Press, 1989. The latter estimates that women (and their dependent children) number up to 80 per cent of refugees and asylees.

37) See David Arnold, *Famine, Social Crisis and Historical Change*, Oxford: Basil Blackwell, 1988, pp 86–95.

38) Some progress toward such recognition was made in the recent admission by France of a Moroccan woman who sought asylum there, having fled the consequences of refusing an arranged marriage.

39) Susan Forbes Martin, ed., *Refugee Women*, London: Zed Books, 1991, Chapter 3, p 17.

40) 'The nightmare continues ... abuses against Somali refugees in Kenya', London: African Rights, 1993; and Mark Huband, *Observer*, 21 November, 1993, p 30. Both reports document the epidemic of rape, mostly gang rape, perpetrated on Somali women who sought refuge in Kenyan camps. The UN response has been completely inadequate, both in apprehending the perpetrators and in affording the women protection.

41) Susan Forbes Martin, ed., *Refugee Women*, London: Zed Books, 1991, contains an especially carefully balanced discussion of the pitfalls and opportunities as well as the special needs and strengths of refugee women, along with numerous recommendations for their assistance.

given the responsibility for allocating and distributing food, it is less likely to be distributed disproportionately to men in authority or diverted to resistance fighters or sale on the black market. (The propensity for food to be used for military and political ends if distributed by male 'community leaders' has been graphically illustrated in the Rwandan refugee camps, where *Medecins Sans Frontières*, ACTIONAID and other NGOs have openly criticized the UN for its distribution policy.) In addition, women trained as health workers are more likely to remain in post.[42]

Refugee status brings burdens as well as occasional opportunities. The duty of shoring up cultures torn apart by war and disaster rests disproportionately on women. In Nadir Bagh camp for widows in Pakistan, for example, when some younger widows refused to be married to relatives of their husbands, the older widows attempted to enforce the tradition. In addition, birth rates in camps often rise, both because of lack of contraceptives suited to camp conditions and from a post-Holocaust wish to replace lost children or other family members, despite conditions so poor that pregnancy and childbirth are the major causes of women's deaths after the original emergency that brought them there.[43]

In Afghan refugee camps the use of purdah has intensified. Programmes designed for refugee women were attacked in 1990, and staff threatened. A mission to help disabled Afghan women was then cancelled. This does not bode well for the prospects of Bosnian Muslim women, who consider themselves fully westernized and European, sent to refugee camps in Pakistan.

Since women (and their children) often have special needs – for food, counselling, education or medical treatment – their voices and views deserve to be, but seldom are, heard apart from those refugee leaders (that is, those who are consulted in the implementation of refugee programmes) who, like other community leaders, are almost invariably men. Sometimes, for example, men may wish to return to the country of origin, but the women, for fear of, or as a result of, violence or because of changes in their values and attitudes toward

---

42) Susan Forbes Martin, ibid, Chapter 4.
43) Women are particularly susceptible to deficiencies in iron, calcium, iodine and Vitamin C. Anaemic pregnant women run the risk of fatal haemorrhages during childbirth. Yet contraception is often in short supply in camps, even when available in the host country (for example, Pakistan). An interesting light was also shed on the problem of pregnancies in dangerous and unpromising conditions for both mother and child by an incident in the Hong Kong refugee detention camps when women there were given depo-provera shots during a rubella epidemic in June, 1988, but the reasons and side-effects weren't adequately explained. This made many women reluctant to go to the family planning clinics, making it appear that women valued continued childbearing beyond their own freedom and their children's welfare and freedom.

traditional practices as a result of their experiences, may not. In other instances, women are more predisposed to returning than men.

Many seldom-noticed differences between male and female refugees were almost incidentally revealed by a recent study by Steven Gold of Vietnamese and Soviet Jewish refugee communities in San Francisco and Los Angeles.[44] Thanks to the criteria under which they are admitted, these refugee communities (like the Cubans in Florida) tend to be both economically and socially conservative. Significantly, the Vietnamese men, but not women, looked back on the traditional Vietnamese patriarchal family with nostalgia. On the other hand, Gold found that the ex-Soviet older women in his study were less satisfied than the men. In Russia they had been vocationally trained and economically active, but in the United States found their skills out of date or otherwise unmarketable and the language difficult to acquire. Coming from positions of professional respect, they are now subject to the particular contempt that Americans, particularly Californians, visit on women past their physical prime and attractiveness.

UNDOCUMENTED WORKERS

The acceptance by the United States and western Europe of workers who are either illegal or semi-legal, insecure, working for low wages and with no employment rights, is extensive and has been highlighted by revelations of the number of prospective US cabinet appointments who have made their lives more convenient and comfortable at little cost by employing such domestic help. Illegal workers are also found in large numbers in agriculture and manufacturing. In Britain, wealthy businessmen and foreign visitors are permitted to bring with them servants who, thanks to their precarious and dependent immigration position, can be kept in a state of virtual slavery to their employers.[45] The British Conservative government's policy of putting government services out to tender, too,

---

44)   S Gold, *Refugee Communities*, London: Sage, 1992.

45)   Robin Hunt, 'Overworked, underpaid and over here', *Guardian*, G2, 5 January, 1994, p 9:

> The Government's compromise was a stamp put on the workers' passports which states they are a visitor, not allowed to undertake paid or unpaid work, but on the next page says they are accompanying their employer ... [E]mployers now see their rights enshrined: of more than 650 women interviewed by Kalayan before and after the 'clarifying' leaflet was produced [by the government], more claimed to have suffered abuse after than before; many said they had been subjected to sexual abuse, forced to sleep on the floor, denied permission to leave the house, had not been paid, had their passport confiscated and been paid less than was in their contract. [sic]

has had the bizarre outcome that agents of the Home Office (which takes care of immigration matters) conduct raids on the Ministries of Defence, Trade and Industry, Education and others, whose cleaning contractors employ illegal workers.[46]

Another particular vulnerability of alien women, including asylum seekers and illegal immigrants, who marry American citizens has been highlighted by recent revelations that these men sometimes neglect to file a document needed for the wives to be granted independent American residence status. Later, the men can use the threat of deportation to persuade their wives to remain in abusive marriages, or report them to immigration officials to avoid prosecution for domestic violence should they complain. 'This is the only crime', as one lawyer observed, 'where the culprit can legally make his victim disappear.'[47]

CONTROLLING PUBLIC OUTCRY

Whatever puts pressure on legal immigration results in a rise of illegal immigration. In several years of the past decade, more than one million illegal entrants to the United States have been apprehended, including everyone from tourists overstaying their visas to Haitian and Chinese boat people washed ashore. Most, however, are Mexican. While some Mexicans and Mexican–Americans still dispute the border and the unfairness of the treaty of Guadalupe–Hidalgo, by which Mexico lost two-fifths of its territory, other Mexican–American citizens are vehemently opposed to the illegal immigrants, claiming they increase the discrimination to which they themselves are subject.

As to the more general question of the economic impact of illegal immigration, the argument over whether 'undocumented workers' take jobs, drive down wages, or simply do jobs that would otherwise be 'uneconomic' to get done at all is still unresolved, as the frequency with which prominent Americans employ undocumented workers

---

46)   These revelations occurred in the course of a BBC2 'All Black' programme on illegal alien workers in Britain (27 August, 1993), the main focus of which explored how easy it is for illegal aliens to get jobs (at low pay), while 3,000,000 people are officially listed as unemployed. The ease of the employment procedure at such sensitive ministries had security implications as well.

47)   It can happen to women from the First World as well as the Third, including a British woman. Commenting on the prospect that deportation meant she would have to leave her children behind, the district director of immigration and naturalization said, 'I'm afraid these things happen.' (Christopher Reed, 'Briton may "lose" three children', *Guardian*, 19 August, 1994, p 9.) In Britain, feminist groups, such as Southall Black Sisters, have campaigned on behalf of a number of women threatened with deportation as a result of the break-up of abusive marriages.

demonstrates. Nevertheless, and despite the findings that illegal immigration makes calls on all types of social service programmes below the levels of both refugees and legal immigrants, political leaders on both sides of the Atlantic continue to reinforce the popular impression that such services are a main purpose of immigration. In Britain, immigration officials speak of the rewards of their jobs as 'protecting the taxpayer', and a 'habitual residence test' has been introduced to block the claims of 'benefit tourists' from other EU countries who can't be stopped at the border. In the first few months after its introduction more than 1000 British nationals failed the test.[48]

In the United States, the governor of California exploited the same belief by complaining that two-thirds of the births in Los Angeles County Hospital are currently to illegal aliens, and, since these children are, potentially at least, American citizens, this entitles their parents to full welfare benefits.[49] Having struck a responsive chord, the issue played an important role in the 1994 American elections in California. The referendum 'Proposition 187', which, probably unconstitutionally, denies to illegal immigrants their few remaining human rights – non-emergency medical care and education for their children – was passed overwhelmingly. In addition, the Republican candidate for the Senate was defeated partly because shortly before the polls he was forced to admit that he, like President Clinton's cabinet nominees two years previously, had employed an illegal immigrant as a servant.

The North American Free Trade Agreement (NAFTA), pushed so enthusiastically by President Clinton and marketed by his environmentalist Vice President Albert Gore, was urged as much as a means of confining potential Mexican migrants to factories south of the border as a promise of increased prosperity for all. In theory, environmental standards for health and safety would be uniformly enforced while Mexican productivity and wages gradually rose to American standards; the immediate increase in low-waged jobs would be enough to stem the immigrant tide. In practice, these factories already exist and are notorious not only for pitiful wages but for the toxic conditions they have produced, conditions already connected with a rise in illness, congenital defects and stillbirths in the women who work and live nearby.[50]

---

48) David Brindle, 'Expat falls into trap set for "benefit tourists"', *Guardian*, 14 December, 1994, p 3.

49) D North, 'Impact of Legal, Illegal and Refugee Migrations on US Social Service Programs', in M Kritz, ed., *US Immigration and Refugee Policy*, Lexington, Mass: Lexington Books, 1983, p 272.

50) See for example P Ghazi, 'America's Deadly Border', *Observer Magazine*, 12 December, 1993, pp 16–20.

The General Agreement on Tariffs and Trade (GATT) and the American Free Trade Agreement are only too likely to provide more of the same, without stemming the migratory tide which increasingly distorts western social policy.[51] Moreover, the 'fortress mentality' and population policies of Northern countries, including the prohibition of legal immigration and blinking of cheaper illegal labour, is spreading to the newly industrializing countries of Asia whose birth rates have recently dropped so precipitately. A new round in the cycle of migration in search of a better life has begun.[52]

51) See Tim Lang and Colin Hines, *The New Protectionism*, London: Earthscan, 1993.
52) See Leah Makabenta, 'Rise of the Fortress NICs', *Terra Viva* (produced for the Cairo conference by Al-Ahram), 6 September, 1994, p 12. The newly industrializing countries have begun to use all the barriers and hypocritical acceptance of undocumented workers (to get dirt cheap and unprotected labour) that European countries use. The migrant workers' own embassies are reluctant to protect their human rights for fear of losing remittances. Host countries include Hong Kong, Malaysia, Singapore, Taiwan and South Korea, of which the worst offender is Malaysia, with 450,000 migrants officially, but NGOs put the real figure at 2.5 million. The migrants come from Bangladesh, Pakistan, Sri Lanka, Indonesia, Thailand and the Philippines. Makabenta's source is Mayan Villalba, director of the Asian Migrant Centre in Hong Kong.

Chapter 11
Afterword: untying assistance

Any real understanding of population issues should begin with an appreciation of the extent to which the ideological and cultural climate in rich as well as poor countries is overwhelmingly pronatal. This is manifest in the ideologies of most religions (often by ignoring or distorting their scriptures), nationalisms and ethnicities. It is also found in popular attitudes to childbirth and abortion, and in the new medical technologies. Parental power in both law and custom constitutes an important pronatalist force as well.

The spread of the sentimental cult of the child is now an important part of western pronatalism. Ideally, children have emotional rather than economic value. Nevertheless, child labour all over the world has not been eradicated, and is in fact increasing. Although the poor do set their children to work, large families are no longer needed nor desired as an economic strategy. Rather, the labour of children profits employers and local economies at the expense of women, themselves, and other children. The strengthening of children's rights is desirable both to protect them from exploitation and as a development out of women's rights.

The pronatalist climate sustains a number of dubious beliefs about the family. Research on the childless, however, indicates that they are neither psychologically nor morally inferior to parents, and are actually less likely to be lonely in old age. Similarly, findings on the single-child family in the United States, Britain, China and Japan indicate that only children are no more selfish, spoiled, or unpopular than other children, but are actually more likely to do well in school.

The pronatalism of western countries has affected the progress and pitfalls of the population policies of India and China, the most populous countries in the world. In these countries, the western debates over contraceptive research and administration, family planning programmes and women's welfare, the effects of the single-child family, lowered fertility without economic development, and demographic competition are all starkly manifested.

The population control policies of the wealthier countries are found in their immigration policies. History shows that they have never been as generous and humane as they are depicted, but have actually been driven by politics and the need to control numbers. Moreover, the increasing numbers of economic migrants and of political and ecological refugees in the world today are at least partly a result of the foreign and economic policies of some of the same wealthy countries, policies which still continue.

Population has always been a political issue. Throughout most of history, large and growing national, religious, ethnic and family groups have meant strength and prosperity to their leaders. Against this belief, still ingrained, many governments have gradually come around to the view that large and increasing populations could eat up territorial resources needed for further economic development, and have adopted fertility-limiting policies within their own borders. Others, whether still clinging to the earlier outlook or where domestic fertility rates have already dropped to near or below replacement, have adopted policies that were either *laissez-faire* or designed to stimulate birth rates.

Recently, many people concerned with local and global ecologies have begun to argue that human numbers are nearing, if they have not already exceeded, the planet's capability of supporting them on a long-term basis. Nevertheless, the assumption that reproduction at the individual and family levels is both desirable and beneficial has never been challenged. It has been the main purpose of this book to do just that, by examining a set of conventional beliefs about religious dogma, medical technology, parental power, childlessness, family size and children's rights and development. These beliefs were then set in the political contexts in which population policies are implemented in both the developed and developing parts of the world.

Since the middle of this century, intense discussions, sometimes taking the form of diplomatic bargaining and sometimes open conflict, have been conducted over how best to manage, allocate and if possible increase available resources. The part played by population size and growth in the 'development' debate has centred around the question of whether economic prosperity must precede or follow declining birth rates. Among the few premises to be generally accepted in the 'environment' debate is that the already 'developed' industrial countries are currently the chief contributors to global resource consumption, pollution generation and environmental degradation. It is therefore sometimes suggested that both development aid and environmental programmes contributed by the North should be used as bargaining chips in exchange for fertility-limiting programmes in the South, whose growing populations are alternately viewed by donor countries as cheap labour, environmental threat and potential immigration.

Many believe that such bargaining is not only unethical – making actions that are necessary, beneficial and overdue in themselves contingent in any way – but entirely unnecessary. Within the past decade, a new factor and a new fact has entered the population equation. The factor is that of gender: the growing insistence of women's groups that women's interests and rights must not be neglected in planning either economic or population policies. (Indeed, some women's groups insist that women's reproductive rights imply the rejection of all population policies.) The new fact is the decline of birth rates in many parts of the world in response to existing family planning programmes even before development, in the industrializing economic sense, has taken place. The reasons for this sometimes precipitate decline are not completely clear, but there is evidence that women on the whole see the aim of bearing and rearing fewer but healthier children as desirable in their own interests, and one which they can realize to the extent that education, economic independence, accessible contraception, improved communications, and lower infant and child mortality permit.

The policy implications of the evidence and arguments presented in this book are that decreasing fertility rates in both developed and developing countries are entirely beneficial, especially to women and children, and are attended by no overbalancing undesirable economic or social effects. Consequently, both aid and domestic policies should be focused on 'social development': the promotion of health, education and well-being in the most disadvantaged women and children of both rich and poor countries, rather than on conventional economic growth, which is unsustainable and threatens the well-being of the whole planet.

Index